# Immigration

Louise I. Gerdes, *Book Editor*

**Bruce Glassman,** *Vice President*
**Bonnie Szumski,** *Publisher*
**Helen Cothran,** *Managing Editor*

CURRENT CONTROVERSIES

**GREENHAVEN PRESS**
*An imprint of Thomson Gale, a part of The Thomson Corporation*

THOMSON
™
GALE

Detroit • New York • San Francisco • San Diego • New Haven, Conn.
Waterville, Maine • London • Munich

*For more information, contact*
Greenhaven Press
27500 Drake Rd.
Farmington Hills, MI 48331-3535
Or you can visit our Internet site at http://www.gale.com

Cover credit: © Greg Smith/CORBIS SABA. A U.S. border patrol officer arrests illegal immigrants at the Mexico-California border.

LIBRARY OF CONGRESS CATALOGING-IN-PUBLICATION DATA

Immigration / Louise I. Gerdes, book editor.
   p. cm. — (Current controversies)
  Includes bibliographical references and index.
  ISBN 0-7377-2779-9 (lib. : alk. paper) — ISBN 0-7377-2780-2 (pbk. : alk. paper)
    1. United States—Emigration and immigration. 2. United States—Emigration and immigration—Government policy. 3. Emigration and immigration.
  4. Emigration and immigration—Government policy. I. Gerdes, Louise I., 1953– .
  II. Series.
  JV6465.I4713 2005
  325.73—dc22
                                       2004061658

Printed in the United States of America

# Contents

# Chapter 2: Are Immigrants Treated Fairly in the United States?

## No: Immigrants Are Not Treated Fairly

## Yes: Immigrants Are Treated Fairly

social practices such as domestic violence are reasonable. Granting asylum to all who suffer as a result of social problems is impractical.

# Chapter 3: How Should the United States Respond to Illegal Immigration?

# Chapter 4: How Should Immigration Be Controlled?

# Foreword

By definition, controversies are "discussions of questions in which opposing opinions clash" (Webster's Twentieth Century Dictionary Unabridged). Few would deny that controversies are a pervasive part of the human condition and exist on virtually every level of human enterprise. Controversies transpire between individuals and among groups, within nations and between nations. Controversies supply the grist necessary for progress by providing challenges and challengers to the status quo. They also create atmospheres where strife and warfare can flourish. A world without controversies would be a peaceful world; but it also would be, by and large, static and prosaic.

## The Series' Purpose

The purpose of the Current Controversies series is to explore many of the social, political, and economic controversies dominating the national and international scenes today. Titles selected for inclusion in the series are highly focused and specific. For example, from the larger category of criminal justice, Current Controversies deals with specific topics such as police brutality, gun control, white collar crime, and others. The debates in Current Controversies also are presented in a useful, timeless fashion. Articles and book excerpts included in each title are selected if they contribute valuable, long-range ideas to the overall debate. And wherever possible, current information is enhanced with historical documents and other relevant materials. Thus, while individual titles are current in focus, every effort is made to ensure that they will not become quickly outdated. Books in the Current Controversies series will remain important resources for librarians, teachers, and students for many years.

In addition to keeping the titles focused and specific, great care is taken in the editorial format of each book in the series. Book introductions and chapter prefaces are offered to provide background material for readers. Chapters are organized around several key questions that are answered with diverse opinions representing all points on the political spectrum. Materials in each chapter include opinions in which authors clearly disagree as well as alternative opinions in which authors may agree on a broader issue but disagree on the possible solutions. In this way, the content of each volume in Current Controversies mirrors the mosaic of opinions encountered in society. Readers will quickly realize that there are many viable answers to these complex issues. By questioning each author's conclusions, students and casual readers can begin to develop the critical thinking skills so important to evaluating opinionated material.

Current Controversies is also ideal for controlled research. Each anthology in the series is composed of primary sources taken from a wide gamut of informational categories including periodicals, newspapers, books, United States and foreign government documents, and the publications of private and public organizations. Readers will find factual support for reports, debates, and research papers covering all areas of important issues. In addition, an annotated table of contents, an index, a book and periodical bibliography, and a list of organizations to contact are included in each book to expedite further research.

Perhaps more than ever before in history, people are confronted with diverse and contradictory information. During the Persian Gulf War, for example, the public was not only treated to minute-to-minute coverage of the war, it was also inundated with critiques of the coverage and countless analyses of the factors motivating U.S. involvement. Being able to sort through the plethora of opinions accompanying today's major issues, and to draw one's own conclusions, can be a complicated and frustrating struggle. It is the editors' hope that Current Controversies will help readers with this struggle.

Greenhaven Press anthologies primarily consist of previously published material taken from a variety of sources, including periodicals, books, scholarly journals, newspapers, government documents, and position papers from private and public organizations. These original sources are often edited for length and to ensure their accessibility for a young adult audience. The anthology editors also change the original titles of these works in order to clearly present the main thesis of each viewpoint and to explicitly indicate the opinion presented in the viewpoint. These alterations are made in consideration of both the reading and comprehension levels of a young adult audience. Every effort is made to ensure that Greenhaven Press accurately reflects the original intent of the authors included in this anthology.

*"For some immigrants . . . assimilation has not come easily, and this difficulty has become central to the immigration debate. When immigrants fail to fully assimilate according to prevailing notions of what assimilation means, conflict erupts."*

# Introduction

America is often described as a melting pot. This metaphor was originally used by British playwright Israel Zangwill, who in 1909 wrote *The Melting Pot* in response to his experience helping settle ten thousand Russian Jews in the United States after horrific massacres of Jews in Russia. An oft-quoted scene from the play describes American attitudes toward immigration at the time:

> There she lies, the great Melting Pot—listen! Can't you hear the roaring and the bubbling? There gapes her mouth—the harbor where a thousand mammoth feeders come from the ends of the world to pour in their human freight. Ah, what a stirring and seething. Celt and Latin, Slav and Teuton, Greek and Syrian—black and yellow—Yes, East and West, North and South, the palm and the pine, the pole and the equator, the crescent and the cross—how the great Alchemist melts and fuses them with His purging flame! Here shall they all unite . . . what is the glory of Rome and Jerusalem . . . compared with the glory of America, where all races and nations come to labor and look forward!

Zangwill's vision of the melting pot assumes that all immigrants in America will assimilate. For some immigrants, however, assimilation has not come easily, and this difficulty has become central to the immigration debate. When immigrants fail to fully assimilate according to prevailing notions of what assimilation means, conflict erupts. Commentators on both sides of the immigration debate—those who want to restrict immigration and those who do not—often use assimilation as a weapon to promote their views. Conflict over assimilation is not confined to America; indeed such problems occur throughout the world.

What exactly it means to assimilate is deeply controversial. Europeans have traditionally defined assimilation fairly rigidly, believing that to assimilate means to abandon original cultural attributes and conform to the behaviors and customs of the majority of the native born population. France, for example, has expelled from its public schools French Muslim girls who insist on wearing chadors (head scarves). French president Jacques Chirac has backed proposals banning the wearing of Islamic head scarves.

Conflict over Muslim immigrants also occurs in German secular schools. Muslim girls are asking to be exempt from coeducational physical education, which is required by German law. According to Marion Berning, director of the

Rixdorfer primary school in Berlin, Germany, "We have Muslim girls who say they don't want to swim with the boys. It's obvious the parents exert pressure on them, but [the parents] have to accept that coeducation is part of German schools." While Germany has generally been more sensitive to Islamic culture than has France, non-Muslim Germans express concern that giving in to Muslims on issues such as physical coeducation will lead to the undermining of their national institutions. According to many analysts, the conflict that the strict interpretation of assimilation has generated in Europe has resulted in national and ethnic disunity, leading to nations dividing into small, often hostile communities.

In contrast to the European conception, assimilation in the United States "has always been much more flexible and accommodating and, consequently, much more effective in achieving its purpose," according to Peter D. Salins, author of *Assimilation, American Style*. Quoting sociologist Henry Fairchild, Salins maintains that American assimilation allows "the United States to preserve its 'national unity in the face of the influx of hordes of persons of scores of different nationalities.'" Unlike in Europe, where immigrants are expected to give up their ethnic identities, in the United States—at least in recent times—immigrants' ethnic identities are actually embraced. It was not until the 1960s, however, that this view—that immigrants should maintain part of their ethnic identity—gained broad intellectual and political support.

During the 1960s the United States adopted the concept of multiculturalism. Philosophy professor Will Kymlicka, author of *Multicultural Citizenship*, explains the concept this way:

> Immigrants are expected to integrate in the sense that they should learn the language of their host society and participate in public institutions so that there's a linguistic and institutional integration, but they're not expected to become indistinguishable from other citizens. It's expected that they will want to maintain a distinct ethnic identity, they'll want to express it, and they'll want public institutions to adapt, to accommodate their distinct identity. So public institutions like schools, hospitals, the police force, the media, should make efforts to reflect and to accommodate the distinctive identities of immigrant groups.

Those who support multiculturalism believe that embracing immigrants' ethnicities respects them as individuals and leads to diversity, which benefits American culture. They argue that to expect immigrants to give up their ethnic identities is racist.

This view of assimilation has not been without its detractors, however. Although American institutions in general support multiculturalism—universities promote multicultural curricula, public offices recruit bilingual employees, and federal, state, and local governments offer pamphlets in many languages—some Americans have come to consider multiculturalism as a threat to American unity. They argue that a multicultural concept of assimilation has led to the racialization of immigrant groups. Commentators such as Sam Francis, a staunch opponent of immigration, claim that some immigrants, particularly Asians and Hispanics, are not assimilating but creating ethnic enclaves. Leaders among these immigrant groups have created political activist organizations that promote what Francis calls "racial crusades" that focus on gaining recognition for their own ethnic groups rather than on what is good for the nation. Francis contends,

> The meaning of the new racial and political consciousness, then, is not that immigrants assimilate but that, once enough immigrants of a particular race, nation or culture arrive, they start thinking in terms of their own group, support political action intended to benefit their own group and forget the interests of the country they've invited themselves to live in. What that leads to is not a melting pot of assimilation but the melted pots of Bosnia and Brazil [where ethnic conflict occurred]. It might be wise for real Americans to think about what mass immigration really means for them and the country they and their ancestors created.

Salins agrees. In his view, because multiculturalism rejects assimilation altogether, it has led to an "ideology of grievance" and thus conflict. "All the nations that have even embraced it, from Yugoslavia to Lebanon, from Belgium to Canada," contends Salins, "have had to live with perpetual ethnic discord."

Another school of thought contends that the conflicts that result from immigration are neither the result of American racism nor the failure of immigrants to assimilate. Analysts such as Peter Skerry claim that immigrants are in fact assimilating. The problem, in Skerry's view, is expecting assimilation to occur without conflict. When different cultures come together, conflict is inevitable, he maintains. For Skerry, the ease with which immigrants assimilate depends on the actions of both immigrant and native. "Both sides of this debate ignore . . . that assimilation and conflict go hand in hand," Skerry argues. "We need to get beyond the romance of immigration enthusiasts as well as the melodrama of immigration alarmists. We need to introduce a sense of realism about how we think about these issues and to face up to the turmoil and strains that mass immigration imposes on our society," he contends.

As those seeking a better life stream across borders worldwide, commentators will continue to debate how best to respond to mass immigration. Whether immigration analysts will meet Skerry's expectations and "face up to the turmoil and strains" associated with assimilation remains to be seen.

# Chapter 1

# Is Immigration a Serious Problem?

# Chapter Preface

One of the issues often ignored in the immigration debate is the impact of immigration on sending countries. Some claim that immigration drains sending nations of their best minds and hurts their economies. Others argue that the money immigrants send to their families left behind and the economic ties they help establish benefit sending nations.

The most obvious loss to sending nations when their citizens emigrate, some analysts contend, is the loss of human capital, often called a "brain drain." People who emigrate are often the brightest and most enterprising. Social geographer Alisdair Rogers maintains that only half of all foreign-born students getting degrees in science in U.S. universities return home. Remzi Lani, director of Albania's Media Institute, contends, "The best brains go and don't come back. We have lost one in six of the population—almost one person per family. There are 8,000 Albanians studying in Italian universities—more than in Tirana University [in Albania]. How many will return? Not more than 5 percent."

Those concerned about immigration's impact on sending nations also point to the loss of tax revenue. In a study of the impact of emigration from India, Mihir Desai of Harvard University found that 1 million Indians lived in the United States in 2001. Although this number comprised only 0.1 percent of India's population, the immigrants' U.S. earnings were equivalent to 10 percent of India's national income. The study concluded that the net fiscal cost to India of losing these taxpayers was nearly 0.5 percent of India's gross domestic product in 2002.

Although many see remittances—the money immigrants send back to their home countries—as a benefit to the sending nations, some authorities claim that even remittances can be harmful. For example, Kimberly Hamilton and Elizabeth Grieco of the Migration Policy Institute maintain, "External communities may organize to fund conflict in [the] sending country (i.e., Eritreans, Tamils) and may foster continued conflict." Still others contend that some remittances are misused by those in sending nations who receive them. Rogers maintains,

> Conventional thinking suggested that such remittances encouraged wasteful expenditure on luxury goods or splendid houses. They made families and villages dependent on unreliable sources of income from outside: in part of rural Mexico, almost half of all families rely for their main source of income on money sent by relatives abroad. Remittances created inequalities between families in the same area. They undermined the ability of rural areas to improve themselves.

Despite these claims, some authorities argue that remittances benefit the economies of sending nations. The *Economist*, a British finance and news magazine, claims, "Developing countries receive more than $60 billion a year in remittances. That is $6 billion more than net official aid from OECD [Organization for Economic Co-operation and Development] countries." In addition, many analysts claim, those who receive remittances spend them on housing, consumer goods, and health care, which benefits communities if the goods and services are locally produced. According to one estimate, the *Economist* maintains, "each dollar sent home generates three to four dollars of economic growth." In some cases, the magazine further asserts, "Immigrants from a particular village team up to pay for a septic tank or a school."

Another benefit of immigration to sending nations is that global trade and business opportunities are often created as immigrants travel back and forth between the host and the sending nation. For example, Aissa Goumidi, who emigrated from Algeria to Marseilles, France, sold all of his textiles to merchants in Algeria. Another Marseilles immigrant, Mohamed Laqhila, an accountant, is bringing people from accounting institutions in the Maghreb countries to discuss business opportunities there with his colleagues in France. A recent phenomenon is the development of what are known as "knowledge networks." Originally created in South Africa, Rogers maintains, "these networks are associations of skilled workers and professionals abroad who are committed to helping their homelands." These networks often use the Internet to create networks of business contacts with similar expertise. According to the *Economist*, the South African Network of Skills Abroad, "embrace[s] people who are not from South Africa but simply interested in the country's development. . . . All aim to offer a way for expatriates to help with development."

Those who have concluded that immigration can have a positive impact on sending nations contend that rather than a "brain drain," immigration can more appropriately be described as "brain circulation." In Silicon Valley, for example, "50% go back at least once a year to their home country on business, and 5% return at least five times a year. Even more telling, 74% of Indian respondents and 53% of Chinese ones said they hoped to start a business back home," claims AnnaLee Saxenian of the Public Policy Institute of California. Some commentators conclude, therefore, that in the modern world, the benefits of immigration outweigh the risks to sending nations. Rogers concludes, "The globalisation of migration, alongside developments in technology, communications and travel, may help redistribute the economic gains of immigration more evenly across the world."

The impact of immigration on sending nations remains subject to debate. The authors in the following chapter debate other issues concerning immigration's impact on societies.

# Immigration Threatens American Culture

## by Lawrence Auster

**About the author:** *Lawrence Auster, a white nationalist, is author of* The Path to National Suicide: An Essay on Immigration and Multiculturalism *and* Huddled Clichés: Exposing the Fraudulent Arguments That Have Opened America's Borders to the World.

The problem of immigration and the changes it is causing in our culture can be approached from many different angles. We could speak about the redefinition of America as a multicultural society instead of as a nation; or the permanent establishment of affirmative action programs for immigrants based on their race; or the town in Texas that declared Spanish its official language; or the thousands of Hispanics at an international soccer match in Los Angeles who booed and threw garbage at the *American* team; or the decline in educational and environmental standards in areas dominated by Hispanics; or the Hmong people from Laos who bring shamans and witch doctors into hospital rooms; or the customs of voodoo and animal sacrifice and forced marriage and female genital mutilation that have been imported into this country by recent immigrants; or the pushing aside of Christianity in our public life to give equal respect to non-Western religions; or the evisceration of American history in our schools because our white-majority American past is no longer seen as representative of our newly diverse population; or the vast numbers of Muslims established in cities throughout this country who sympathize with the Muslim terrorists and dream of turning America into an Islamic state; or *our own leaders* who, even *after* [the terrorist attacks of] September 11 [2001], keep telling us that the Muslims are all patriotic and tolerant, keep warning *us* against our supposed anti-Muslim bigotry, and continue letting thousands of people from terror supporting countries to immigrate into America.

At bottom, each of these phenomena and many more like them are happening

Lawrence Auster, "Mass Immigration: Its Effect on Our Culture," *The Social Contract*, vol. 12, Spring 2002. Copyright © 2002 by The Social Contract Press. Reproduced by permission.

for one reason and one reason only—the 1965 Immigration Act which opened U.S. immigration on an equal basis to every country in the world, rather than, as in the past, favoring our historic source nations of Europe. Of course many of the recent immigrants from non-European countries have fitted into America and made good contributions here. It is the unprecedented scale of this diverse immigration that is the problem.

I could easily devote the rest of this article to making a detailed case that the post-1965 immigration is indeed changing our culture in negative ways. But here I want to ask a different question: Why have *we Americans* allowed this to occur? Why are we *continuing* to let it happen? And why, even when we gripe and complain about some aspects of it, do we feel *helpless* to do anything to stop it?

## The Surrender of the American Mainstream

Many have argued, most recently [conservative political figure] Patrick Buchanan, that these things are happening because of the cultural left that hates America and wants to destroy it. There is no doubt that the cultural left hates America and wants to destroy it; and there is also no doubt that the left sees mass immigration from Third-World countries as a handy way of achieving that. But that argument leaves unanswered a more disturbing question—why has there been no significant opposition to this leftist agenda? Presumably, the Republican party does not hate America and want to destroy it. Presumably, the conservative movement does not hate America and want to destroy it. Presumably conservative Protestants and parents' groups that have fought against Whole Language teaching and homosexual indoctrination in the schools do not hate America and want to destroy it. Yet nowhere among these legions of mainstream conservatives and the organizations that represent them have there been any serious calls to reduce this immigration from the non-Western world and the inevitable cultural transformations it is bringing.

> *"Patriotic conservatives acquiesce in [an immigration] policy that is so obviously dividing and weakening our nation."*

Nor is the fear of political correctness [PC] an adequate explanation for this conservative surrender. Whatever the power of PC in our society, it cannot account for the fact that tens of millions of mainstream conservatives ranging from Rush Limbaugh fans to conservative evangelicals either support the current immigration policy or fail to speak up against it—even in the relative privacy and safety of their own organizations.

## A Startling Paradox

We are thus left with a remarkable paradox—that the patriotic and Christian Right supports exactly the same immigration policy that is supported by the anti-American, atheistic left—an immigration policy, moreover, that spells the permanent eclipse of the Republican party and the victory of big government, since most of the recent immigrants vote Democratic.

Indeed, our conservative Christian President [George W. Bush], when he's not busy embracing so-called "moderate" Muslim leaders who are allies of terrorists, wants to expand Third-World immigration even further. But that's not all. Unlike Republicans in the past such as Ronald Reagan, who supported Third-World immigration on the hopeful if naive assumption that the immigrants were all assimilating,

*"Tens of millions of people from alien cultures whose exercise of their individual right to come to America will mean the destruction of our cultural goods."*

President [George W.] Bush actively promotes the growth and development of foreign languages and unassimilated foreign cultures in this country. In a speech in Miami during the 2000 campaign, he celebrated the fact that American cities are becoming culturally and linguistically like Latin American cities:

> We are now one of the largest Spanish-speaking nations in the world. We're a major source of Latin music, journalism and culture. . . . Just go to Miami, or San Antonio, Los Angeles, Chicago or West New York, New Jersey . . . and close your eyes and listen. You could just as easily be in Santo Domingo or Santiago, or San Miguel de Allende. . . . For years our nation has debated this change—some have praised it and others have resented it. By nominating me, my party has made a choice to welcome the new America.

As president, Mr. Bush has not only left in place [former president Bill] Clinton's executive order requiring government services to be provided in foreign languages, he has started his own bilingual tradition, delivering a Spanish version of his weekly national radio address. Even the White House Web site is now bilingual, with a link accompanying each of the president's speeches that says "*En Español*" and points to a Spanish translation of the speech.

Yet, with the exception of one or two conservative columnists, these steps toward the establishment of Spanish as a quasi-official public language in this country have been met with complete silence on the right, even though opposition to bilingualism used to command automatic agreement among conservatives. If conservatives are no longer willing to utter a peep of protest in defense of something so fundamental to America as our national language, is there anything else about our historic culture they will defend, once it has been abandoned by a Republican president?

What all of this suggests is that mass immigration and the resulting multiculturalism are not—as many immigration restrictionists tend to believe—simply being imposed on us by the anti-American left. Rather, these destructive phenomena stem from *mainstream beliefs* that are shared by most Americans, particularly by conservatives. Of course economic and political forces, and the birthrate factor, are pushing this process in a variety of ways, but on the deepest level the cause is not material, it is philosophical and spiritual. The reason Americans cannot effectively oppose the transformation of our culture is that they subscribe to the belief system that has led to it.

## The Credo That Has Left America Defenseless

What is that belief system? At its core, it is the quintessentially American notion that everyone is the same under the skin—that people should only be seen as individuals, with no reference to their historic culture, their ethnicity, their religion, their race. Now there is a great truth in the idea of a common human essence transcending our material differences. But if it is taken to be literally true in all circumstances and turned into an ideological dogma, it leads to the expectation that all people from every background and in whatever numbers can assimilate equally well into America.

This explains why patriotic conservatives acquiesce in a policy that is so obviously dividing and weakening our nation. Since the end of World War II, and especially since the 1960s, conservatives have tended to define America not in terms of its historic civilization and peoplehood, but almost exclusively in terms of the *individual*—the individual under God and the individual as an economic actor. For modern conservatives, what makes America is not any inherited cultural tradition from our past, but our belief in the timeless, universal, God-granted right of all persons in the world to be free and to improve their own lives. Therefore conservatives don't believe there can be any moral basis to make distinctions among prospective immigrants based on their culture.

We cannot say, for example, that a shaman-following Laotian tribesman, or a Pakistan who believes in forced marriage, is less suited for membership in our society than an Italian Catholic or a Scots-Irish Presbyterian. And we can't make such distinctions because, from the point of view of pure individualism, our inherited culture does not reflect any inherent or higher truth, and therefore cannot be the object of our love and protection. The only value that reflects higher truth and is deserving of our energetic defense is the freedom and sacredness of each individual. In practical terms this translates into the equal right of all individuals to make their own choices and pursue their own dreams, even if we are speaking of tens of millions of people from

> *"We started letting in all these other cultures at the very moment that we had* defined our own culture out of existence.*"*

alien cultures whose exercise of *their* individual right to come to America will mean the destruction of *our* cultural goods.

In theory, multiculturalism is the opposite of liberal individualism. In practice it is the direct result of pursuing liberal individualism to its logical extreme. The 1965 Immigration Act was not about multiculturalism. No lawmaker said in

1965: Hey, we *need* Third-World cultures, we *need* female genital mutilation in our country, we *need* Shiite Islam and Wahabbi Islam to fulfil the meaning of America. The 1965 legislators voted to open our borders to the world, not because of a belief in the equal value of all cultures, but because of a belief in the equal rights of all individuals; the single comment most frequently heard in the Congressional debate was that prospective immigrants should be chosen solely on the basis of their "individual worth." But this noble-sounding sentiment was an illusion, because, in the real world, most of the people admitted into America under the new law did not come just as individuals. They came as part of the largest mass migration in history, consisting largely of family chain migration, and inevitably brought their cultures with them.

> *"Having cast aside our own culture, we had no choice but to yield, step by step, to the elevation of other cultures."*

## Abandoning American Culture

Thus, in passing the 1965 Immigration Act, we did two fateful things. We announced that we had no culture of our own except for the principle of non-discrimination toward people of *other* cultures—*and* we began admitting millions of people from those other cultures. We started letting in all these other cultures at the very moment that we had *defined our own culture out of existence.*

This delusional act led to the next stage of our self-undoing. In the late 1970s and 1980s, we began waking up to the fact that those other cultures were here, that they were very different from our own, and that they were demanding to be recognized and given rights as cultures. But at that point, what basis did we have to resist those demands? We had already said that the only thing that defines us as a people is non-discrimination toward other peoples; we thus had no justification for saying that maybe it's not such a great idea to import people adhering to radical Islam or Mexican nationalism into the United States. Having cast aside our own culture, we had no choice but to yield, step by step, to the elevation of other cultures. This is how America, through an indiscriminate and unqualified belief in individualism, ended up surrendering to its opposite—to multiculturalism.

## Is Immigration Restriction Immoral or Un-Christian?

What has been said up to this point will offend many conservatives, particularly Christians. For one thing the Christian church consists of people of every culture and race, so why can't a nation? The answer is that the church is a heavenly organization, it is not responsible, as a nation is, for the defense and preservation of a particular earthly society. Mexico and Nigeria, for example, are largely Christian, but in cultural terms are radically different from the United States.

To believe that all peoples on earth should join our country is the very idea that God rejected at the tower of Babel. God said he did not want all men to be united in one society, because that would glorify human power. If I may presume to say so, God had a more modest idea of human life on earth. He wanted men to live in distinct societies, each speaking its own tongue, developing its own culture, and expressing God in its own way. This is the true diversity of cultures that constitutes mankind, not the false diversity that results from eliminating borders and coercively mixing everyone together, which destroys each country's distinctive character. Consider how today's multicultural London has lost much of its Englishness, and increasingly resembles multicultural New York.

So I would respectfully suggest that when Christians translate the spiritual idea of the unity of people under God into the political ideology that people from all cultures should be allowed to come en masse to America and other Western countries, that is not the traditional teaching of the Christian church, that is a modern liberal idea, that is the *Religion of Man*, which has been infused into the Christian church over the past fifty years.

But if this is the case, how can we reconcile our spiritual unity as human beings under God with our actual cultural differences? The answer is that in individual and private relationships, people of different backgrounds can relate to each other as individuals, without discrimination of culture and ethnicity. But on the group level, on the level of entire peoples and nations and mass migrations, cultural differences do matter very much and cannot be safely ignored.

## Thinking and Acting Anew

It would therefore be a tragic error to limit our thinking about immigration to technical matters such as law enforcement against illegal aliens and security measures against terrorists, as vitally important as those things are. Beyond the immediate threat of mass physical destruction, we face a more subtle but no less serious threat to the very survival of our civilization. As Daniel Pipes writes in the [Spring 2002] issue of *Commentary:*

> To me, the current wave of militant Islamic violence against the United States,
> however dangerous, is ultimately less consequential than the non-violent effort
> to transform it through immigration, natural reproduction, and conversion.

Of course I agree with Mr. Pipes. But, as I've tried to demonstrate, we cannot hope to stop or significantly slow that immigration unless we abandon this contemporary idea that America is defined by *nothing* except individual freedom and opportunity—the idea that America has no particular culture of its own that is worth preserving. Rethinking these beliefs and rewriting our immigration laws accordingly will not be easy, but if we fail to make the attempt, we will simply continue sliding, slowly but surely, toward the dissolution of our culture and our country.

# Immigration Spreads Disease and Threatens Public Health

by Wayne Lutton

**About the author:** *Wayne Lutton, a policy analyst and historian, is editor of the* Social Contract, *a quarterly journal advocating immigration limits, assimilation, and the preservation and promotion of a shared American language and culture. Lutton is coauthor with Robert J. Howard of* Immigration and the Public Health Crisis.

One of the areas where the United States and other Western nations progressed dramatically during the late 19th through 20th centuries was in the area of public health. Swamps were drained, sanitation and personal hygiene improved, vaccines were discovered. All of these contributed to the improvement of health to the point where, by the late 1970s and early 1980s, many once common diseases all but vanished from the United States.

Historically, the United States government enforced health standards for immigrants. Even today, under section 212 of the Immigration and Nationality Act (8 U.S. Code 1182), the Attorney General is not to admit aliens if they are afflicted with certain mental or physical conditions, any "dangerous contagious disease," or any defect, disease or disability that may affect their ability to earn a living. Public Health Service regulations include infectious leprosy, active tuberculosis, and venereal diseases among the dangerous infectious diseases disqualifying someone from migrating to the United States.

## A Change in U.S. Policies

A turning point in the U.S. government's policy toward the entry of persons infected with contagious diseases came on March 15, 1980, when the Attorney General, acting on a request from the State Department to expedite the processing of Indochinese refugees, decided to lower the health qualifications for admitting designated refugees to our country. From this point on, refugees have been permitted to enter and settle in the United States who earlier would have been excluded, including people afflicted with active tuberculosis, mental retardation, and infectious leprosy. During the Clinton Administration, people carrying the deadly AIDS/HIV virus were permitted to legally enter the United States.

> *"Mass immigration . . . has contributed to a new threat to our nation's health. Diseases once practically eradicated are breaking out again."*

Mass immigration—a consequence of the 1965 Immigration Act (which opened the door to large-scale immigration from the Third World), the Refugee Act of 1980, and refusal by federal authorities to control illegal immigration—has contributed to a new threat to our nation's health. Diseases once practically eradicated are breaking out again. Tropical diseases, previously unheard of in the United States, but prevalent in Third World countries, are appearing. Medieval ailments are resurfacing. The immigration/disease relationship demolishes the claims that high immigration levels, with hundreds of thousands of people entering the U.S. uninspected every year, is entirely benign.

## Warnings Unheeded

In recent years, health professionals have tried to alert government authorities and the general public about certain of the newly emergent health dangers. During the Reagan Administration, J. Michael McGinnis, deputy assistant secretary of the U.S. Department of Health and Human Services, warned of problems in the American Southwest originating in Mexico, "Along the border we have a prevalence of diseases that we shouldn't be seeing much of in modern Western society. We have higher rates of such things as malaria, tuberculosis, measles, rubella, rabies, and pertussis (whooping cough)." He added that physicians trained in the United States where such diseases are not prevalent, have difficulty recognizing them in new patients.

The 1995 Ebola virus outbreak in Zaire drew new attention to the emergence of drug-resistant forms of tuberculosis, whooping cough, and pneumonia. Interviewed by *Fox Morning News*, Dr. Nils Daulaire of the U.S. Agency for International Development was asked if he was trying to sound an alarm here about infectious diseases? Dr. Daulaire replied,

> Yes. There's a real serious issue that has gone unnoticed by a lot of people in this country, and that is that we are no longer secure as we were in the 1950s and '60s and '70s from the threats of these diseases. At that time we thought we had the problem basically licked. We had good vaccines, we had good antibiotics for a lot of the bacteria, tuberculosis was on a steep decline and we thought basically we could move out of the area of infectious diseases into

things like heart disease and diabetes, the chronic diseases. . . .

We're had a very severe reminder over the last several years with the emergence of the Ebola, with tuberculosis spreading rampant in much of the Third World and in inner cities in the U.S. and with the development of antibiotic resistance.

Asked the cause of these developments, Dr. Daulaire, continued:

First of all, as human populations expand and move into areas of tropical rain forest, which are the most biologically diverse areas on earth, we're having face-to-face contact between species that really haven't had contact or significant contact before. And so we're getting increased spread of new pathogens, new microbes that haven't been in the human population, like Ebola. . . . And they are being brought out in developing countries, in places where populations are growing tremendously. And then, and this is the part that is particularly worrisome for the U.S., there's no place in the world anymore that's more than 24 hours travel from any port of entry in the U.S., so these things can move very quickly to the U.S. where they pose a real risk.

*Fox News:* "Some people say, 'Oh, come on, these are Third World problems. We don't have to worry about that . . . it can't happen here."

Dr. Daulaire: "Well, that was true a hundred years ago, it was probably even true 40 years ago. But with the amount of travel and international commerce that takes place now, in fact, one-third of the tuberculosis in the U.S. is foreign-born, so there's a lot of importation."

> *"Tuberculosis reemerged in the United States in the late 1980s, carried by immigrants and refugees from Third World countries."*

The National Science and Technology Council (NSTC) issued a report in September 1995, *Infectious Disease—A Global Health Threat*, which spurred demands for a new national public health policy for dealing with ominous threats of emerging and reemerging infections. This prompted the White House to convene a Committee on International Science, Engineering, and Technology (CISET), chaired by then Vice President Al Gore. CISET issued their own report, which confirmed that HIV (AIDS), the periodic outbreaks of new and reemerging infections, and the realities of drug-resistant tuberculosis and of many nosocomial infections, are irrefutable confirmation of those threats.

Why, the CISET report asked, "are infectious diseases reemerging as major threats to human health?" Answers included population growth, unprecedented travel, and other movements of population (migration and immigration). Both CISET and NSTC concluded that high among the needed responses was global surveillance and security against infection, requiring closer scrutiny of "persons, animals or material" traversing our borders.

In late 1996, the *Journal of the American Medical Association* again warned that the United States was "importing tropical illnesses." The publication cited remarks made by Om Sharma, M.D., professor of medicine at the University of California, Los Angeles, School of Medicine, to attendees of the annual meeting of the American College of Chest Physicians. *JAMA* reported, "like vagabonds hopping the next freight train, infectious diseases once confined to the tropics and subtropics are traveling the globe via tourists, business travelers, and immigrants." Dr. Sharma noted that disease killers accompanied by respiratory symptoms can turn up anywhere in the world. Among them are malaria, paragonimiasis (often mistaken for TB), and schistomiasis (often found in patients with lung disease and associated liver or urinary tract disease).

Marsha Goldsmith, writing in *JAMA* in 1998, cautioned,

> Travel is broadening. Unfortunately, it may also be diarrhetic, emetic, toxic . . . that is to say, a vehicle for exposing the body to unfamiliar ills even as it opens up new vistas for the mind.

She went on to observe that physicians in the U.S. and other developed countries

> are finding their diagnostic acumen challenged by diseases that have disappeared from, or were never common in, the places where they practice. . . . Medical professionals in North America and Europe are also encountering patients who visit or migrate from their native countries, sometimes leaving behind everything but their endemic illnesses.

## Diseases Cross U.S. Open Borders

Alarms raised by health care and national security professionals have not led to the policy changes required to secure our country from foreign threats. There are 301 official air, land, and sea ports of entry into the U.S. On a typical day, over 1.1 million passengers enter, over 57,000 trucks and containers and 323,622 other motor vehicles are processed, 580 vessels hove into ports, and 2,459 aircraft land. The Division of Global Migration & Quarantine of the federal National Center for Infectious Diseases currently has a staff of 39 employees in the field and 42 at its Atlanta-based headquarters administration. Field officers have the power to detain, medically examine, or conditionally release individuals and wildlife suspected of carrying an infectious disease. But with examiners stationed at barely one-tenth of our ports of entry, it is clear that the federal government has all but abandoned any pretense of properly screening overseas visitors, immigrants, and refugees.

*"Immigrants and illegal aliens . . . have helped circulate [HIV/AIDS]."*

Overseas screening of visitors, immigrants, and refugees is likewise inadequate. In a system rife with fraud, prospective entrants to the U.S. submit certification of health. Inspections by visa officials and at U.S. ports of entry are cursory, often taking less than 5 seconds. These procedures are rarely able to detect foreigners carrying contagious diseases and parasitic infections, nor identify persons with other personal problems, such as mental illness, mental retardation, alcohol and drug addiction, and many other major health problems, including heart and kidney disease, diabetes, and cancer.

What are some of the contagious diseases—a number long thought to have been eradicated, or never before seen in the United States? . . .

## The Problem of Tuberculosis

Tuberculosis reemerged in the United States in the late 1980s, carried by immigrants and refugees from Third World countries. Once dubbed the "white plague," TB was the leading cause of death for young adults in the early part of the 20th century. By the 1970s, many experts thought TB was conquered in the United States, even as it remained a major health problem in Third World countries. The steady decline in the incidence of TB in the U.S., from 101.5 cases per 100,000 people to 18.3 in 1970, came to a halt in the mid-1980s.

> *"Most of those infected [with leprosy] in the U.S. are immigrants from such global leprosy hot spots as Brazil, the Caribbean, and India."*

By the early 1990s, public health officials were issuing new warnings about the danger of resurgent TB. Representative of the reporting on this issue was a story in the *Chicago Tribune*, "TB Makes A Deadly Comeback," Feb. 20, 1992. The newspaper revealed that "the number of new cases has risen steadily. . . . Illinois has the fifth-highest number of drug-resistant cases, among the 13 states where these forms of the disease have been diagnosed." John Kuharik, head of Chicago's TB program, declared, "We are looking at the possibility of an explosive outbreak if the people who have the drug-resistant strains are not treated and infect other people."

In 1993, the Centers for Disease Control revealed that TB was tied to immigration, with 53 percent of the new cases in the United States centered in four states that are magnets for immigrants—California, New York, Texas, and Florida. The highest number of reported TB cases was in California, with 61 percent of them among the foreign born. Dr. Sarah Royce, chief of the TB control branch of the California Department of Health Services, emphasized, "Anybody can catch tuberculosis. It's an airborne infection, and any person untreated can spread it to others. It's something everybody needs to be concerned about. It's totally preventable. We need better screening." CDC officials noted that TB statistics represent only reported cases. They don't know how many illegal aliens may be carrying and spreading the disease.

By 1995, the number of foreigners living in the U.S. with TB rose 55 percent from 1986, as a growing number of infected immigrants entered the country, the CDC reported. Most were people from Mexico, the Philippines, and Vietnam. Dr. Patrick Zuber of the CDC's Division of Tuberculosis Elimination admitted that people entering the country, as non-residents were not required to be tested for TB before obtaining a visa to enter the U.S. "We would like to find a way to more effectively identify persons who enter the U.S. with tuberculosis. We may have to re-evaluate the criteria of inclusion for persons who have to be screened."

Despite concerns expressed by public health officials, TB continued to rise among foreign-born persons living in the U.S. In 2000, CDC revealed, "Immigration is a major force sustaining the incidence of tuberculosis in the United States." Six states (California, New York, Texas, Florida, New Jersey, Illinois) reported 73.4 percent of the foreign-born cases. Approximately two-thirds of these cases were originally from Mexico, the Philippines, Vietnam, India, China, Haiti, and South Korea.

Many immigrants do not know they are infected when they enter the U.S. Others come here for the purpose of obtaining treatment at American taxpayers' expense. The prevalence of TB in the countries from which most immigrants to the U.S. originate is 10 to 30 times greater than in this country. A study conducted by health officials along the Texas-Mexico border discovered that among the 17,651 illegal aliens apprehended in the Port Isabel, Texas region in 1999, 49 percent tested positive for the TB bacterium. The rate of full-blown tuberculosis in the lower Rio Grande Valley is triple the national average, according to the U.S. Public Health Service in Port Isabel. On average, a person with active TB infects 20 others annually. At the high end, a boy adopted from the Marshall Islands infected 56 persons in a small North Dakota town. Lax screening of legal immigrants and refusal to halt illegal immigration triggered the return of this deadly disease.

## The Spread of HIV/AIDS

HIV/AIDS is a deadly virus that originated in Africa and spread throughout the Caribbean (especially Haiti), Latin America, and parts of Asia. Immigrants and illegal aliens from these areas have helped circulate the disease. In 1992, U.S. Surgeon General Antonia Novello confirmed that Hispanics, then 8 percent of the U.S. population, accounted for more than 16 percent of reported AIDS cases.

> *"Funds diverted to cover the medical expenses of foreigners are leading to severe cutbacks in services available to U.S. citizens."*

Ten years later, George Lemp, director of the AIDS Research Program at the University of California, said that a study of men aged 18–29 years old indicated that young Hispanic men in the border area of San Diego and Tijuana, Mexico, have AIDS/HIV infection rates three to four times higher than the rates in other California cities (18.5 percent in Tijuana and 35 percent in San Diego). Nationwide, Hispanics represented 13 percent of the U.S. population in 2000, but accounted for 19 percent of the total number of new reported AIDS cases (many cases go unreported). Overall, the AIDS incidence rate per 100,000 persons was 22.5 among Hispanics, more than 3 times the rate for Whites (at 6.6), but lower than the rate for Africans living in America and American Blacks (58.1). In Minnesota, where African "refugees" and new immigrants have been settling, Africans drove up the state's HIV rate by 6 percent in 2002. African immigrants make up less than 1 percent of Minnesota's population, but account for 20 percent of new HIV infections.

## New and Re-Emerging Diseases

Cholera is a communicable disease that re-emerged in South America in the early 1990s and entered the United States by Latino migrants. It usually comes from drinking, bathing or washing with water contaminated by fecal matter. Eric Niiler, in *Scientific American*, reported, "In addition to exposing themselves, the migrants (from central and southern Mexico), may be exposing others—in the fields, factories and restaurants where they find work. The Centers for Disease Control and Prevention found that California has twice the rate of infections of two foodborne pathogens associated with human sewage—campylobacter and shigella—of any other state tested.". . .

Malaria was eradicated in the United States by the early 20th century. In the mid-1990s it re-emerged as a serious health problem, with new cases springing up from Texas to New York and New Jersey. The New York metropolitan cases were the first in more than four decades. "Nearly all those cases have involved *vivax* parasites carried by Mexican and Central American immigrants," according to Dr. Anne Barber of the CDC malaria branch.

> *"The refusal of federal officials to reduce immigration levels has made it much more difficult to reduce the size of the uninsured population."*

In 1995, mosquito-transmitted malaria was discovered in Michigan. The CDC noted that sources of mosquito infection include imported cases of malaria in Michigan, and unrecognized or unreported cases among immigrants, migrant workers, and travelers from malaria-endemic countries.

West Nile virus was discovered in the African country of Uganda in 1937. It made its first appearance in the United States in 1999, when 8,200 people residing in the New York metropolitan area (most of them foreign born) came down with West Nile encephalitis. The virus is carried by birds and transmitted to humans via mosquitoes. It is thought that humans can carry this disease. West Nile virus has spread from New York to other parts of the East Coast, with the first death from the disease in Georgia reported in the fall of 2001. Health officials expect it to spread throughout the Southwest and on into Mexico and Central America. . . .

Leprosy is a Biblical disease often spread by coughing, as the bacteria pass through the respiratory droplets of an infected person. Untreated infections can lead to serious complications, including the loss of toes or limbs. Forty years ago the U.S. had 900 reported cases. In February 2003, health officials said there are more than 7,000 people living in America who have leprosy and health officials have declared it now endemic to the Northeastern United States for the first time in our nation's history. Most of those infected in the U.S. are immigrants from such global leprosy hot spots as Brazil, the Caribbean, and India. Officials in New York have encountered cases of leprosy from people who have contracted the disease in the United States.

Severe Acute Respiratory Syndrome (SARS) is a deadly, pneumonia-like ailment imported to the United States from China and Hong Kong in early 2003. It is easily spread, and U.S. health care workers have contracted SARS through patient contact. In one of the first cases of the disease reported outside of Mainland China, a doctor who caught the illness in a Guangdong hospital traveled to Hong Kong in mid-February 2003. Within a short time, people staying or visiting on the same floor of a hotel where he was staying contracted SARS. In turn, they carried the disease to Vietnam, Singapore, and Canada.

## The Costs to American Taxpayers

Exposure to imported illnesses not only endangers Americans' physical well-being, it costs taxpayers billions of dollars. Additionally, funds diverted to cover the medical expenses of foreigners, are leading to severe cutbacks in services available to U.S. citizens in areas enduring especially high rates of immigration.

The total dollar costs for health services provided to foreigners nationwide is not available. Rice University economist, Professor Donald Huddle, calculated the 1996 cost of Medicaid for legal and illegal immigrants to be a net $14.5 billion. Legal immigrants are estimated to account for more than 80 percent of the net cost of Supplemental Security Income (SSI), which pays for disability and medical conditions not covered by Medicaid. . . .

## The Health Insurance Crisis

Mass immigration is contributing to the ranks of the uninsured. According to a study prepared by the Center for Immigration Studies, immigrants who arrived between 1994 and 1998 and their children accounted for 59 percent of the growth in the size of the uninsured population since 1993 (2.7 million persons). Nearly a third of persons living in immigrant households lacked health insurance, more than twice the 13.9 percent of native citizens. The refusal of federal officials to reduce immigration levels has made it much more difficult to reduce the size of the uninsured population. . . .

States across the country report that their Medicaid/Medicare support systems have reached the disaster level, with massive budget shortfalls projected for years to come. The budget crises come not only from the cost of spending hundreds of millions of dollars on patients who are foreign nationals. The system is rife with fraud perpetrated by foreigners operating in the United States.

For example, in September 2003, Surinder Singh Panshi, a Pakistani, was sentenced to 16 years in state prison for using Southern California clinical laboratories to cheat the Medi-Cal program out of an estimated $20 million. Labs controlled by Panshi ran a black market for blood and stole the identities of patients and doctors. They billed Medi-Cal for thousands of false tests sometimes performed on blood drawn on unsuspecting patients or purchased from runaway children, the homeless, and drug addicts. The California Attorney General's Bureau of Medi-Cal Fraud reports that Medi-Cal fraud is a multi-billion dollar problem and is responsible for a huge chunk of the state budget deficit.

> *"New diseases and escalating costs incurred by legal and illegal immigrants is compelling evidence that the United States should . . . reduce legal immigration."*

In Arizona, the state Department of Health and Human Services uncovered an elaborate Medicare fraud that netted over $15 million. Twenty defendants, most of them Nigerian nationals, pled guilty. Nigerians set up more than two-dozen stores in Arizona and other states dealing in prescription medical supplies, such as wheelchairs, hospital beds, and diet supplements. Going under the name Dona Medical Distributors Inc., they fraudulently secured patient names and manufactured false documents, and then billed Medicare for supplies that were either not delivered or were grossly overpriced. Doctors' signatures were forged thousands of times, and a nurse was hired to create false medical histories.

In Miami Federal Court, Alfredo Omar Rodriguez pled guilty to masterminding a $20 million Medicare fraud, one of the largest scams in South Florida history. Rodriguez controlled 18 shell corporations that billed health providers for unnecessary or excessive knee braces, charging over $1,200 apiece. Rodriguez attempted to move cars, yachts and other assets to Costa Rica before authorities arrested him and over 20 other accomplices.

The cases cited here are just the tip of the iceberg. Federal and state authorities are understaffed and often stumble across cases long after millions of dollars have been stolen. As one Nigerian criminal remarked, "I love Americans . . . they are so trusting!"

The importation of new diseases and escalating costs incurred by legal and illegal immigrants is compelling evidence that the United States should take effective measures to sharply reduce legal immigration, halt illegal immigration to the greatest extent possible, and expel the estimated population of 8 to 11 million illegal aliens residing in our country.

- Health inspectors should be on duty at all ports of entry. People exhibiting signs of illness should be detained for further examination.
- Visas should not be issued without proof of insurance.
- The federal government should seek reimbursement from foreign countries

for the uninsured medical bills of their citizens.

• The Citizen-Child loophole which grants citizenship status to the American-born children of non-citizens (and thus access to a host of benefits, including education and health care) should be closed.

Americans have worked hard since the founding of this nation to provide a clean, safe environment for themselves and their families. All of that progress is being threatened because federal officials refuse to curtail mass immigration. Unless swift action is taken, the United States is in danger of experiencing a public health calamity.

# Immigration Leads to Income Inequality

**by the Federation for American Immigration Reform**

**About the author:** *The Federation for American Immigration Reform is a national, public interest organization whose goal is to reform America's immigration policy by improving border security, halting illegal immigration, and promoting controlled immigration levels.*

Over the decade of the 1990s, the number of middle-income households in the United States decreased by more than 13.6 million—an enormous 30.3 percent decline. This major societal change is inextricably linked with the rapid rise in the immigrant population—both legal and illegal—as was shown in an earlier study of 1990 Census data. The more recent income and immigration data, like that in the previous study, demonstrate convincingly that the current wave of immigrant settlement is inextricably linked to this erosion of the American middle class.

## Findings from the 2000 Census

A change in income distribution is neither bad nor good, per se. If the number of low-income households were falling, while the numbers of middle-income and high-income households were increasing, this would be a welcome change. And, while an increase in the number of high-income households may be a sign of prosperity, it may also portend societal problems if, at the same time, the number of low-income households is not declining. That is precisely what the 2000 Census data show. While the number of middle-income households was dropping precipitously, and the number of high-income households was increasing, the number of low-income households was also increasing—by 5.3 households—a 14 percent increase.

The increase in the number of well-off families in 2000 comes both from some middle-income households in 1990 improving their earnings as well as the arrival of well-paid foreign professionals. In fiscal year 2000, about 14 percent of immigrants admitted for permanent residence aged 20–64 was composed of professionals, executives and management. The increase in low-income households in 2000 is fueled largely by the influx of relatively unskilled and unschooled foreigners, both legally and illegally in the country. The 2000 Census data show that more than 70 percent of the society was composed of the wealthy and the poor, and poor households (41.5%) outnumbered the wealthy (29%). This greater economic polarization coincides with changes in the pattern of immigrant settlement.

With immigrants disproportionately swelling the numbers of households at the bottom of the socio-economic structure, this may have significant societal implications beyond the fiscal burden that it represents. This growing stratification in our society is making it resemble more the economic disparity in Third World countries, except, of course, that the well-off population here is much broader than in the Third World. It should be kept in mind that, in many of these stratified societies, this inequality has engendered resentment towards the wealthy by those who make only a fraction of the wages. In the United States, there is also evidence of increasing political mobilization, and in some cases criminality, among those who see only a limited prospect for upward mobility and by children who see their parents failing to achieve the American dream.

> *"The current wave of immigrant settlement is inextricably linked to [the] erosion of the American middle class."*

One approach to analyzing income inequality focuses on the difference between the extremes of the wealthy and the impoverished. The Gini index is a mathematical tool developed to measure the difference between these extremes. Our focus is not, however, on the extremes of high- and low-income households, but rather on what is happening to the middle class and how that relates to changes in the concentration of immigrants. Nevertheless, it should be noted that the Gini index has documented a steadily rising trend in inequality from a low point in 1968 up to the present. That trend in greater inequality coincides with the upward trend in immigrant settlement—both legal and illegal—unleashed by the Immigration Act of 1965. Recent research has shown the connection between increased immigrant settlement and increased income inequality as measured by the Gini index.

## Changing the National Income Structure

Immigration is one of the factors fueling the change in the income structure in our country. As noted in the seminal study of the effects of immigration by the National Research Council (NRC), immigration is composed largely of some high-wage earners and many more low-wage earners. For that reason, it tends to add to the high-wage earning population as well as the ranks of low-wage earners. In addition, the NRC study concluded that immigration tends to boost the wealth accumulation by the wealthiest, while undermining the wages of the nation's poorest workers. As the supply of labor available for a specific job increases, there is less incentive for employers to offer higher wages to attract new workers, and wages tend to stagnate or fall.

As the NRC's press release on the study noted: "Wages of native-born Americans with less than a high school education who compete with immigrants may have fallen some five percent over the past 15 years because of this competition." This trend of wage depression or suppression is well documented in sectors of the economy such as seasonal crop agriculture, food processing and janitorial services, and it is marked by employers increasingly claiming that they cannot find Americans to do these jobs as the wages fall.

In a study of the relationship between immigration and income inequality in California, Public Policy Institute of California researcher Deborah Reed concluded that, "Of the factors examined . . . rising returns to skill and immigration account for 44 percent of the rising income inequality in California." Furthermore, the study noted that there is greater income inequality in California in comparison to the rest of the country and it concluded that, "The study found that virtually all of the difference in income inequality between the state and the rest of the nation in 1989 was due to immigration."

To examine the interrelationship between changes in middle-income households and immigration, we looked at Census data for the country as a whole [and] at the trend among the 50 states and the District of Columbia. We found evidence of the coinciding trends of increasing immigrant shares and declining middle-income household shares in each of these analyses.

## Immigrant Shares of Income

When 2000 Census data for Washington, D.C., and the 27 states with foreign-born population shares higher than five percent are arranged in order of ascending middle-income shares, a trend becomes evident. The states with the larger foreign-born shares tend to be the same states with the smaller middle-income shares of their population (i.e., higher immigration coincides with lower middle-income households).

*"Greater economic polarization coincides with changes in the pattern of immigrant settlement."*

As the array of middle-income shares among the 28 localities rises from 24.8 percent (District of Columbia) to 34.1 percent (Utah), the trend is downward in the corresponding foreign-born shares of the population. The range drops from about 16 percent, coinciding with the lowest middle-income shares, to about five percent, coinciding with the highest middle-income shares.

In other words, where the lowest middle-income shares of the population are found, the highest immigrant shares of the population are also likely to be found. The question then is, does this trend also hold true in reverse? Where the highest immigrant shares are found, does that result in the lowest shares of the middle-income population?

It does. This same trend may be seen in reverse when the data are arranged by descending order for the foreign-born share for the same 28 localities. As the foreign-born share decreases from 26.2 percent (California) to five percent (Idaho), the trend in the middle-income household level rises, from about 28 percent to about 32 percent of all households (i.e., lower immigration coincides with higher middle-income shares).

> *"Immigration is one of the factors fueling the change in the income structure in our country."*

The fact that lower middle-income shares tend to coincide with higher immigrant concentrations, and vice versa, does not necessarily mean that one caused the other. It is possible that immigrants may be attracted to areas of relatively high concentrations of low-income households, although this seems unlikely if the object of the illegal immigration is to seek job opportunities. Nevertheless, it could result when newly arriving immigrants are drawn to areas where there are already concentrations of earlier immigrants, or where localities encourage illegal residents to settle by the adoption of policies that accommodate them, e.g., providing hiring halls or driver's licenses. However, because most illegal residents and many newly arriving immigrants work in low-wage jobs, it is clear that the settlement of these immigrants contributes to the increase in the share of low-income households.

The 2000 Census data for the states show the inverse relationship between immigrant shares and mid-level income shares. Large immigrant population concentrations tend to coincide with smaller middle-income population shares, and vice versa. This suggests that during a period of rapidly increasing immigrant settlement, like the present, it could be expected that there would be a decrease in the share of middle-income households.

## Changes in the Middle-Income Share

When Census data for middle-income household shares in 1990 are compared with the similar, inflation-adjusted shares for 2000, it may be seen that the middle-income shares tend to rise in both years as the foreign-born share becomes smaller.

In 2000, as the foreign-born share decreases (from California to Kansas), the trend for the middle-income share rises from less than 28 percent to about 32 percent. In 1990, the corresponding trend in the middle-income share was an increase from about 33 percent to about 35 percent of the households.

It is noteworthy that the middle-income household shares are consistently lower in 2000 than in 1990 after each of these 28 jurisdictions had experienced an increase in foreign-born settlement. It also may be seen that the decrease in middle-income household shares between 1990 and 2000 tended to be some-what greater in states where the increase in both the foreign-born share and the number largest.

The data reveal that while all states experienced a drop in the share of middle-income earners, states with higher levels of immigration had more dramatic de-creases. The amount of decrease in the middle-income shares tended to be greater among the states already with large foreign-born populations (averaging a 4.5% drop in middle-income household shares among the top ten high foreign-born share states) than it was among states with lower shares (averaging a 3.9% drop in middle-income shares for the ten lowest with the lowest foreign-born shares).

## Low-Income Households

A look at the change in the shares of low-income households between 1990 and 2000 shows that the segment of the population did not fare as well in high-immigration states as in low-immigration states. When the share of households in the low-income range (less than about two times the poverty level) is com-pared using 1990 and 2000 Census data, the high-immigration states show an increase not only in the number of low-income households but also in the share of such households (i.e., more immigration coincides with more low-income families).

On average, the high-immigration states increased the average share of low-income households by about one percentage point and the number of such households by more than 2.5 million (15.6%). Conversely, the low-immigration states saw the average share of low-income households decrease even though the number of low-income households was increasing.

In 1990, the ten states with the highest immigrant shares had smaller shares of low-income households than the states with the lowest immigrant shares (38.6% compared to 40.5%).

By 2000 the number of low-income households in the high-immigration states had increased by 18.5 percent, and the share of those households had increased to an average of 39.5 percent of all households. Over the same period, the share of low-income households in the ten states with the lowest immigration shares had fallen to 39.6 percent even though the num-ber of those low-income households had increased by 11 percent (i.e., lower immigration coincided with less increase in low-income households).

> *"Immigration tends to boost the wealth accumulation by the wealthiest, while undermining the wages of the nation's poorest workers."*

The data show that the share of the foreign-born population increased across the board between 1990 and 2000. The low-income share of the population decreased in six of the ten low-immigration states. Over the same period, the share of low-income households rose in states with the largest immigrant populations, but fell in others with lower immigrant shares. The low-income share rose overall because the increase was greater in states that had large low-income shares than in states that had smaller low-income shares.

Nationally, between 1990 and 2000, the number of lower-income households increased by 5.3 million. More than half (50.3%) of that increase occurred in seven states: California (709,209), Florida (538,128), Texas (442,008), New York (362,899), North Carolina (219,601), Georgia (208,832), and Arizona (196,680). An additional ten states had increases of more than 100,000 lower-income households, and, when they were added to the first seven, the 17 accounted for nearly three-quarters (74.1%) of the national total increase in lower-income households. The additional ten were: Pennsylvania (157,195), Virginia (157,151), New Jersey (146,900), Tennessee (142,809), South Carolina (123,210), Maryland (113,559), Ohio (111,126), Washington (110,607), Massachusetts (104,932), and Nevada (101,510).

The bulk of the increase in the foreign-born population over the 1990s occurred in the same states. The seven states that accounted for the largest increases in low-income households also accounted for more than three-fifths (60.9%) of the 11.3 million increase in immigrant residents over the decade. The additional ten states, when added to the first seven, together accounted for nearly four-fifths (79.1%) of the total increase in immigrants. There were, however, exceptions to this parallel trend. Colorado, Illinois, Michigan, Minnesota, and Oregon all had increases of more than 100,000 in their foreign-born populations during the 1990s. And, while each of them also had increases in the number of low-income households, unlike the above 17 states they experienced decreases in the share of low-income households over the decade. . . .

> *"Low-income households . . . did not fare as well in high-immigration states as in low-immigration states."*

## Drawing Conclusions

The above analysis and the earlier study of 1990 Census data indicate that the trend of a decreasing share of middle-income households is likely to continue as long as mass immigration and lax immigration law enforcement continue.

While the increase in the immigrant population could be curbed by stemming the flow of illegal immigration, now estimated to add about a half-million new illegal residents each year, there is little indication that the Bush Administration or Congress are prepared to deal with this problem any more seriously than the Clinton Administration did earlier. In fact, the prospect of the Administration's support for a new guest-worker program that would legitimate the status of illegal alien workers seems likely to attract still others to follow the example of their relatives, friends, and neighbors who earlier came illegally, thus exacerbating the problem. The platforms of all of the contenders for the Democrat nomination suggest an even greater readiness to bend the immigration laws to accommodate aliens illegally in the country.

> *"The unpleasant truth is that the present rate of legal immigration has been a boon to employers and a disaster for low-income workers."*

Similarly, there is little evidence that either the Administration or the Congress is prepared to deal with the nation's currently out-of-control legal immigration structure. After choosing to lay aside the 1995 recommendations of the U.S. Commission on Immigration Reform—the Jordan Commission—for a restructuring and reduction in legal immigration, the Congress has shown little indication of being prepared to address the issue.

Immigration has grown to immoderate proportions since being unleashed in 1965. From averaging less than 300,000 per year in the early 1960s, immigration—legal and illegal—has zoomed to about 1.4 million per year (more than one million legal admissions in both fiscal years 2001 and 2002). Some of this increase is due to amnesty-type provisions for groups of illegal immigrants and programs such as the visa lottery system. Another contributing factor is the numerically uncapped family reunification immigration.

If neither the expanding immigrant settlement nor the composition of it is changed, characterized by large numbers of poorly educated and largely unskilled persons, it is reasonable to expect that this immigrant flow will also continue to add to the ranks of low-income households

What this trend means in terms of the workforce is a greater separation between high-education, high-skills, high-wage workers on the high end of the scale and the limited-education, limited-skills, low-wage workers on the low end of the scale. The erosion of the middle ground between these extremes means fewer opportunities at a seamless upward mobility.

In a society that continues to espouse egalitarian principles and hold upward mobility as an opportunity for all, a growing abyss between the shibboleth and the practice of upward mobility may lead to increasing resentment and frustration. The growing settlement of foreign newcomers who compete for job opportunities with earlier immigrants and others in the nation's most disadvantaged segment of the population, increased social tensions and conflict may be expected.

As UCLA Professor William A.V. Clark has commented, "Conflict takes many forms, from disagreement generated by prejudice to tensions arising from conflict over jobs and political power. At the extreme, the 1992 [Los Angeles] riots were a volatile manifestation of minority/majority conflict and of interethnic conflict. Race and ethnic relations are much more complicated today than they were in the 1960s and 1970s, when the debates revolved around outlawing segregation and creating equal opportunities for blacks. Today's conflict has four subdimensions: cultural differences, racial and interethnic tension, economic conflict, and political power struggles. Each of these is intertwined with recent immigration."

Finally, it must be noted that the trend of increasing legal and illegal immigration and a declining middle class need not be accepted as inevitable. To the extent that today's mass immigration is contributing to the greater income stratification, that process can be arrested and reversed by changing the nation's immigration policy. Such a change is long overdue. The American public has long believed that illegal immigration must be stopped and that legal immigration should be lowered. The blue-ribbon Jordan Commission offered a detailed blueprint for bringing immigration policy more into line with the public's expectations. But Congress has yet to adopt the document verification system the Commission recommended as the key reform to deny jobs to illegal workers and, thereby, deter illegal immigration, and it has yet to seriously address the issue of legal immigration reform and reduction.

Advocacy of lower immigration is not a partisan position, nor is it either conservative or liberal. It does tend, however, to segment along socio-economic lines, with better-educated, and wealthier Americans favoring the status quo. As shown above, they are the ones who are benefiting from the current trend, to the disadvantage of middle and lower income segments of the population.

Author, and social commentator Michael Lind noted in 1998 that, "The unpleasant truth is that the present rate of legal immigration has been a boon to employers and a disaster for low-income workers. It is time for progressives to take the issue back . . . and advocate an immigration policy that keeps the interests of the working class, not the business class, in mind."

Lind's focus was on immigration's impact on working class families, but the trend he identified affects middle-income families too, and immigration reformers must keep that in mind.

# Canadian Immigration Contributes to International Terrorism

by John Berlau

**About the author:** *John Berlau is an investigative writer for* Insight, *a news-magazine.*

On Sept. 19, 2001, in the Chicago suburb of Justice, Ill., U.S. authorities made the first major arrest in connection with the [September 11, 2001, terrorist] attacks on the World Trade Center and the Pentagon. Nabil al-Marabh technically was taken into custody on the basis of immigration and parole violations, but authorities believe he may have played a major role in coordinating the terrorist strikes.

Telephone records showed al-Marabh made telephone calls to at least two of the 19 members of [terrorist leader] Osama bin Laden's al-Qaeda [terrorist] team who commandeered the planes used to kill more than 3,000 people. According to newspaper reports, al-Marabh also is suspected of providing the terrorists with cash and fake IDs. He had been a coworker at a Boston taxi company and shared a residence with Raed Hijazi, an alleged al-Qaeda operative now in prison in Jordan on charges that he planned to bomb a luxury hotel in Amman [Jordan] during the 2000 millennium celebration. Sketches of an airport flight line, including aircraft and runways, were found at a Detroit [Michigan] apartment al-Marabh had shared with three other men who also were arrested, according to the Cox News Service.

This wasn't the first time al-Marabh, apparently born in Kuwait in 1966, had been arrested in the United States. In fact, in an incident that has terrorism experts shaking their heads, he had been in custody less than three months before his Sept. 19 arrest. On June 27, 2001, a U.S. border guard in Niagara Falls, N.Y., found al-Marabh in the back of a tractor-trailer trying to sneak across the border with a fake Canadian passport.

# Facing Justice?

How did the U.S. government bungle this one? To a large extent, another government mostly is to blame. The biggest U.S. mistake appears to have been sending al-Marabh back across the border to face "justice" in Canada. Despite the fact that he had been deported from Canada in 1994, had been found guilty of stabbing a man in the leg in Boston and had known ties to al-Qaeda's Hijazi, a Canadian judge released him after his uncle posted bail of $7,500 Canadian currency, or about $4,500 U.S. Al-Marabh did not so much as attend his deportation hearing and found his way back to the United States.

Even after Sept. 11, Canada's minister of immigration, Elinor Caplan, defended the judge's decision and said it was in line with Canada's policies. "We do not detain people on whispers or innuendo," she told Detroit television station WDIV a month after the terrorist attacks.

# A Haven for Terrorists

Terrorism experts and a growing number of concerned Canadians contend that the al-Marabh incident is just one more indication of why Canada has become a haven for terrorists. "We've got a lot of blood on our hands worldwide," says David Harris, former chief of strategic planning for the Canadian Security Intelligence Service (CSIS), Canada's top intelligence agency. Harris tells *Insight*, "If some can say the Americans were asleep at the switch prior to the 11th of September, we've been in a coma."

In 1998 the director of CSIS told a special committee of the Canadian Parliament that members of more than 50 international terrorist groups were living there. "With perhaps the singular exception of the United States, there are more international terrorist groups active here than in any other country," testified CSIS Director Ward Elcock. "Terrorist groups are present here whose origins lie in virtually every significant regional, ethnic and nationalist conflict there is."

The CSIS elaborated in 1999. "For a number of reasons, Canada is an attractive venue for terrorists," said a CSIS report. "Long borders and coastlines offer many points of entry which can facilitate movement to and from various sites around the world, particularly the United States."

But there is another reason experts say Canada has become attractive to terrorists—one which went unspoken by the CSIS. That is, Canada's highly permissive immigration and refugee policies. With a population of about 30 million, Canada takes in about

*"Canada has become a haven for terrorists."*

300,000 newcomers per year, which per capita is twice the rate at which immigrants are admitted to the United States. And there virtually are no restrictions on the countries from which they come.

According to Harris, now president of Insignis Strategic Research, "The tidal wave of new people coming here, the vast majority of whom are going to be great contributors to the country one assumes, has got to statistically include a really significant number of very, very dangerous people in today's world who cannot possibly be screened out in any meaningful sense. We are presenting ourselves year after year with a building danger and menace, and if we refuse to deal with the menace represented by the sheer statistics, we're going to inevitably find ourselves in a situation where the government will have to impose more and more restrictions on our civil liberties."

## Raising Funds to Support Terrorism

Terrorists also find Canada an ideal place for raising funds, critics say, because before the al-Qaeda attacks on the United States there were very few laws there to prevent the funneling of money to extremist organizations in foreign lands. "Before Sept. 11, you could have opened up a storefront in Toronto and said, 'I'm raising money for bin Laden; and you could have collected money, and nobody could have charged you because that was not against the law," Stewart Bell, a reporter for the Toronto-based *National Post*, tells *Insight*. Bell, who has broken many stories about terrorist connections through Canada, says: "There was no law against raising money for terrorism. Now there's a law, but it's not being used yet."

> *"Terrorists . . . find Canada an ideal place for raising funds."*

This means that, even without crossing the border, terrorists still can use Canada as a base from which to damage the United States and other countries.

Some of the most damaging support for terrorists that al-Marabh is alleged to have provided may have been conducted in Canada. According to the Canadian television network CTV, authorities say the unemployed Islamist moved about $15,000 from a Canadian bank account to at least three of the hijackers. He is believed to have made fake IDs for the hijackers at a Toronto print shop where he worked. Authorities found similarities between the fake IDs left at the hijackers' homes and the paper stock, laminates and ink seized from the print shop, CTV reported.

## A Lax Refugee Policy

Like many other Canadian residents connected with acts of terrorism, al-Marabh arrived in the country as a refugee claimant, and some say his case illustrates what is wrong with the immigration system there. Immigration scholars such as George Borjas have praised Canadian policy for actively seeking skilled immigrants who can help the national economy, although some Canadians dispute just how many are "skilled" as advertised and how much their presence benefits the economy. The problem, Harris and others say, is that Canada admits practically anyone who claims to be a refugee and does so in unlimited numbers. "We take a lot of people that no one else would accept," Martin Collacott, Canada's former ambassador to Syria and Lebanon and a senior fellow at the Vancouver-based Fraser Institute, tells *Insight:* "We have stretched the definition [of refugee] far beyond the original intent in the U.N. Convention on Refugees. We also have the most generous system of perks."

Because of a Canadian Supreme Court decision in the mid-1980s, everyone who comes to Canada and claims to be a refugee is entitled to a hearing, even if they have no documentation. The Canadian government provides them with a free lawyer and, while awaiting the government's decision,

> *"Canadian connections have been found in a host of terrorist incidents."*

refugee claimants are eligible for welfare and/or employment, are covered by Canada's national healthcare system, may attend school and only rarely are detained, as they often are in the United States.

The generosity of these perquisites combined with freedom of movement has attracted the attention of terrorists targeting the United States. The process for determining refugee status can take years. And even if a refugee claim is denied, claimants often stay in Canada by declaring that a return to their country of origin will put them in danger. Al-Marabh came to Canada in 1988. His refugee claim wasn't denied until 1994 and he had no trouble reentering in 2001.

Mahmoud Mohammad is a convicted terrorist and murderer from the Popular Front for the Liberation of Palestine who hijacked an Israeli airliner, served time in Greece and was released as part of demands by another group of hijackers. Then he entered Canada in 1986 with a false identity. He soon was arrested and ordered deported, but he filed suit and remains in Canada today—16 years later—and runs a small candy store in Ontario.

The number of refugee claimants in Canada has doubled from 22,000 in 1998 to 44,000 in 2001. The *Toronto Sun* reports that official records show as many as 60 percent of refugee claimants have unsatisfactory documents or none at all. Many just "disappear" and are believed to have entered the United States illegally. In a paper for the U.S.-based Center for Immigration Studies, James Bissett, the former executive director of Canada's immigration service, reports that 20 percent of refugee claimants in Canada never even show up for their asylum hearings, and there are more than 25,000 outstanding arrest warrants for them. "It is evident, therefore, that the chances of remaining in Canada despite a negative ruling [for refugee status] are favorable," Bissett writes, with dry wit. "Naturally, this is a major selling point" for terrorists.

## The Canadian Connection

Canadian connections have been found in a host of terrorist incidents. Conspirators who had lived in Canada were involved in the first World Trade Center bombing in 1993 and the Khobar Towers bombing in Saudi Arabia in 1996. A Canadian-refugee claimant also played a role in a foiled plot that could have been as devastating as the attacks of Sept. 11. In 1994 Ahmed Ressam came to

Montreal as a refugee claimant, using a fake French passport. After failing to show up for his refugee hearing and "disappearing" he was arrested by a U.S. Customs agent in December 1999 as he tried to cross the U.S. border from Vancouver with 100 pounds of explosives in his car trunk.

Ressam turned out to be a member of an Algerian terrorist group with close ties to bin Laden and planned to bomb Los Angeles International Airport during celebrations for the year 2000. He was convicted in a Los Angeles courtroom in April 2001.

Terrorism experts say Canadian law enforcement is not the problem. The CSIS and the Royal Canadian Mounted Police courageously have warned about the threat of terrorism and provided crucial help going after al-Marabh, says Steven Emerson, executive director of the Investigative Project, a counter-terrorism think tank in Washington. The problem is that they're being handcuffed by politicians afraid of offending voters in ethnic communities, he argues. "There's a tremendously polarized situation between the 'refugee lobby,' which includes advocates of some of the government policies, versus the law-enforcement and intelligence services."

> *"Many [Canadian] leaders ... appear to be in denial about their country's contribution to international terrorism."*

And many of the leaders from Canada's ruling Liberal Party still appear to be in denial about their country's contribution to international terrorism. Longtime Prime Minister Jean Chretien stood in the House of Commons shortly after Sept. 11 and proclaimed, "I am not aware at this time of a cell known to the police to be operating in Canada with the intention of carrying out terrorism in Canada or elsewhere." Perhaps the many CSIS reports and lengthy testimony documenting the terrorist presence in Canada did not reach his desk.

When members of the conservative Canadian Alliance Party ask questions in Parliament about refugee policies that contribute to terrorism, they are shouted down as anti-immigrant and racist by Liberal Party members. This is despite the fact, as Bell has documented in the *National Post*, that ethnic communities sometimes are the first victims of terrorist shakedown and extortion efforts to raise money.

## Changing Canadian Policies

After Sept. 11, under pressure from the United States and a shocked Canadian public, Parliament finally attempted to outlaw terrorist fund-raising. The government responded by banning fund-raising only for Hezbollah's military purposes but not for its "social" and "political" wings, a distinction many say is without a difference. [The terrorist group] Hezbollah, based in Lebanon, takes credit for suicide bombings in Israel and it bombed U.S. Marine barracks in Lebanon in 1983. It is formally cited as a terrorist organization by both London and Washington. But Canada's foreign-affairs minister, Bill Graham, explained in Parliament in April [2002] that "there is a civil dimension" to Hezbollah, adding: "We will continue to work with all parties with whom we can get peace."

Meanwhile, Hezbollah is free to funnel money from its "charitable contributions" in Canada to its worldwide terrorist activities. Says Harris, "The Canadian Boy Scouts have a demonstrably favorable record of good works, but if some arm of that group ever starts blowing up major public buildings, I reserve my right to question their entitlement to collect funds on Canadian territory. It's this kind of thing that's surely got to be raising significant questions among our allies."

Since Sept. 11, Canada has allocated $200 million to improve its screening of foreigners, a fact that Canada's leaders point to when called on the carpet by victims of terrorism. But former immigration-service head Bissett says the ongoing policy of generous perks plus freedom of movement for refugee claimants with shoddy paperwork essentially is unchanged. In fact, he says, a recently passed law advertised as streamlining the process may make it even more generous to potential terrorists.

Before the new law was passed, the Canadian courts had the discretion to choose which refugee cases would be heard on appeal if a claimant was denied refugee status. But under the Immigration and Refugee Protection Act, appeals now will be heard automatically, adding another layer to the already-lengthy process to deport terrorists and other inappropriate immigrants. "It's just made the whole process a hell of a lot easier for a claimant to make his claim and be accepted, and extremely difficult to get rid of them once they're here," Bissett tells *Insight*. He says the new law "reflects an attitude of complacency and cynicism on the part of a government that appears less concerned about the security of its citizens than in satisfying the demands of special interests."

# Immigration Benefits America

## by Daniel T. Griswold

**About the author:** *Daniel T. Griswold, associate director of the CATO Institute's Center for Trade Policy Studies, specializes in the economic effects of international trade and immigration.* His articles have appeared in the Wall Street Journal, *the* Los Angeles Times, *and other major publications.*

Immigration always has been controversial in the United States. More than two centuries ago, Benjamin Franklin worried that too many German immigrants would swamp America's predominantly British culture. In the mid-1800s, Irish immigrants were scorned as lazy drunks, not to mention Roman Catholics. At the turn of the century a wave of "new immigrants"—Poles, Italians, Russian Jews—were believed to be too different ever to assimilate into American life. Today the same fears are raised about immigrants from Latin America and Asia, but current critics of immigration are as wrong as their counterparts were in previous eras.

Immigration is not undermining the American experiment; it is an integral part of it. We are a nation of immigrants. Successive waves of immigrants have kept our country demographically young, enriched our culture and added to our productive capacity as a nation, enhancing our influence in the world.

## Providing an Economic Edge

Immigration gives the United States an economic edge in the world economy. Immigrants bring innovative ideas and entrepreneurial spirit to the U.S. economy. They provide business contacts to other markets, enhancing America's ability to trade and invest profitably in the global economy. They keep our economy flexible, allowing U.S. producers to keep prices down and to respond to changing consumer demands. An authoritative 1997 study by the National Academy of Sciences (NAS) concluded that immigration delivered a "significant positive gain" to the U.S. economy. In testimony before Congress [in 2001], Federal Reserve Board Chairman Alan Greenspan said, "I've always argued that this country has benefited immensely from the fact that we draw people from all over the world."

Contrary to popular myth, immigrants do not push Americans out of jobs. Immigrants tend to fill jobs that Americans cannot or will not fill, mostly at the high and low ends of the skill spectrum. Immigrants are disproportionately represented in such high-skilled fields as medicine, physics and computer science, but also in lower-skilled sectors such as hotels and restaurants, domestic service, construction and light manufacturing.

> *"Immigration is not undermining the American experiment; it is an integral part of it."*

Immigrants also raise demand for goods as well as the supply. During the long boom of the 1990s, and especially in the second half of the decade, the national unemployment rate fell below 4 percent and real wages rose up and down the income scale during a time of relatively high immigration.

Nowhere is the contribution of immigrants more apparent than in the high-technology and other knowledge-based sectors. Silicon Valley and other high-tech sectors would cease to function if we foolishly were to close our borders to skilled and educated immigrants. These immigrants represent human capital that can make our entire economy more productive. Immigrants have developed new products, such as the Java computer language, that have created employment opportunities for millions of Americans.

Immigrants are not a drain on government finances. The NAS study found that the typical immigrant and his or her offspring will pay a net $80,000 more in taxes during their lifetimes than they collect in government services. For immigrants with college degrees, the net fiscal return is $198,000. It is true that low-skilled immigrants and refugees tend to use welfare more than the typical "native" household, but the 1996 Welfare Reform Act made it much more difficult for newcomers to collect welfare. As a result, immigrant use of welfare has declined in recent years along with overall welfare rolls.

## The Numbers

Despite the claims of immigration opponents, today's flow is not out of proportion to historical levels. Immigration in the last decade has averaged about 1 million per year, high in absolute numbers, but the rate of 4 immigrants per year per 1,000 U.S. residents is less than half the rate during the Great Migration of 1890–1914. Today, about 10 percent of U.S. residents are foreign-born, an increase from 4.7 percent in 1970, but still far short of the 14.7 percent who were foreign-born in 1910.

Nor can immigrants fairly be blamed for causing "overpopulation." America's annual population growth of 1 percent is below our average growth rate of the last century. In fact, without immigration our labor force would begin to shrink within two decades. According to the 2000 Census, 22 percent of U.S. counties lost population between 1990 and 2000. Immigrants could help revitalize demographically declining areas of the country, just as they helped revitalize New York City and other previously declining urban centers.

## The National Security Question

Drastically reducing the number of foreigners who enter the United States each year only would compound the economic damage of [the terrorist attacks of] Sept. 11 [2001] while doing nothing to enhance our security. The tourist industry, already reeling, would lose millions of foreign visitors, and American universities would lose hundreds of thousands of foreign students if our borders were closed.

Obviously the U.S. government should "control its borders" to keep out anyone who intends to commit terrorist acts. The problem is not that we are letting too many people into the United States but that the government has failed to keep the wrong people out. We can stop terrorists from entering the United States without closing our borders or reducing the number of hardworking, peaceful immigrants who settle here.

We must do whatever is necessary to stop potentially dangerous people at the border. Law-enforcement and intelligence agencies must work

> *"Immigrants represent human capital that can make our entire economy more productive."*

closely with the State Department, the Immigration and Naturalization Service (INS) and U.S. Customs to share real-time information about potential terrorists. Computer systems must be upgraded and new technologies adopted to screen out the bad guys without causing intolerable delays at the border. More agents need to be posted at ports of entry to more thoroughly screen for high-risk travelers. We must bolster cooperation with our neighbors, Canada and Mexico, to ensure that terrorists cannot slip across our long land borders.

In the wake of Sept. 11, longtime critics of immigration have tried to exploit legitimate concerns about security to argue for drastic cuts in immigration. But border security and immigration are two separate matters. Immigrants are only a small subset of the total number of foreigners who enter the United States every year. Only about one of every 25 foreign nationals who enter the United States come here to immigrate. The rest are tourists, business travelers, students and Mexicans and Canadians who cross the border for a weekend to shop or visit family and then return home with no intention of settling permanently in the United States.

The 19 terrorists who attacked the United States on Sept. 11 did not apply to the INS to immigrate or to become U.S. citizens. Like most aliens who enter the United States, they were here on temporary tourist and student visas. We could reduce the number of immigrants to zero and still not stop terrorists from slipping into the country on nonimmigrant visas.

## Patrolling U.S. Borders

To defend ourselves better against terrorism, our border-control system requires a reorientation of mission. For the last two decades, U.S. immigration policy has been obsessed with nabbing mostly Mexican-born workers whose only "crime" is their desire to earn an honest day's pay. Those workers pose no threat to national security.

Our land border with Mexico is half as long as our border with Canada, yet before Sept. 11 it was patrolled by 10 times as many border agents. On average we were posting an agent every five miles along our 3,987-mile border with Canada and every quarter-mile on the 2,000-mile border with Mexico. On the Northern border there were 120,000 entries per year per agent compared with 40,000 entries on the Southwestern border. This is out of proportion to any legitimate fears about national security. In fact terrorists seem to prefer the Northern border. Let's remember that it was at a border-crossing station in Washington state in December 1999 that a terrorist was apprehended with explosives that were to be used to blow up Los Angeles International Airport during the millennium celebrations.

At a February 2000 hearing, former Sen. Slade Gorton (R-Wash.) warned that "understaffing at our northern border is jeopardizing the security of our nation, not to mention border personnel, while in at least some sections of the southern border, there are so many agents that there is not enough work to keep them all busy."

We should stop wasting scarce resources in a self-destructive quest to hunt down Mexican construction workers and raid restaurants and chicken-processing plants, and redirect those resources to back potential terrorists and smash their cells before they can blow up more buildings and kill more Americans.

For all these reasons, President George W. Bush's initiative to legalize and regularize the movement of workers across the U.S.-Mexican border makes sense in terms of national security as well as economics. It also is politically smart.

> *"Immigrants could help revitalize demographically declining areas of the country."*

In his latest book, *The Death of the West*, Pat Buchanan argues that opposing immigration will be a winning formula for conservative Republicans. His own political decline and fall undermine his claim. Like former liberal Republican Gov. Pete Wilson in California, Buchanan has tried to win votes by blaming immigration for America's problems. But voters wisely rejected Buchanan's thesis. Despite $12 million in taxpayer campaign funds, and an assist from the Florida butterfly ballot,[1] Buchanan won less than 0.5 percent of the presidential vote in 2000. In contrast, Bush, by affirming immigration, raised the GOP's share of the Hispanic vote to 35 percent from the 21 percent carried by Bob Dole in 1996. If conservatives adopt the anti-immigrant message, they risk following Buchanan and Wilson into political irrelevancy.

It would be a national shame if, in the name of security, we closed the door to immigrants who come here to work, save and build a better life for themselves and their families. Immigrants come here to live the American Dream; terrorists come to destroy it. We should not allow America's tradition of welcoming immigrants to become yet another casualty of Sept. 11.

1. A butterfly ballot refers to a ballot paper that has candidate names down both sides with punch holes in the center. Some Florida voters claimed the ballot design was confusing.

# The Benefits of Immigration Outweigh the Disadvantages

**by Frances Cairncross**

**About the author:** *Frances Cairncross, an expert on technology and its impact on society, is senior editor at the* Economist, *chair of Britain's Economic and Social Research Council, and author of* The Death of Distance, *a study of the economic and social effects of the global communications revolution.*

"With two friends I started a journey to Greece, the most horrendous of all journeys. It had all the details of a nightmare: barefoot walking in rough roads, risking death in the dark, police dogs hunting us, drinking water from the rain pools in the road and a rude awakening at gunpoint from the police under a bridge. My parents were terrified and decided that it would be better to pay someone to hide me in the back of a car."

This 16-year-old Albanian high-school drop-out, desperate to leave his impoverished country for the nirvana of clearing tables in an Athens restaurant, might equally well have been a Mexican heading for Texas or an Algerian youngster sneaking into France. He had the misfortune to be born on the wrong side of a line that now divides the world: the line between those whose passports allow them to move and settle reasonably freely across the richer world's borders, and those who can do so only hidden in the back of a truck, and with forged papers.

Tearing down that divide would be one of the fastest ways to boost global economic growth. The gap between labour's rewards in the poor world and the rich, even for something as menial as clearing tables, dwarfs the gap between the prices of traded goods from different parts of the world. The potential gains from liberalising migration therefore dwarf those from removing barriers to world trade. But those gains can be made only at great political cost. Countries

Frances Cairncross, "The Longest Journey," *The Economist*, vol. 365, November 2, 2002. Copyright © 2002 by The Economist Newspaper Ltd., www.economist.com. All rights reserved. Reproduced by permission.

rarely welcome strangers into their midst.

Everywhere, international migration has shot up the list of political concerns. The horror of [the terrorist attacks of] September 11th [2001] has toughened America's approach to immigrants, especially students from Muslim countries, and blocked the [immigration] agreement being negotiated with Mexico. In Europe, the far right has flourished in elections in Austria, Denmark and the Netherlands. In Australia, the plight of the *Tampa*[1] and its human cargo made asylum a top issue [in 2001].

## The Forces Favoring Immigration

Although many more immigrants arrive legally than hidden in trucks or boats, voters fret that governments have lost control of who enters their country. The result has been a string of measures to try to tighten and enforce immigration rules. But however much governments clamp down, both immigration and immigrants are here to stay. Powerful economic forces are at work. It is impossible to separate the globalisation of trade and capital from the global movement of people. Borders will leak; companies will want to be able to move staff; and liberal democracies will balk at introducing the draconian measures required to make controls truly watertight. If the European Union admits ten new members, it will eventually need to accept not just their goods but their workers too.

Technology also aids migration. The fall in transport costs has made it cheaper to risk a trip, and cheap international telephone calls allow Bulgarians in Spain to tip off their cousins back home that there are fruit-picking jobs available. The United States shares a long border with a developing country; Europe is a bus-ride from the former Soviet bloc and a boat-ride across the Mediterranean from the world's poorest continent. The rich economies create millions of jobs that the underemployed young in the poor world willingly fill. So demand and supply will constantly conspire to undermine even the most determined restrictions on immigration.

For would-be immigrants, the prize is huge. It may include a life free of danger and an escape from ubiquitous corruption, or the hope of a chance for their children. But mainly it comes in the form of an immense

> *"The potential gains from liberalising migration . . . dwarf those from removing barriers to world trade."*

boost to earnings potential. James Smith of Rand, a Californian think-tank, is undertaking a longitudinal survey of recent immigrants to America. Those who get the famous green card, allowing them to work and stay indefinitely, are being asked what they earned before and after. "They gain on average $20,000 a

---

1. On August 28, 2001, the Norwegian cargo-carrier *Tampa*, which also contained a load of 438 refugees of Afghan, Iraqi, and Iranian origin, sought to enter Australian territorial waters. In breach of its international obligations, the Australian authorities detained the *Tampa* refugees, then transferred them to the small island state of Nauru.

year, or $300,000 over a lifetime in net-present-value terms," he reports. "Not many things you do in your life have such an effect."

Such a prize explains not only why the potential gains from liberalising immigration are so great. It explains, too, why so many people try so hard to come—and why immigration is so difficult to control. The rewards to the successful immigrant are often so large, and the penalties for failure so devastating, that they create a huge temptation to take risks, to bend the rules and to lie. That, inevitably, adds to the hostility felt by many rich-world voters.

## A Shift in Attitudes

This hostility is milder in the four countries—the United States, Canada, Australia and New Zealand—that are built on immigration. On the whole, their people accept that a well-managed flow of eager newcomers adds to economic strength and cultural interest. When your ancestors arrived penniless to better themselves, it is hard to object when others want to follow. In Europe and Japan, immigration is new, or feels new, and societies are older and less receptive to change.

Even so, a growing number of European governments now accept that there is an economic case for immigration. This striking change is apparent even in Germany, which has recently been receiving more foreigners, relative to the size of its population, than has America. [In 2001] a commission headed by a leading politician, Rita Sussmuth, began its report with the revolutionary words: "Germany needs immigrants." Recent legislation based on the report

> *"Demand and supply will constantly conspire to undermine even the most determined restrictions on immigration."*

(and hotly attacked by the opposition) streamlines entry procedures.

But there is a gulf between merely accepting the economic case and delighting in the social transformation that immigrants create. Immigrants bring new customs, new foods, new ideas, new ways of doing things. Does that make towns more interesting or more threatening? They enhance baseball and football teams, give a new twang to popular music and open new businesses. Some immigrants transform drifting institutions, as Mexicans have done with American Catholicism, according to Gregory Rodriguez, a Latino journalist in Los Angeles. And some commit disproportionate numbers of crimes.

They also profoundly test a country's sense of itself, forcing people to define what they value. That is especially true in Europe, where many incomers are Muslims. America's 1.2–1.5 million or so Muslim immigrants tend to be better educated and wealthier than Americans in general. Many are Iranians, who fled extremist Islam. By contrast, some of the children of Germany's Turks, Britain's Pakistanis and France's North Africans seem more attracted to fundamentalism than their parents are. If Muslims take their austere religion seriously, is that deplorable or admirable? If Islam constrains women and attacks homosexuality, what are the boundaries to freedom of speech and religion? Even societies that feel at ease with change will find such questions hard.

## The Challenges of Immigration

Immigration poses two main challenges for the rich world's governments. One is how to manage the inflow of migrants; the other, how to integrate those who are already there.

Whom, for example, to allow in? Already, many governments have realised that the market for top talent is global and competitive. Led by Canada and Australia, they are redesigning migration policies not just to admit, but actively to attract highly skilled immigrants. Germany, for instance, tentatively introduced a green card of its own [in August 2000] for information-technology staff—only to find that a mere 12,000 of the available 20,000 visas were taken up. "Given the higher wages and warmer welcome, no Indians in their right minds would rather go to Germany than to the United States," scoffs Susan Martin, an immigration expert at Georgetown University in Washington, DC.

> *"Governments must persuade [voters] that [immigration] is being managed in their interests."*

Whereas the case for attracting the highly skilled is fast becoming conventional wisdom, a thornier issue is what to do about the unskilled. Because the difference in earnings is greatest in this sector, migration of the unskilled delivers the largest global economic gains. Moreover, wealthy, well-educated, ageing economies create lots of jobs for which their own workers have little appetite.

## The Economic Composition of Immigrants

So immigrants tend to cluster at the upper and lower ends of the skill spectrum. Immigrants either have university degrees or no high-school education. Mr Smith's survey makes the point: among immigrants to America, the proportion with a postgraduate education, at 21%, is almost three times as high as in the native population; equally, the proportion with less than nine years of schooling, at 20%, is more than three times as high as that of the native-born (and probably higher still among illegal Mexican immigrants).

All this means that some immigrants do far better than others. The unskilled are the problem. Research by George Borjas, a Harvard University professor whose parents were unskilled Cuban immigrants, has drawn attention to the fact that the unskilled account for a growing proportion of America's foreign-born. (The same is probably true of Europe's.) Newcomers without high-school education not only drag down the wages of the poorest Americans (some of whom are themselves recent immigrants); their children are also disproportionately likely to fail at school.

These youngsters are there to stay. "The toothpaste is out of the tube," says Mark Krikorian, executive director of the Centre for Immigration Studies, a think-tank in Washington, DC. And their numbers will grow. Because the rich world's women spurn motherhood, immigrants give birth to many of the rich world's babies. Foreign mothers account for one birth in five in Switzerland and one in eight in Germany and Britain. If these children grow up underprivileged and undereducated, they will create a new underclass that may take many years to emerge from poverty.

For Europe, immigration creates particular problems. Europe needs it even more than the United States because the continent is ageing faster than any other region. Immigration is not a permanent cure (immigrants grow old too), but it will buy time. And migration can "grease the wheels" of Europe's sclerotic labour markets, argues Tito Boeri in a report for the Fondazione Rodolfo Debenedetti [a European public policy foundation], published in July [2002]. However, thanks to the generosity of Europe's welfare states, migration is also a sort of tax on immobile labour. And the more immobile Europeans are—the older, the less educated—the more xenophobic they are too.

The barriers need to be dismantled with honesty and care. It is no accident that they began to go up when universal suffrage was introduced. Poor voters know that immigration threatens their living standards. And as long as voters believe that immigration is out of control, they will oppose it. Governments must persuade them that it is being managed in their interests.

# Immigrants Are Vital to the U.S. Economy

## by the American Immigration Lawyers Association

**About the author:** *The American Immigration Lawyers Association is a national association of attorneys and law professors who practice and teach immigration law and whose goal is to educate the American people and elected leaders on the many benefits that immigration and immigrants bring to our society and economy.*

Immigrants have been important to the U.S. economy in the past, including the very recent past, and will continue to be vital in the future. Immigrants retain a key role today in America in starting businesses, spending on goods and services that employ natives and immigrants, and working in high technology, hospitality industries, health care, construction, agriculture, and other areas. However, it is particularly important to take a longer-term perspective to understand the vital role that immigration plays in the U.S. economy. In fact, the current discussion about a jobless recovery, or of job losses, obscures recent history and the projected future of American jobs. While the number of jobs has contracted in the past few years, the civilian labor force remains far higher today than it was in 1990, having risen by 15 million between 1990 and 2003, according to the Bureau of Labor Statistics.

It is important to understand that there is no such thing as a fixed number of jobs with everyone competing for and against each other. Immigrants fill jobs but they also create jobs through entrepreneurship, innovations, and purchases of food, housing, cars, and other consumer items. That is why the entry of an immigrant into the labor force should not be viewed as harming a native-born person's employment prospects. Filling jobs in the niches at the low and high end of an economy are one of the characteristics of immigrants. While it is well-known that the U.S. economy will continue to create high-skilled jobs, few realize that current data indicate substantial job growth in occupations that require limited education or training.

# Chapter 1

## The Economic Contributions of Immigrants

While some critics concede that immigration has been beneficial in the past, they argue that it harms the economy today and will do so in the future. However, this allegation ignores that the economic benefits of immigration do not change with fluctuations in the business cycle. . . . In areas such as homeownership, entrepreneurship, and consumer spending, immigrants are assets to the U.S. economy. Census data show that more than 60 percent of immigrants live in owner-occupied homes within 20 years of arriving in America. "In thirteen of the fifteen most populous immigrant groups, two out of three households were owner-occupied after twenty-six years of residence in

> *"Immigrants have been important to the U.S. economy in the past . . . and will continue to be vital in the future."*

the U.S.," according to the National Immigration Forum. Immigrants are as likely or more likely as natives to be self-employed, further creating jobs in the economy. *Inc. Magazine* reported in 1995 that immigrants were overrepresented as owners of the fastest growing corporations, with 12 percent of *Inc.* 500 companies started by immigrants.

Consumer spending is a vital part of the U.S. economy. Datamonitor Consumer Markets projected that Hispanic consumer spending, much of it by recent immigrants, would increase by $340 billion between 2000 and 2007, "to reach at least $926 billion—a 60 percent increase." A study by New America Strategies Group and DemoGraph Corporation "projected Asian Americans to increase average spending 17.7 percent from 1995 to 1998 . . . while Hispanic expenditure growth was 15.5 percent. Whites, meanwhile, spent only 13.7 percent more over the three-year period."

## Examining Economic Studies

The overall economic benefits to the U.S. economy of immigration also have been documented by a variety of studies. Immigrants increase the Gross National Product by $200 billion a year and provide a net economic benefit to natives of $10 billion annually, according to the 1997 National Academy of Sciences (NAS) *New Americans* study. However, that $10 billion figure may be understated. In Congressional testimony, Rand Corporation economist James P. Smith, the chair of the NAS study, stated that "The $10 billion gain is an annual figure. . . . The net present value of the gains from those immigrants who arrived since 1980 would be $333 billion." Net present value (NPV) is "an important assessment which calculates the current value of a future cash flow. NPV is a very useful tool for corporations and government alike in that it allows for a comparison of current costs to . . . potential benefits."

With the downturn in the U.S. economy, . . . some have turned to blaming the foreign-born for diminished job opportunities. There is no empirical evidence to support the belief that immigrants raise the unemployment rates of natives. In releasing the 1997 report, the National Academy of Sciences concluded that "Immigration benefits the U.S. economy overall and has little negative effect on the income and job opportunities of most native-born Americans." The National Academy of Sciences study, while finding there may be some impact of immigration on some African Americans locally, concluded that "While some have suspected that blacks suffer disproportionately from the inflow of low-skilled immigrants, none of the available evidence suggests that they have been particularly hard-hit on a national level."

Several studies have also shown that wage impacts on natives are minimal or isolated. In her study on immigration's impact on the wages and employment of black men, the Urban Institute's Maria E. Enchautegui concluded, "The results show that in the 1980s black men were not doing worse in areas of high immigration than in other areas and that their economic status in high-immigration areas did not deteriorate during that decade." A recent 4-page report from the UCLA Chicano Studies Research Center concluded that Latinos, primarily earlier immigrants, may experience "wage penalties" for being in "brown-collar occupations," those occupations that have a significant percentage of Latinos, including recent Latino immigrant men. However, the policy brief does not explain whether some recent immigrants enter jobs with declining prospects because those are easier jobs to obtain for someone with little or no English language skills or whether there is proof that the entry of the immigrants caused the lower wages. Since the policy brief is based on a longer paper that has yet to be released, it is not possible to draw conclusions as to the validity of the report's findings. Still, the study's author [Lisa Catanzarite] does not call for new immigration restrictions but rather for legalization of undocumented immigrants and states that "The findings . . . by no means endorse the notion that immigration harms natives generally."

> *"In areas such as homeownership, entrepreneurship, and consumer spending, immigrants are assets to the U.S. economy."*

## Answering Questions About Visas

While there has been very little call to restrict legal immigration in the face of the recent economic slowdown, some have complained that corporate outsourcing has increased and that, as a result, some Americans may have lost jobs to foreign-born individuals on temporary visas. The cases have been anecdotal and there is no indication of widespread abuse. In a few of the instances it has been alleged that a U.S. company outsourced information technology (IT) functions to an Indian company that used at least some individuals on L-1 intra-company transfer visas (individuals employed overseas by the foreign company and brought into the United States for a period of time).

L-1 visa holders enter the U.S. on a temporary basis either on an L-1(A) visa for executive or managerial positions or on an L-1(B) visa which requires the employee to possess specialized or advanced knowledge that generally is not found in the particular industry. (Where the specialized knowledge relates to the company's operations, products, procedures, and services, it must be noteworthy or uncommon knowledge.) The L visa is of particular benefit for American business owners who need to transfer employees from foreign affiliates to the United States. Using an L visa to send a foreign national to the United States to work alongside the workforce of a third party, under the control of the third party, performing the same kind of work done by the third entity's employees and displacing U.S. employees is prohibited. Some L visas recently were granted in which the visa holder was assigned at a third party site and was not using specialized knowledge or under the control of the petitioning employer. These visas were erroneously granted and are prohibited by current law and Department of State guidance. In the wake of these erroneously issued L-1 visas, several bills have been introduced that would substantially restrict the use of this visa, which appears to be an overreaction. To the extent a problem exists it appears to be narrow. "It will hurt employment in the United States if we impede the ability of legitimate users to transfer managers and specialists between different affiliates of international organizations," according to attorney Daryl Buffenstein. At a recent Senate Immigration Subcommittee hearing he called for Congress and the Administration to use a "surgical instrument," not a sledgehammer, in crafting any action in this area.

## Labor Force Needs in the United States

Immigration critics allege that the U.S. economy no longer produces jobs that require less than an undergraduate degree. In fact, . . . data show this is far from the truth. Jobs that require only brief or moderate training will constitute a large percentage of jobs to be filled in the United States throughout this decade. Two related factors will contribute to the growth of these types of jobs. First, the aging of the U.S. workforce will leave openings for skilled positions, which will lure more individuals into these higher-paying jobs. Second, at the same time, the aging of the country will create more openings for entertainment, health care, construction and other less skilled jobs.

*"Immigration is a key to solving . . . labor skill shortages."*

It follows that contrary to predictions of the disappearance of lesser and semi-skilled jobs, between 2000 and 2010, more than 33 million new job openings will be created in the United States that require only short-term or moderate-term (1–12 months) training, according to the Bureau of Labor Statistics. This growth will represent 58 percent of all new job openings.

Examples of jobs that will grow significantly in the coming years that require only *short-term training* include nursing aides, orderlies, home health aides, and restaurant workers. Jobs projected for large increases that require only *moderate-term training* include medical assistants, customer service representatives, and drivers of trucks and heavy machinery. Manual labor jobs in construction are projected to increase by 17 percent, with over 200,000 total job openings between 2000 and 2010. Other construction-related jobs, including equipment operators, will increase substantially as well, according to the Bureau of Labor Statistics. Future immigration to the United States will be a key component in filling these and other job needs.

> *"Immigrants have shown an ability to fill manufacturing jobs important to U.S. economic growth."*

## Averting Labor Shortages

The Bureau of Labor Statistics projections are supported by other economic analyses. "During the next 30 years, more than 61 million Americans will retire," according to a report by the Employment Policy Foundation. "If present trends continue, America will experience a labor shortage of 4.8 million workers in 10 years; 19.7 million in 20 years and 35.8 million in 30 years."

The Employment Policy Foundation identified needs at both the high and low end of the job spectrum. "College educated, highly skilled workers also will be in short supply. In 10 years, the labor force will be short 3.6 million workers who will need at least a bachelor's degree. In 20 years, the number will be 10.5 million. In 2031, the workforce could be short as many as 20.4 million college-educated workers."

The Employment Policy Foundation warns of serious ramifications if steps are not taken to address this issue. "Unless these high levels of labor and skills shortage can be averted, the United States will be unable to maintain its historic rate of economic growth." The report goes on to state: "Failure to close the labor supply gap will lower gross domestic product (GDP) growth from its projected levels by at least 3 percent in 10 years and at least 17 percent in 30 years. The result will be lower average per capita income of $47,000 in 30 years instead of $57,000 if current rates of GDP growth are maintained."

Immigration is a key to solving these labor skill shortages. The Employment Policy Foundation concluded that:
- Between 1994 and 2000, the total U.S. labor force grew by 10 million, with nearly 4.7 million supplied by foreign-born residents.
- Today, foreign-born workers provide 12 percent of the total hours worked in a week. Without their contributions, the output of goods and services in our nation would be at least $1 trillion less.
- Foreign- and native-born workers complement each other in the job market. As native-born Americans seek better education and careers, they tend to

avoid jobs in the manual labor service industries. Thus, immigrants fill a growing share of low-skill jobs. About 1.1 million new lower-skilled immigrants in the labor force have filled the gap since 1994 as the native-born population attracted to such jobs has declined from 9 million to 7.6 million.

- Immigrants also provide an important resource to meet the growing demand for highly skilled college-educated managers, technical specialists and professionals. Since 1994, the number of foreign-born college graduates in the labor force has increased 43.8 percent to 4.6 million.
- Future economic growth will depend on having enough immigrant workers with the needed skills and education.

A comprehensive review of immigration policy to facilitate the entry of immigrants and those on temporary visas to work in the United States is a key recommendation of the Employment Policy Foundation study.

## The Looming Manufacturing Labor Force Crisis

In an important but largely overlooked report released in the Spring of 2003, the National Association of Manufacturers (NAM) concluded "It may seem contradictory, but at a time when manufacturing has lost jobs for 32 consecutive months . . . we face a looming shortage of skilled manufacturing employees. The stark reality is that this trend presents a real and growing threat to the ability of the United States to compete in the world marketplace."

Despite the job losses in manufacturing, NAM and its co-authors, the Manufacturing Institute and Deloitte & Touche, found that demographics and the perceived lack of desirability of jobs in manufacturing are creating a potential disaster for American companies. This is particularly the case since economists expect that U.S. manufacturing will emerge from its present cyclical downturn. "Demographic reality tells us that a seasoned manufacturing workforce will soon be passing from the scene, a process greatly accelerated by the current manufacturing slump. Yet a new generation of skilled workers is not at hand to replace these retiring baby boomers once the economy returns to solid growth."

The study's authors view a crisis on the horizon. "The result is an alarming mix of conditions that could transform the talent shortage of the 1990s into a genuine labor crisis. This shift could foreshadow a significant decrease in manufacturing's competitiveness, accelerate the transfer of American productive capacity and well-paid manufacturing jobs overseas—and deliver a decisive blow to the nation's long-term economic prospects."

## Explaining Labor Shortages

The study found that manufacturing will not be lacking people as much as qualified employees, concluding that, in the medium- and long-term, immigration is the primary source of new skilled workers for manufacturing. "The result is a projected need for 10 million new skilled workers by 2020."

This should not be surprising. In the 1990s, "A growing number of the nation's manufacturers, especially in the Northeast region, were very dependent on new immigrants to fill many of the blue-collar production jobs, including highly skilled as well as semi-skilled positions," according to the Business Roundtable.

American youth are "turned off" by modern manufacturing, say experts. Nor are they encouraged by their teachers or counselors to consider a career in the field. This creates an enormous pipeline problem as retirements mount due to age and discouragement with the cyclical downturns in manufacturing.

The study concludes that the current availability of unemployed manufacturing workers "is not a solution to manufacturing's long-term workforce problems." While immigration can be only part of the solution to this looming problem, it is clear that historically—and more recently—immigrants have shown an ability to fill manufacturing jobs important to U.S. economic growth.

## Immigrants and the 1990s Experience

Politics often enter into discussions about jobs with regard to who is to be blamed or praised for the country's economic performance. While politicians have argued over who should receive credit for the substantial growth of jobs in the 1990s, economists are now pointing to a group of people few have credited—immigrants. "The national jobs boom of the 1990s clearly would not have been possible in the absence of these new record waves of immigrant workers, especially men," concluded Northeastern University economists Andrew Sum, Neeta Fogg, and Paul Harrington in a study for the Business Roundtable. "The Great American Job Machine was largely fueled by new immigrant labor, a finding that has received insufficient attention from most economic and labor market analysts." Overall, the economists concluded,

> *"Immigrants are an important source of labor and economic growth for entire sectors and geographic areas of our nation."*

"New immigrants have been a key demographic force underlying growth in the nation's labor force and its employed population during the past decade."

The growth of jobs and the economy during the 1990s shows that, far from being a drain on the economy, as some opponents of immigration have alleged, immigrants are an important source of labor and economic growth for entire sectors and geographic areas of our nation. Generally speaking, in order to sustain economic growth, a country needs both productivity growth and labor force growth. Without these, it risks stagnation. "New immigrants accounted for 50% of the growth in the nation's civilian labor force over the 1990–2001 period," note the authors of the Business Roundtable study. "One of every two net labor force participants in the U.S. over the past eleven years was a new foreign immigrant."

The impact on certain states is even more profound. All of the growth in the labor force in the Northeast (including Connecticut, Maine, and New Hampshire) between 1990 and 2000–2001 was due to immigrants. "In fact, in the absence of new foreign immigration, the Northeast region's labor force would have declined by more than 1.3 million over the past 11 years. Within the West, new foreign immigration generated one-half of the region's labor force growth."

Northeastern University economists Andrew Sum, Neeta Fogg, and Paul Harrington found that male immigrants contributed 79% of the male labor force growth between 1990 and 2000–2001. "These findings clearly suggest that in the absence of the growth of the immigrant male labor force the nation's entire male labor force would have grown only marginally (by only 1.15 million) over the past decade, and male labor shortages would likely have been widespread in many areas of the country, especially in the Northeast and Pacific regions."

The authors note that "a fairly high fraction" of the new immigrant workers, particularly those in jobs requiring fewer skills, were undocumented immigrants. This fact undermines the allegations that undocumented immigrants cause economic problems, as opposed to those directing criticism at the lack of an effective immigration system to bring such workers into the country through legal channels. "Our national immigration policies have largely been a failure in reducing undocumented immigration, and our work force needs are being met by a group of workers who possess few rights," note Sum, Fogg, and Harrington.

Immigrants have been particularly important in the private sector, since only one in 20 new immigrants work for a local, state, or federal government agency, compared to one in 7 native-born Americans. The study concludes "Given the full employment labor market conditions prevailing throughout the nation at the end of the decade, it is difficult to argue that new immigrants were displacing any substantive numbers of native-born workers from jobs. . . . The so-called "New Economy" of the U.S. in the 1990s was overwhelmingly dependent on male immigrant workers for its employment growth."

Immigrants are a key part of the U.S. economy and will become an increasingly important element in America's economic growth and development in the future. Middle- to longer-term projections show a significant need to fill new jobs at all levels of the skill spectrum, with new immigrants playing a vital role in filling these jobs. Over the next two decades immigrants will be an essential element of labor force growth in American manufacturing and service sectors, as well as the U.S. economy as a whole. Today, immigrants continue to fill niches in the labor market, create jobs through entrepreneurship and consumer spending, and aid economic growth and the funding of the baby boom generation's retirement. A review of recent economic studies emphasizes the need for comprehensive immigration reform that would address the reality of the marketplace and the future labor force needs of the U.S. economy and American employers.

# Immigration Strengthens Canada

## by Rudyard Griffiths

**About the author:** *Rudyard Griffiths is executive director of the Dominion Institute, a Canadian charity that promotes Canadian history and citizenship. The institute gained attention when on the eve of Canada Day in 1997, newspapers across Canada published the institute's "Youth & Canadian History Survey," in which barely half of young Canadian adults could name Canada's first prime minister. The institute publishes one or more surveys each year.*

Immigration: its effect on our collective identity is one of the most compelling and often contentious issues facing Canada today. But so much of our thinking about the subject is framed by debate about its impact on the economy. As someone who spends his working life dealing with Canadian history—but who likes to look to the future as well—I'd like to make another point about the subject of new people coming to our shores: far from diluting Canada's identity, as some critics like to suggest, immigrants offer our best hope for the future of strengthening it.

The problem, before we even get to my thesis, is the degree to which all discussion about immigration seems to revolve around economic considerations. Consider the preliminary findings of the 2001 census, which showed that new immigrants were mostly responsible for the four-per-cent growth in the population of Canada since 1996. From Jean Chretien on down, government officials recited the mantra that increased immigration is key to future economic development. This argument encourages us to see immigration primarily as an economic good. But when you start to talk about cultural consequences of immigration, politicians invariably discuss official multiculturalism, a 30-year-old policy that is increasingly unpopular with Canadians for its promotion of a hyphenated national identity.

Canadian attitudes towards immigration mirror and then diverge from the government line. A . . . Leger Marketing survey indicates that three-quarters of Canadians think immigrants make an economic contribution to the country. But the same poll finds that half of Canadians feel we accept too many immigrants. Forty per cent think Canada is too open to political refugees. Alongside polite support for immigration, many of us wouldn't mind a less competitive job market, or living in communities where people look like "us," eat the same foods and speak the same language. The Leger poll suggests that our commitment to immigration is skin-deep—self-interest and economic preservation still trump social tolerance.

> *"Immigrants bring unique experience of what it means to be Canadian."*

## The Contributions of Immigrants

Those figures imply that anti-immigrant sentiment still runs high. One way to change that is to make the point that the closer you look, the more you realize that immigrants, despite their disparate cultural interests, strengthen our common values in very deliberate and specific ways. In fact, we should double immigration rates not for economic reasons, but to ensure the preservation of a common set of Canadian values and way of life.

In five years of exhaustive polling by my organization—the Dominion Institute, a history advocacy organization—the data has consistently shown that immigrants know more about Canada and Canadian history than natural-born citizens. That applies not only to knowledge of Canada's civic institutions and the way government functions, but also to such issues as Confederation and the patriation of the constitution. Some argue that this is mere trivia—the product of newcomers having to write a basic citizenship exam. But this kind of knowledge represents cultural capital that makes our society work: it allows us as citizens to talk intelligently together about the public good.

Immigrants bring unique experience of what it means to be Canadian. For most immigrants, coming to Canada is the result of a rational choice. It may sometimes be an ambiguous one, where memories of a lost homeland mix with the problems of integrating into a new society, but it's still a conscious decision. Because they're the emotional product of both their homeland and adopted country, they constantly question what it means to be Canadian.

By contrast, those of us born here often take Canada for granted. We assume that the country as we have known it in our lifetimes will continue: our contribution to that process is to vote and, perhaps, renew our passport every five years.

A healthy dose of self-examination is good for everyone. In the next decade, many of the traditional hallmarks of the Canadian identity—things like universal health care, an independent military, and border controls between our country and the United States—could be either abolished or radically reworked by the forces of continental integration. As these institutions diminish or disappear, we'll have to rebuild our collective identity around a set of commonly held values that define what it means to be Canadian. While it's hard to predict the composition of those new values, the self-examination that immigrants bring will be essential to figuring out who we are as a nation—and what we hope to accomplish together.

# Chapter 2

# Are Immigrants Treated Fairly in the United States?

# Chapter Preface

In 2002 more than 150 million people lived outside the country of their birth. Nearly 22 million of these immigrants, nearly half of whom are children, seek refuge or asylum from persecution in their homelands. At the end of the last millennium, hundreds of thousands of ethnic Albanians fled atrocities in Kosovo. Hundreds of thousands of Sierra Leoneans, 1.5 million Colombians, three-quarters of the population of East Timor, and 155,000 Chechens also fled their homelands, uprooted by violent conflict and the threat of ethnic cleansing and other human rights abuses. Many of these refugees will seek asylum in Western European nations, where some claim their persecution continues. While Europeans once welcomed refugees and asylum-seekers, policies toward these immigrants have begun to change; human rights groups claim that these changes have led to unfair policies.

Traditionally, Western Europeans welcomed refugees and asylum seekers. After World War II, 1 million refugees fled to Europe. However, most of those who settled in Europe during this time had beliefs and customs similar to Western Europeans, and most assimilated with relative ease. During the 1990s, the number of refugees seeking asylum in Europe grew dramatically. According to journalist Maria Margaronis, "In the 1990s, more than 4 million asked for asylum in Europe, most of them from Asia, the Middle East and the Balkans—an increase of two and a half million over the previous decade." Many of these asylum seekers have customs and values different from those of their host countries, and opposition to liberal refugee policies has begun to grow. The editors of the *Economist*, a British newsmagazine, point out that mass immigration "changes the neighbourhood. People in the street speak odd languages; the neighbours' cooking smells strange. So immigration often meets passionate resistance."

The cultural differences have also made it difficult for refugees themselves, and this new wave of asylum-seekers has experienced more difficulty assimilating into European culture than refugees did in the past. As a result, whether by choice or by necessity, many have settled into ethnic enclaves, creating tension and increasing economic divisions within European nations. According to editorial columnist Jeremy Harding, "Everyone pays grudging homage to the American model of cultural diversity, but European governments of all persuasions are dour about its advantages and alert to its dangers: cities eroded by poverty and profit; the cantonisation of neighbourhoods; urban and rural societies doubly fractured by ethnicity and class." These tensions and divisions have further inflamed European resistance to those seeking asylum in Europe.

The sudden increase in the number of refugees at the end of the 1990s and the cultural tension and division that followed have been compounded by fears of terrorism. Those who oppose immigration have used these fears to fuel anti-immigrant sentiment in Europe. Their success is evident in European elections, in which far-right parties in France and Austria and traditionally tolerant countries such as Denmark and the Netherlands have run successfully on anti-immigrant stands. As a result of this political influence, European refugee and asylum policies have begun to change. In Great Britain, for example, the number of asylum applicants allowed to remain in the country fell from 80 percent in 1987 to 20 percent in 1996. France and Italy exclude victims of civil wars and sectarian violence, thus turning away large numbers of refugees escaping violence in Africa and Asia.

Human rights and humanitarian groups claim that these policies are unfair to refugees. They claim that many asylum-seekers are refused based on their failure to overcome petty legal hurdles. Margaronis claims, for example, that "increasing numbers are refused on grounds of 'noncompliance'—that is, for errors in filling out the long form that must be completed in English within ten working days of application or failure to attend an interview many miles away." Those who claim refugee policies are unfair also assert that the requirements are often absurd. In one instance, Margaronis maintains, a Sudanese woman was denied asylum because she was publicly flogged on only one occasion, which was not deemed to be persecution. "If Jesus Christ came to Britain," an immigration lawyer told Margaronis, "he would not be given asylum."

The United States too feels the strain of increasing numbers of refugees and asylum seekers. As Harding notes, Americans generally tout the virtues of cultural diversity. However, in the wake of the terrorist attacks of September 11, 2001, and in the face of mass immigration of those with conflicting values, a number of Americans, like their European counterparts, have come to question their nation's immigration policies, including those concerning refugees. At the same time, those who think restrictive refugee policies are unfair continue to fight to protect refugee rights in America. In the following chapter authors debate the fairness of these policies.

# Immigration Laws Do Not Treat Immigrants Fairly

## by William G. Paul

**About the author:** *William G. Paul, former president of the American Bar Association, practices law in Oklahoma City.*

Like Alice following the white rabbit, thousands of immigrants to the U.S. are trapped in the confusing and all-powerful legal net of . . . harsh laws, which the Immigration and Naturalization Service (INS) is required to administer. These Federal statutes do not comport with due process standards or the fundamental fairness inherent in the American justice system that protect our citizens. Clearly, there is a double standard for immigrants.

## Facing Deportation

For example, about the time the controversy over [the immigrant status of] Elian Gonzalez—the six-year-old boy plucked from the coastal waters off Florida after an escape attempt from Cuba took the lives of his mother and several others—first reached fever pitch, a young Chinese girl, captured while trying to enter the U.S. after she fled her homeland, appeared at a review hearing. She was unable to understand English and terribly frightened, and, as tears rolled uncontrollably down her cheeks, she could not wipe them away because her arms were chained to her waist. She must have been in terror, having fled oppression only to be jailed and hauled in chains before strangers, where she understood nothing. She faces deportation.

Moreover, consider the compelling stories of two mothers also subject to deportation. The first is a young German woman who was adopted and brought to Georgia. Now the mother of two, she recently applied for citizenship. Instead, she was ordered deported because, as a teenager, she had entered a guilty plea to charges stemming from pulling the hair of another girl over the affections of a boy.

The second, a young mother in Falls Church, Va., faces deportation and separation from her children because she called the police after being brutally beaten by her husband. Instead of coming to her defense, police arrested her because she bit her husband as he sat on her and repeatedly hit her. Incredibly, both mothers face deportation, while their children—all born here—can remain.

How can a hair-pulling or biting incident be grounds for deportation? Equally important, how has the U.S. become a country that tears apart families or denies due process to those trying to obtain freedom, safety, and prosperity for themselves and their families?

## Changing the Rules

Answers to both questions are in the Illegal Immigration Reform and Immigrant Responsibility Act (IIRAIRA) and the Anti-Terrorism and Effective Death Penalty Act. Adopted in 1996, these tough laws are at the crux of the problem. They have changed the legal rules for newcomers, making them subject to harsher penalties for infractions than are citizens.

These laws reclassify past infractions retroactively so that they become deportable offenses, even in cases when no prison time was ordered or where there is evidence of rehabilitation. They have widely expanded the definition of aggravated felony to include minor crimes. Noncitizens convicted of aggravated felonies are now not only deportable, but ineligible for a waiver from deportation or for judicial review.

IIRAIRA undermines one of the principles underlying the Constitution—the separation of powers—by removing the historic role of the courts as protectors of individuals from government overreaching. Harsh laws permit those administering them to take harsh action. The INS [Immigration and Naturalization Service] and its individual agents are authorized by law to detain and deport anyone attempting to enter the U.S. if there is suspicion of fraud, and there is no appeal from these decisions.

The laws have permitted the summary return of victims of torture and persecution to their persecutors, and vested INS agents with the power to banish for 10 years legitimate travelers entering the U.S. on the basis of unsubstantiated allegations of misrepresentation. IIRAIRA also requires imprisoning thousands at great expense to taxpayers. Largely due to this law, the INS has the fastest-growing prisoner populations in the nation. In 1994, it held about 5,500 people. Currently, 17,400 individuals are being held by the INS, which warehouses immigrants in state and local facilities because of the overflow. The INS estimates that, by [the end

> *"Clearly, there is a double standard for immigrants."*

of 2002], it could be detaining upwards of 23,000 individuals.

INS Commissioner Doris Meissner has testified before Congress that the agency is housing more immigrant detainees than its budget will support. She has openly questioned whether the INS should be in the large-scale prison business.

## Denying Due Process

The American Bar Association, alarmed about the far-reaching impact of immigration reform and lack of due process for those in INS custody, has held a series of meetings with representatives of the White House, the Justice Department, and the INS. They have resulted in the promulgation of standards for those being held in INS facilities. The standards guarantee access to lawyers, telephones, legal rights presentations, and a limited legal library. However, the INS is unwilling to extend these same standards to local and state facilities, where 60% of all detainees are being held. . . .

Detainees often are held in facilities far from their families, support groups, and lawyers, if they are fortunate enough to have legal representation. There have been cases of detainees being transferred from one facility to another without their paperwork, arriving without their jailers knowing the reason for their incarceration. Detainees have been transferred without such personal belongings as their address books, money, and eyeglasses.

The INS routinely refuses to notify a detainee's attorney about his or her transfer. In one case, a lawyer, who had been representing an individual for years, only learned that her client had been moved 1,000 miles and three states away when she went for

> *"Expedited removal [of immigrants] violates . . . our nation's principles of justice, fairness, and decency by giving INS agents full authority to be prosecutor, judge, and jury."*

a routine visit and could not find him. Immigrant advocates maintain that their clients frequently are moved without their advocate being notified. These immigration reform laws have created such havoc in the lives of thousands of families that they demand examination.

## The Harshness of Expedited Removal

Unlike Elian Gonzalez, who received special treatment, children and their parents arriving legitimately at ports of entry can encounter one of the most harsh mechanisms put in place by the 1996 law—expedited removal. This gives a low-level government official the right to deport anyone based on mere suspicion of attempted illegal entry, with no appeal.

How does this work? After waiting in long lines, international passengers have their passports examined by a uniformed INS agent, who enters their information into a computer and then makes a cursory comparison of the passport picture to the traveler before waving him or her through. Those agents have the power to deport people summarily and ban them from reentering the country for up to 10 years if an INS agent believes the documents "don't look right" or if there is something "suspicious" about a traveler.

Additionally, those fleeing oppression and arriving in the U.S. without any papers at all are arrested, imprisoned, and may ultimately be sent back to the country they fled. Moreover, once the decision has been made, there is no appeal—even when the agent is proven wrong. Expedited removal violates the very fundamentals of our nation's principles of justice, fairness, and decency by giving INS agents full authority to be prosecutor, judge, and jury, and stripping away the right to due process.

> *"Mandatory detention can trap many [immigrants] in . . . limbo."*

Take the case of Sonia, who arrived at Miami International Airport from Venezuela shortly after the new immigration laws were enacted. She expected to use her visitor's visa to visit her children, who are students, as she had done in the past. Instead, Sonia was detained for 36 hours, humiliated, mistreated, subjected to strip searches, fed nothing, and then forced to sign papers that banned her from entering the country for five years—all without legal representation. "This was the most shameful and humiliating day that I have ever had," she recalled. "That horrible, dark, and gloomy day came with no mercy at all."

As part of the expedited removal process, Sonia was held without counsel for three days and denied access to a telephone. She was deported despite having a valid visa issued by the U.S. Embassy in Caracas. Finally worn out and worn down, Sonia signed documents admitting that she had attempted to enter the U.S. fraudulently, even though her papers were valid.

Sonia does not blame the U.S. "I know what a totalitarian regime is—where the people are only trash and where they have no rights to anything," she said. "I know that [America] is not a country like this."

Individuals can be imprisoned for life if the U.S. has no relations with the country they left. These "lifers" become stuck in jail limbo, as were the Cubans who took hostages in 1999 in Louisiana after spending more than a dozen years in captivity. In an isolated act, the U.S. negotiated a highly unusual agreement during the zenith of the Elian Gonzalez frenzy, in which the Cuban government accepted those Cubans back, then imprisoned them upon their return.

While no one condones hostage-taking, harsh laws can prompt harsh reactions. In Florida, outside the Krome Detention Center near Miami, a hunger strike was launched by the desperate and frustrated mothers of Cuban lifers who had been locked away for years, far from family and community support. After several weeks, and with growing public support, the INS responded to the mothers' demands and ordered their sons transferred back to Florida. Five were eventually released.

Mandatory detention can trap many in this limbo. It requires that all INS detainees awaiting deportation must be held, making them the only prisoners in the U.S. with no right to an individual bond hearing. Under the American legal system, even people charged with a capital offense have a right to a bond hearing. Applied in conjunction with other immigration reform laws, mandatory detention has tripled the number of individuals being held by the INS.

Another provision of IIRAIRA is aggravated felony, which reclassifies past crimes of noncitizens to more serious and deportable offenses, even if they have already served their time for the infractions, have been rehabilitated, or never spent a day in jail.

There have been many cases of people being stopped at U.S. borders as they attempt to enter to conduct business. For some of these individuals, when INS agents check their passports and computerized information, they may find a past infraction—now reclassified retroactively to a more serious offense. These people can no longer enter, or—as in the case of a Canadian businessman found to have passed a few bad checks 20 years earlier—they are jailed.

## Reexamining the Law

Rep. Sheila Jackson Lee (D.-Tex.) has questioned the soundness and constitutionality of mandatory detention. She maintains that any individual who has family ties, is not a danger to the community, is not likely to abscond, and has posted bond should be released. Jackson Lee asserts that restoring discretion to the INS on whether to detain or deport individuals would not only ensure fairness, but alleviate the INS burden. She is not alone in reexamining the harsh 1996 legislation. Several bills are pending in Washington to amend portions of the law.

Rep. Bill McCollum (R.-Fla.), once a staunch IIRAIRA supporter, wants another look. "The 1996 law went too far," maintains McCollum, who has introduced remedial legislation. "We are a just and fair nation and must strike a just and fair balance in our immigration laws." [H.R. 5062 passed the House on September 19, 2000, and remains without action in the Senate.]

Reps. Barney Frank (D.-Mass.), Martin Frost (D.-Tex.), and Lincoln Diaz-Balart (R.-Fla.) have introduced amendments to provide long-term legal residents a day in court. Among other changes, the proposed amendments would provide a chance to consider an individual's family life, length of residency, community contributions, and military service before requiring deportation. [The bill was referred to a House subcommittee on April 30, 1999, and no further action has been taken.]

> *"The U.S., a nation of immigrants, cannot be free if it takes freedom from those who believe in the promise of justice for all."*

When originally considering IIRAIRA, some of its supporters maintained that minor crimes such as shoplifting would not be grounds for deportation. Tell that to Olufolake Olaleye, a Nigerian living in Atlanta. This mother of two was ordered deported because of a conviction on charges of shoplifting baby clothes worth $14.99.

Olaleye entered the U.S. legally in 1984, becoming a permanent resident in 1990. She worked as a gas station cashier and never asked for, or received, public benefits. In 1993, while attempting to return baby outfits without a receipt, Olaleye was accused of shoplifting, given a citation, and told to appear in court. Faced with a problem she considered a misunderstanding, Olaleye appeared without a lawyer.

After explaining the circumstances to the judge, she entered a guilty plea she said was to put a quick end to the matter. She was fined $360 and received a 12-month suspended sentence and 12 months probation, which was terminated two months later when she paid the fine. At the time, there were no negative immigration consequences for Olaleye. She was accepted for citizenship and awaited a swearing-in date. Subsequently, IIRAIRA became law and the INS reopened her file. She was ordered deported as an "aggravated felon."

Or how about the case of the young woman from Sri Lanka, having fled civil war and torture, only to arrive in Chicago and have her child taken away from her? This woman, who speaks no English, was jailed. For weeks, unable to communicate with those around her, she was frantic to learn the fate of her child. Amnesty International caught wind of her case and asked local advocates to investigate. They did and found the child unharmed in foster care.

"This is a country that respects people's rights. I come here because this country is a freedom country for me to raise my family," Bi Meng Zheng said while in the INS Detention Center in San Pedro, Calif. He fled China for the promise of freedom. Instead, he was jailed after he missed his first immigration court hearing.

Zheng, who never committed a crime, spent four years locked behind bars after he was ordered deported because China refused to accept him back. He was released only after human rights advocates campaigned zealously for his freedom.

Let us hope his life in a free country meets his expectations. More importantly, let us hope his new nation meets its promises of freedom and a better way of life.

This article recounts the stories of just a few caught in a trap after pursuing the dream of freedom. It gives them faces, resonance, and sympathy. What about the lives and the plight of thousands of others being jailed and deported? What does it say about us, that we cannot promise them a fair hearing? The U.S., a nation of immigrants, cannot be free if it takes freedom from those who believe in the promise of justice for all.

IIRAIRA has taken us down the wrong path. We must set out on a new and better course.

# Battered Women Seeking Asylum Are Not Treated Fairly

**by Lydia Brashear Tiede**

**About the author:** *Lydia Brashear Tiede, a San Diego lawyer, represents battered immigrant women, asylum seekers, and immigrants in detention.*

Domestic violence victims suffer unspeakable horrors at the hands of their abusers throughout the world. Two often-overlooked groups of domestic violence victims are women who are abused in their home countries and seek to immigrate to the United States and immigrant women living in the United States who are abused in this country. How the circumstances of the abuse are interpreted as well as how the available legal standards are applied in these cases depend exclusively on whether the victim is fleeing domestic violence that occurred in her home country or domestic violence occurring within the United States. Immigration law deals with these two groups of women separately. Each group must fulfill different legal requirements and evidentiary burdens.

## Abuse Is Abuse

Women subjected to domestic violence in their home countries confront social, familial, and legal systems that refuse to acknowledge the seriousness of the problem or to protect the victim. In many countries, the voices of the victims go unheard, drowned out by age-old traditions that perpetuate the idea that women should serve their husbands no matter how they are treated. Often, the victims' own families do nothing to help the victim of spousal abuse and force her to "endure"—as generations of women have done.

Outside the family network, women also find little assistance in the legal system. Many countries do not codify domestic violence as a separate crime, and some countries regard domestic violence as strictly a family issue to be dealt with in a private manner. In many countries, the law fails to recognize rape by a spouse, a policy that was prevalent in many U.S. states not so long ago. Few countries recognize domestic violence as a crime or have enacted protections for domestic violence victims. And, measures that have been enacted all too often fall short due to little or no enforcement. Calling the police in many countries does not ensure any real protection for the victim.

Battered immigrant women in the United States face similar traumas due to both the culture and traditions in which they have been raised. The victim often does not know protection is available, or how to seek it. Many immigrant victims do not speak English and are uninformed about U.S. criminal and immigration laws and systems. Some victims lead very isolated lives in the United States; if they are undocumented, they live secret lives in which they literally have no legal identity and few if any ties to social services, friends, or family. Abusers often compound their abuse by threatening to call the Immigration and Naturalization Service (INS) and have the victim deported if she dares complain about the abuse. The impact of such threats is not exaggerated; undocumented victims know that they are constantly at risk of deportation and fear leaving their children in the United States with the abusing spouse and facing a hostile society upon return to their home country. For example, in many Latin American countries, a woman who returns to her village without her husband and children is ostracized, making it difficult to survive.

## The Battered Asylee

As stated above, immigration relief available to battered immigrant women depends on where the abuse occurred. A woman fleeing her country due to domestic violence can, when she enters the United States, seek the remedy of political asylum based on the domestic violence. This makes her subject to asylum law, which derives from U.S. treaty obligations under the United Nations Protocol Relating to the Status of Refugees. To qualify for asylum, an individual must establish that he or she is a "refugee," defined in the Immigration and Naturalization Act [INA] as any person who is unable or unwilling to return to his or her home country due to persecution or a well-founded fear of persecution for one of five reasons: race, religion, nationality, membership in a particular social group, or political opinion.

> *"Gender-based asylum claims include rape, female genital mutilation, forced abortion, and domestic violence."*

Asylum claims related to woman are often referred to as "gender-based" asylum claims and include any type of persecution that is inflicted on women solely due to their gender. Gender-based asylum claims include rape, female genital mutilation, forced abortion, and domestic violence. Generally, gender-based asylum claims rely on the theories of membership in a social group or political opinion that are found in the definition of a "refugee."

U.S. law recognizes persecution due to gender-related abuse as a basis of asylum. International standards include the United Nations Declaration, the United Nations High Commissioner of Refugee Standards, and the Convention on the Elimination of All Forms of Discrimination Against Women, as well as gender-related persecution guidelines adopted in Canada in 1993. The INS issued its own guidelines, Considerations for Asylum Officers Adjudicating Asylum Claims from Women, in May 1995. They specifically address types of persecution suffered by women and discuss legal arguments tying gender-related persecution to membership in a social group and/or political opinion.

The issue of asylum based on domestic violence took on new significance in the 1999 Board of Immigration Appeals (BIA) decision in *In re Matter of R-A* (Interim Decision 3403, BIA 1999). A Guatemalan woman was subjected to extreme domestic violence at the hands of her husband, who beat and raped her repeatedly. He dislocated her jaw, kicked her in the stomach when she was pregnant, whipped her with an electrical cord, and wielded a machete while threatening to cut off her limbs and leave her to spend the rest of her life in a wheelchair. The victim in this case argued that she qualified for asylum because she was persecuted, as evidenced by the domestic violence, based on both a social group and political or imputed political opinion theory.

Although the Immigration Court (an administrative court) granted the victim asylum in the first court proceeding, the BIA reversed the decision, denying the victim's claim on both theories. Especially troubling is that not only did the BIA appear to disregard the INS guidelines and previous gender-based asylum case law, but it also added additional requirements to the asylum standard.

> *"Battered immigrant women living in the United States face a much easier standard than their counterparts fleeing abuse in their home countries."*

The BIA found that the victim was not a member of a particular persecuted social group, defined as "Guatemalan women who have been involved intimately with Guatemalan male companions, who believe that women are to live under male domination." In rejecting the victim's social group argument, the BIA required that the victim not only prove that she was hurt due to her membership in a group but also that her social group was "cognizable" or easily recognized in society and that there existed a "nexus" between the victim's abuse and the social group. In other words, the BIA required the victim to prove that her spouse specifically abused her due to her membership in a recognized persecuted group.

Under the imputed political opinion theory, the BIA was equally restrictive and denied the victim's asylum claim, stating that she failed to prove that her husband hurt her due to her specific political beliefs. After efforts made by immigration and woman's rights advocates, U.S. Attorney General Janet Reno, on

December 7, 2000, issued proposed rules to amend the INS regulations dealing with political asylum and social groups. The drafters recognized that gender could be a basis for a particular social group in an asylum determination and that due to the decision in R-A, the issue of women and asylum requires further examination. The regulations allowed for a commentary period through January 2001. Subsequently, Reno ordered the BIA's decision in R-A to be vacated and remanded the case back to the BIA for reconsideration with instructions to rehear the case after the proposed regulations become final. It is unclear what form the final law regarding gender-based asylum will take and how this will ultimately affect the decision in R-A.[1]

> *"If legislators are serious about domestic violence . . . they should work to protect victims of domestic violence regardless of where the abuse occurs."*

## Battered Immigrant Women Living in the United States

The treatment of domestic violence in the asylum context is starkly different from the treatment of domestic violence suffered by immigrant women in the United States. A comparison reveals a double standard in which battered immigrant women living in the United States face a much easier standard than their counterparts fleeing abuse in their home countries.

In 1994, Congress recognized that battered immigrant women who were undocumented, living in the United States, and married to U.S. citizens or legal permanent residents warranted special protection. Traditionally, these women relied on their husbands to petition for their legal status, and had to remain in their good graces. This situation gave the petitioner even more control over his spouse, because her entire immigrant status and ultimate identity in American society depended on his cooperation in signing an affidavit of financial support and attending an interview with his spouse—sometimes years after the application had been filed. The process encouraged undocumented women to stay with their abusers.

Legislation enacted by Congress in 1994 recognized the vulnerability of these battered women. As part of the Violence Against Women's Act (VAWA), Congress amended the INA, allowing battered women who meet certain requirements to seek legal immigration status through a self-petitioning process that does not require the assistance of their abusive spouses. Under this legislation, women must prove the following requirements: (1) legal marriage to a U.S. citizen or legal permanent resident; (2) residence in the United States with the abuser; (3) abuse or extreme cruelty occurring within the U.S.; (4) good moral character of the victim; and (5) extreme hardship if deported. Under this law,

---

1. The proposed regulations did not become final. As of July 2004, Attorney General John Ashcroft, who in March 2003 indicated he would reconsider the Alvarado case, has not yet done so.

women or their attorneys compile the above proof and submit it to the INS. If their self-petitions are approved, the women can immediately apply for work authorization and can eventually apply for legal permanent residency.

In the fall of 2000, the U.S. Congress amended VAWA significantly. The changes allow even more women to qualify for benefits under the law.

## A Double Standard

These differing approaches reflect an indefensible double standard. The asylee who flees her country may be held to extraordinarily stringent evidentiary and legal standards. In contrast, the undocumented victim in the United States who meets the requirements is assured protection and legal status by virtue of the fact that the abuse occurred in the United States and that the victim was married to a U.S. citizen or legal permanent resident. If legislators are serious about domestic violence, which the amended VAWA legislation indicates is so, they should work to protect victims of domestic violence regardless of where the abuse occurs. The recent events regarding the proposed gender-based asylum regulations as well as Janet Reno's vacating of the decision in R-A may provide parity to these two groups of victims. A double standard serves no one's interests.

# Immigrant Students Are Not Treated Fairly

**by Chaiti Sen**

**About the author:** *Chaiti Sen is a writer, researcher, and teacher from New York City.*

Part of the government's "new and improved" xenophobic hysteria is now to step up its plans to control foreign students in this country. The Bush Administration announced in early May [2002] that they are accelerating the implementation of a computerized system called the Student and Exchange Visitor Information System (SEVIS). In December 2001, Congress approved $36.8 million to build and refine SEVIS and has given the INS [Immigration and Naturalization Service] until January 2003 to have it in full operation [a deadline that the INS in fact met]. Using this system, colleges and universities must report the names, addresses, enrollment status, and majors of all foreign students. The system includes methods of tracking all the classes that foreign students take, supposedly to catch students who violate their visas by enrolling in classes less than half-time. SEVIS will open up all sorts of possibilities for spying on foreign students, especially those who are politically active on campus or involved in academic pursuits or cultural and social clubs deemed "suspicious."

## Arrested Education

We don't know if any colleges are currently turning over information leading to the arrests of current detainees, such as the thousands detained in the months following [the terrorist attacks of] September [11, 2001]. But there are rumors among staffers in administration offices that the FBI has already viewed student records at Hunter College, although the City University of New York (CUNY) system denies handing over any records. Chris Day, manager of the Student Resource Center at Hunter, says he saw two suited men who "looked like they were straight out of central casting FBI" in the company of campus security officials during the fall [2001] semester. "The first time I saw them, they were being led around by the head of Hunter security. They went to the Muslim Students Association Office, they came here, checking things out. Later they came to a rally on immigrant tuition hikes." When Day asked a top CUNY security official who they were, he was told that they worked for CUNY security.

With the shroud of secrecy that keeps most facts about INS detentions a mystery, there are only a few known cases of students who have been arrested and held. About 20 FBI agents arrested Reem Khalil, a senior biochemistry major at the City College of New York, and her family, according to the *CUNY Messenger*, early in the morning on February 27 [2002].

> *"Undocumented students cannot attend public colleges at in-state tuition rates, even if they have been living in that state for their entire lives."*

After being separated and questioned in relation to unfounded terrorism charges, Khalil, her mother, father, and two teenaged brothers were all turned over to INS and held in separate detention for two and a half months. The Khalils are Syrian and have been living in the U.S. for years, but they are undocumented. Apart from her two youngest siblings, who were born in the U.S., Khalil and the rest of her family now face the threat of deportation.

Yazeed Al-Salmi is a legal resident from Saudi Arabia who enrolled at Grossmont Community College in eastern San Diego County. He was arrested in September [2001] and detained for 17 days without charges. Two other students were arrested May 30 [2002]: activists Ahmed Bensouda in Urbana, Illinois, and Jaoudar Abouazza in Cambridge, Massachusetts. As is typical with INS arrests, it took several days to locate Bensouda, and both the INS and FBI have questioned him repeatedly. When a small group of supporters tried to attend his first immigration court hearing, the judge asked them to leave, saying it was a closed hearing. His next immigration hearing, when the judge will hear secret evidence, is also closed. On recent visits with Bensouda, friends say that he was behind glass with chains around his wrists and ankles. Although the official word is that he is being held for a visa violation, the government's real case against him and their secret evidence will not be subject to public scrutiny.

## Restricting Access

Foreign students have already been on a heightened state of alert for many months now. Since September 11, many universities and colleges that had once resisted the proposed tracking system since the 1996 passage of the Illegal Immigration Reform and Immigrant Responsibility Act have now complied. The INS has also been using this time to develop SEVIS and prepare for its implementation and enforcement. The 1996 legislation includes another measure that many schools have not used until now. Due to restrictions of benefits for undocumented immigrants, students who are not legal residents or student visa holders cannot receive higher education assistance. This means that undocumented students cannot attend public colleges at in-state tuition rates, even if they have been living in that state for their entire lives. Undocumented students whose families had been working in low-wage service jobs and contributing to the New York economy for more than 10 years told us they've had to rethink their plans for an education, something that they had counted on for many years.

City University of New York has long been known as one of the best educational options for both documented and undocumented immigrant students. CUNY was one of the few schools to knowingly allow an undocumented student to be admitted or not require proof of legal status. They also allowed immigrant students to pay in-state tuition, which is half the amount of foreign student tuition. However, the administration sent letters to all the students they knew to be undocumented, informing them that they will be charged foreign student tuition starting in the spring semester of 2002. The letter advised them to discuss their immigration status with specific officials, but many undocumented students stayed away from the immigrant "help centers" mentioned in the letter. As one Colombian immigrant student, a New York City resident for the last 18 years, said, "Which undocumented student do you think will go to talk to them? If they can increase our tuition, do you think we will trust them?" Another student said that she and other immigrants she knew would not go to a help center for fear of being deported.

The spring [2002] semester has seen a declining number of immigrant enrollments. Although the administration has not released an official number, estimates range from around 1,000 to 2,600 CUNY students who have not returned in the spring semester. But the numbers do not tell the whole story. According to City College Professor William Cram, a vocal oppo-

> *"[The Student and Exchange Visitor Information System] can potentially turn the United States educational system into a network of spies."*

nent of the immigrant tuition hikes, many students took a hardship deferral but cannot continue if proposed state legislation to allow in-state tuition does not pass in their favor. Still others have enrolled in fewer classes and will take longer to graduate. Some students have also transferred to community colleges. The increased scrutiny is deterring countless numbers of undocumented immigrants who may no longer view higher education as possible.

There is no question that the experience of immigrant students has been markedly different since September [2001]. Hunter College's Muslim Students Association [MSA] has . . . graffiti posted on their door. The first one came shortly after September 11, a cartoon depicting suicide bombers. Others include "Remember 9/11" with a picture of a cross, drawn on the door with marker. The latest one read "God Bless America." One MSA officer said the graffiti is so frequent that they don't bother reporting it to the administration anymore. And although many Muslim students say they feel less isolated at CUNY than they might on other campuses, the threatened tuition hikes and new tracking system have put a chill in the air.

The Palestine/Israel conflict and the U.S. war on Afghanistan have also polarized student opinion on campuses. One incident erupted at Hunter College when a woman angrily tore down anti-war flyers and a Muslim student challenged her right to do so. A Brooklyn College Muslim student named Saba Gilani was targeted for disciplinary action after she tried to stop flyers from being torn down, which led to a charge of physical assault. Even though no physical altercation occurred, Brooklyn College officials tried to convince her to admit to pushing another student.

## Anti-Immigrant Agenda

Although officials say SEVIS and the immigrant tuition hikes are unrelated, these policies point to an overall anti-immigrant agenda. A steady procession of anti-immigrant proposals has come down the policy conveyer belt since September [2001] from tuition hikes to military tribunals to the recent Justice Department proposal to fingerprint thousands of Muslim and Middle Eastern visa holders. To the Bush Administration, immigrants represent a potentially dangerous force, offering an international perspective that directly counters the sentiment of the president's September 20 speech: "Every nation, in every region, now has a decision to make. Either you are with us, or you are with the terrorists." With campuses a possible hotbed of activism, it is especially in the government's interest to limit potential anti-war influences among students.

Legally, there are few barriers to stop the Justice Department and INS from arresting students based on information provided by their institution and holding them without due process. The importance and impact of SEVIS should not be underestimated. This tracking system can potentially turn the United States educational system into a network of spies, and without a united, diverse, and determined movement to resist the repression being carried out in the name of national security, there is no reason to think that the arrests and detentions will stop or slow down.

# Same-Sex Immigrant Couples Are Not Treated Fairly

**by Susan Hazeldean and Heather Betz**

**About the authors:** *Susan Hazeldean, a staff attorney with the Peter Cicchino Youth Project of the Urban Justice Center in New York City, provides free legal representation to Lesbian, Gay, Bisexual, and Transgender (LGBT) and HIV-positive young people. Heather Betz, director of the Lesbian and Gay Refugee Advocacy Project at the Lesbian and Gay Immigration Rights Task Force, represents immigrants seeking asylum based on sexual orientation, gender identity, and HIV status.*

When Richard Adams applied to sponsor his Australian partner for immigration to the United States in 1975, the Immigration and Naturalization Service [INS] sent him the following response: "Your visa petition . . . for classification of Anthony Corbett Sullivan as the spouse of a United States citizen [is] denied for the following reasons: You have failed to establish that a bona fide marital relationship can exist between two faggots."

Had Richard Adams's life partner been a woman, she could have received a green card and eventually become a U.S. citizen based on their relationship. But, like the thousands of lesbian, gay, bisexual, and transgender (LGBT) Americans in relationships with a same-sex partner from another country, Richard Adams was out of luck. His loving, committed relationship to Anthony Sullivan did not matter under immigration law, and his attempts to secure legal immigration status for his partner were greeted with nothing but scorn.

One might expect that things would have changed radically since Richard Adams filed his immigration application in 1975. After all, hundreds of same-sex couples have now entered into civil unions in Vermont, and thousands of companies across the country offer domestic partner benefits to their employees. . . .

But for the thousands of U.S. citizens like Richard Adams with foreign same-sex partners, nothing has changed. Americans may take it for granted that if they fall in love with a foreigner, they will be able to sponsor their partner for residency in the United States, but there is no such option for same-sex couples. It simply does not matter how long a couple has been together or how devoted they are to each other; if the partners are the same sex, their relationship is irrelevant for immigration purposes.

President George W. Bush has said that our immigration system should "recognize the importance of families and . . . help to strengthen them." Family reunification is certainly supposed to be the primary goal of U.S. immigration policy. Americans can sponsor fiances or fiancees, spouses, parents, children, and siblings for residency in the United States, but no such provision is available for same-sex partners. Yet every day thousands of LGBT people are separated from their loved ones by our immigration laws. Imagine building a family and a life with the person you love only to have your partner barred from the country or forcibly removed from it.

## Broader Policies Worldwide

This situation is even more outrageous when one compares the United States to the rest of the world. Sixteen nations around the globe have reformed their immigration policies to ensure that LGBT citizens can sponsor same-sex partners for immigration. Many of these countries have had such policies in place for many years. In fact, several nations enacted additional legislative or policy reforms to make it even easier for citizens to sponsor same-sex partners. All the while, the United States has changed nothing.

Nine countries (Denmark, Finland, France, Germany, Iceland, the Netherlands, Norway, Portugal, and Sweden) grant immigration benefits to same-sex couples as part of a broader partnership-recognition policy. In 1989 Denmark was the first country to enact legislation granting lesbian and gay couples marriage-like benefits. The Danish Registered Partnership Act created an institution similar to marriage except that it was restricted to same-sex couples and omitted access to church weddings, adoption, and reproductive technology. Since then, Finland, Iceland, the Netherlands, Norway, and Sweden have passed similar legislation allowing same-sex couples to become registered partners and enjoy most of the rights and benefits of marriage, including immigration benefits. On

> *"Americans can sponsor fiances or fiancees, spouses, parents, children, and siblings for residency . . . but no such provision is available for same-sex partners."*

April 1, 2001, the Netherlands went a step further and became the first jurisdiction in the world to allow same-sex couples full access to marriage, with Belgium allowing marriages effective [in 2003]. Many countries are also revisiting the few limitations imposed on registered partners.

France grants gay and lesbian couples immigration rights through a less comprehensive partnership scheme called the Pacte Civil de Solidarite (PACS). The PACS is open to opposite-sex couples as well as same-sex couples and is not intended to be parallel to marriage; it does not change a person's civil status from single to married, nor is a formal proceeding similar to a divorce required to terminate the relationship. It does, however, confer immigration rights.

Germany and Portugal enacted legislation similar to the French scheme. Germany passed a Registered Life Partnership Law in November 2000, which grants participating same-sex couples a limited number of legal rights including inheritance, tenancy, and immigration. Portugal passed a similar statute in March 2001, creating an institution called a registered union that grants same-sex couples a limited number of rights, including the ability to sponsor a foreign partner for immigration.

South Africans have been able to sponsor same-sex partners for immigration benefits since February 12, 1999, when the country's Constitutional Court handed down its decision in *National Coalition for Gay and Lesbian Equality v. Minister of Home Affairs.* Previously, the South African government granted immigration benefits only in heterosexual marriage relationships. The court unanimously held that failing to treat same-sex life partners equally was a violation of the South African Constitution's equality clause.

> *"Including same-sex partners in our immigration laws would cost the American public nothing."*

Even countries that fail to recognize same-sex relationships in other contexts have given couples immigration rights. Australia, Canada, Israel, New Zealand, and the United Kingdom reformed their immigration policies to recognize same-sex couples without granting the right to marry or creating an alternative partnership scheme.

These countries' policies have proved so successful that many subsequently reformed their policies to make it even easier for same-sex couples to qualify for immigration benefits. Canada initially permitted foreign same-sex partners to apply for residency under the humanitarian and compassionate grounds exception but now simply includes same-sex couples in its "family" immigration category. Australia, New Zealand, and the United Kingdom initially required evidence of long-term cohabitation before same-sex couples could qualify for immigration benefits based on the relationship. All three countries adapted their policies by reducing cohabitation requirements and probationary periods.

The European Parliament of the fifteen-member-state European Union/Community most recently illustrated the international trend toward greater immigration equality for same-sex couples. On February 11, 2003, it approved a directive guaranteeing same-sex couples freedom of movement among member states equal to that of married heterosexual couples, where those same-sex relationships are recognized. Justification for the legislation was unambiguous: the European Union declared it must "reflect and respect the diversity of family relationships that exist in today's society" by including same-sex couples.

## Introducing Permanent Partner Policies

Given the pride that Americans take in our identity as a nation of immigrants, it is anomalous that the United States lags so far behind so many other countries on this issue. Fortunately, the needs of bi-national same-sex couples are at last beginning to attract some attention. On February 14, 2000, Representative Jerrold Nadler (D-NY) took an important step toward ending this discrimination by introducing the Permanent Partners Immigration Act (PPIA), which would grant same-sex couples the same rights as married heterosexual spouses under current immigration law. On February 13, 2003, the PPIA was reintroduced in the House of Representatives (H.R. 832). As of May [2003], the bill had 107 cosponsors in the House, and plans are under way to introduce a companion bill in the Senate during the [108th] Congress. [S.1510 was introduced in the Senate in July 2003 and remains in the Judiciary Committee.]

> *"Failing to acknowledge same-sex relationships for immigration purposes is cruel, unnecessary, and unacceptable."*

By inserting the words "permanent partner" next to "spouse" throughout much of the Immigration and Nationality Act (INA), the PPIA creates a mechanism by which U.S. citizens and permanent residents (green-card holders) may sponsor a same-sex partner for immigration. Because the PPIA's intent is to remedy the unequal treatment of same-sex partners, it would not affect unmarried heterosexual couples, who have the option to marry and seek relief under the INA.

To qualify a person as a "permanent partner," the couple must meet the following conditions: be in a "committed, intimate relationship"; not be married or in a "permanent partnership" with anyone else; intend a lifelong commitment to each other; and demonstrate that they are financially interdependent. To prevent fraudulent applications, the application process includes many of the same requirements that currently apply to heterosexual spouses. Before the foreign partner can obtain a green card, the partners must establish that they are in a bona fide relationship. Immigration authorities typically decide whether a marriage is bona fide by questioning spouses about their home life, habits, and history to determine whether the couple are truly committed in the long term, or whether they are engaged in a sham marriage. Permanent partners would be subject to a similar inquiry. The sponsoring "permanent partner" would also have to commit to providing financial support before the other partner could obtain immigration benefits based on their relationship. These requirements ensure that the PPIA protects same-sex couples in committed relationships while preventing fraudulent immigration applications.

By law, the costs of administering immigration programs in the United States must be completely covered by application fees collected from immigrants themselves. Including same-sex partners in our immigration laws would cost the American public nothing, nor would it create additional fiscal burdens for the federal government.

The United States adopted family reunification as the guiding principle of its immigration system so that Americans would not be separated from their loved ones. Failing to acknowledge same-sex relationships for immigration purposes is cruel, unnecessary, and unacceptable. It is time for the United States to stand with the sixteen countries around the globe that already recognize same-sex couples for immigration purposes. LGBT Americans deserve a legal regime that will keep their families together instead of tearing them apart.

# Closed U.S. Borders Protect Illegal Immigrants

by Phyllis Schlafly

**About the author:** *Phyllis Schlafly, editor of the monthly newsletter the* Phyllis Schlafly Report, *is a conservative columnist and representative of the pro-family movement.*

How many people will die before the Bush Administration realizes that the most humane act it can take is to close our southern border to illegal traffic and eliminate the incentive to unscrupulous smugglers who take the calculated risk that financial profits outweigh the costs of getting caught? The death from dehydration and heatstroke of 19 out of 100 people crammed into a tractor-trailer that was discovered near Houston in May [2003] was only the latest in a long series of similar tragedies.

The profitable racket of smuggling illegals into the United States in sealed trucks has been going on for years, and only death makes it newsworthy. Trucks ought to be inspected when they cross the border, for the illegal aliens' protection as well as for American sovereignty.

Smugglers reap millions of dollars in profits. They collect their fees up front ($800 to $2,500 per person), then often abandon their clients in desert areas without food or water, or hold them hostage in "drop houses" for ransom from relatives. Last year [2002], 145 illegals died horrible and painful deaths in the Arizona desert. Smuggling is accompanied by a huge increase in violent crimes, including murder, rape, robbery and kidnapping.

Yet, only 140 new federal agents were assigned to the U.S.-Mexico border in Arizona this year [in 2003]. That's a pitiful response compared to the tens of thousands who invade our territory every year. Congress and the Administration are toying with plans to use state-of-the-art technology to monitor the activities of law-abiding Americans, and are now using camera-equipped, unmanned spy planes in Afghanistan to hunt for terrorists. When are we going to use advanced technology on *our* border, including surveillance planes, electric fences, and, yes, U.S. troops to protect the states against "invasion" as required by Article IV of the U.S. Constitution?

## The Tragic Consequences of Smuggling

The leader of a ring that smuggled about 900 illegal aliens during the 1990s was convicted in April [2003] after two of his passengers died in a sweltering tractor-trailer near Dallas. Each week, the smuggler would bring up to five loads of aliens to safe houses in El Paso where they would be picked up to be hauled to eager U.S. employers nationwide.

A Florida farm labor contractor was sentenced in April for luring illegal aliens into a smuggling operation that left 14 dead and 11 others to suffer in the Arizona desert after they were abandoned by their smugglers, called coyotes. [In 2002], 94 people were prosecuted in Colorado for smuggling illegal aliens.

A Tijuana restaurant owner pled guilty to running a smuggling ring that brought illegal aliens, mostly from Lebanon, through Mexico into San Diego.

People-smugglers are bringing people from Pakistan and the Middle East into the United States for as much as $30,000 a person.

*"Trucks ought to be inspected when they cross the border, for the illegal aliens' protection as well as for American sovereignty."*

The leader of a ring that smuggled over a thousand Ukrainians into the United States through Mexico was sentenced in March to 17 years in prison. The smuggling operation began in Kiev, Ukraine, where people (referred to as "merchandise") paid fees of $5,000 to $7,000 each, were provided with Mexican tourist visas, coached to say "United States citizen" without a Russian accent, flown to Mexico and escorted to Los Angeles.

Accidents are a common occurrence, even on highways far from the border, when vans carrying illegal aliens crash because of high speeds, incompetent drivers going the wrong way, or inability to read English signs. The injured have to be cared for in local hospitals at U.S. taxpayers' expense.

In San Diego in December [2002], 6 illegals were killed and 16 injured in a wrong-way lights-off head-on crash on the interstate, and 2 were killed and 20 injured in another crash in March [2003]. In Bowie, Kansas, in February, a van rolled over killing 3 and hospitalizing 15.

Near Fort Smith, Arkansas, in March, 5 aliens were hospitalized after a head-on crash. A tractor-trailer driven by an illegal alien jackknifed and crashed in the new Boston Big Dig tunnel in May, and the cost to the taxpayers will be $500,000.

In populated areas of California and Arizona, the illegal traffic often moves through tunnels, of which U.S. officials say there may be "at least 100, if not several hundreds." A truck will park over the U.S. end of the tunnel, and bundles of drugs are handed up through a hole in the trailer's floor.

On April 4 in a parking lot near San Diego, U.S. authorities found a sophisticated tunnel with electricity, ventilation and a million-dollar pulley system. It was the fifth secret passageway discovered along that county's border in the past 14 months.

The federal government has appropriated $695,000 to clean up the trash and waste in southeast Arizona to cope with the environmental damage caused by this human traffic. Arizonans say they need $62.9 million and 93 more employees to repair the damage and to protect against the threat of wildfires from mountains of trash.

We certainly can't depend on Mexico to stop this invasion of illegals. U.S. authorities estimate that smugglers will pay $500 million this year in bribes and payoffs to Mexican military and police to protect this illicit traffic.

## The Crimes of Illegal Immigrants

How many policemen will die because of our government's failure to stop illegal entry into the United States? One of the worst aspects of our government's open borders policy is the repeated re-entry of alien criminals who were previously deported but easily return to commit more crimes.

In May, an illegal alien criminal and documented gang member, with four previous felony convictions and who had been deported several times, sneaked back into the United States and committed a cold-blooded crime. When Oceanside (Calif.) police officer Tony Zeppetella stopped Adrian Camacho for a traffic violation, the alien pulled out a gun and killed the policeman with three shots.

Saul Morales-Garcia alias Javier Duarte Chavez shot Las Vegas police officer Enrique Hernandez six times in December. The alien had previously been deported, but he illegally re-entered the United States.

Zeppetella had served six years in the Navy and Hernandez eight years in the Marines. Both had a wife and infant child, and friends of both officers said their childhood ambition was to be a policeman.

In June, Enrique Sosa Alvarez was arrested in San Jose and charged with dragging a nine-year-old girl from her home and raping her repeatedly for three days before releasing her. A fingerprint check identified him as David Montiel Cruz who had previously been convicted of auto theft.

> *"One of the worst aspects of our government's open borders policy is the repeated re-entry of alien criminals who were previously deported but easily return to commit more crimes."*

Police don't know for sure who he is, but we do know for sure he should have been deported after his earlier crime. The ease with which criminals change their names and come back across the border shows the folly of accepting Mexico's *matricula consular* as a valid I.D.

Illegal alien Walter Alexander Sorto was repeatedly picked up for driver's license violations and for not having insurance, but Houston police were barred from reporting his illegal status to federal authorities. In March [2003], he and a companion abducted, raped and killed three Houston women.

Maximiliano Esparza, who raped and killed a Bellevue, Washington, nun [in 2002], had earlier been in a California prison and the court had ordered him deported. But our government didn't deport him; it merely asked him to sign an I-210, a simple promise to depart, widely known as a "catch-and-release" document.

Before the [September 11, 2001, terrorist attacks], ringleader Mohamed Atta was ticketed in Florida for driving without a license, and his accomplice Ziad Samir Jarrah was ticketed for speeding in Maryland, and both were on expired visas. Chalk that up to missed opportunities to prevent 9/11. . . .

Under a final order of deportation are 314,000 absconders, illegal aliens whom our government can't deport because we can't find them, including 4,800 from nations where Al Qaeda terrorists are active. Only a fraction of them have been entered on the National Crime Information Center database, the Department of Justice's listing of outstanding warrants and fugitives.

Only the brutal gang rape of a Queens, New York, woman in December [2002] by four illegal aliens has produced a governmental response. Three of those four criminals already had long rap sheets from previous arrests and should have been deported.

## Shackling Law Enforcement

The House Judiciary subcommittee on immigration was spurred to hold a hearing in February [2003] to question New York and Houston officials about their so-called "sanctuary" ordinances that deter or even prohibit local police from reporting illegal aliens to federal authorities. New York was under such an executive order issued in 1989 by then-Mayor Edward Koch.

On May 30, New York City Mayor Michael Bloomberg signed Executive Order 34 *permitting* city employees to ask people seeking government services about their immigration status *if* that is relevant to their eligibility. Bloomberg said his order was necessary to put the city into compliance with federal law, and even Koch came out in support of the Bloomberg order. Bloomberg's order, however, has limitations. He said in a written statement that he will never let police or city agencies become an arm of the INS "under my administration."

*But why not?* State and local police, of whom we have at least 670,000, are our first line of defense against criminals (not the minuscule 2,000 federal investigators assigned to immigration enforcement). But local police are being shackled by city officials.

Twenty cities, including Los Angeles, San Francisco, Chicago, Miami, Denver, Seattle and Portland, Maine, have adopted "sanctuary" ordinances banning police from asking people about their immigration status unless they are suspected of committing a felony, are a threat to national security, or have been previously deported. But how are the police going to know if they have previously been deported unless they first ascertain who they are?

> *"Local police should be allowed to preempt vicious crimes by checking the citizenship status of persons arrested for minor as well as major crimes."*

What happens when alien criminals complete their prison terms? The Justice Department's inspector general admitted that our government released 35,318 criminal aliens into the general population in 2000, and nobody knows how many then committed other serious crimes.

The famous case of the sniper who terrorized the Washington, D.C., area for weeks [in 2002] is a good example both of the importance of the role of the local police and of the irresponsible way that federal immigration authorities release aliens instead of deporting them. Lee Malvo was picked up and fingerprinted the previous year by a Bellingham, Washington, police detective and west coast Border Patrol agent. They turned Malvo over to federal immigration officials, who had the duty under our laws to deport him immediately because he came to the United States as a Jamaican stowaway on a ship that docked in Miami. But Seattle district immigration officials released Malvo, who subsequently went across the country on a killing spree with John Muhammad, who was financed by the $60,000 he made selling forged U.S. driver's licenses and birth certificates.

In fairness to our local police, they repeatedly complain that they get no cooperation from federal immigration officials when reporting illegal aliens—unless a major felony is involved. Attorney General John Ashcroft should make sure that all police know about his October 8 [2002] speech to the International Association of Chiefs of Police wherein he promised that federal agents will respond when local officers notify them of immigration violators.

If the United States can wage a preemptive war against Iraq, local police should be allowed to preempt vicious crimes by checking the citizenship status of persons arrested for minor as well as major crimes, and then reporting illegals to federal authorities. All sanctuary ordinances should be rescinded.

# Political Asylum Laws That Exclude Battered Women Are Reasonable

**by Daniel A. Stein**

**About the author:** *Daniel A. Stein is director of the Federation for American Immigration Reform, a national public interest organization whose goal is to reform America's immigration policy by improving border security, halting illegal immigration, and promoting controlled immigration levels.*

On their way out the door, top officials of the Clinton Justice Department unveiled a new category of people who can be granted political asylum in the United States. Under this parting proposal, women around the world who are battered by their spouses would be eligible to receive protection in this country. Already, this legal provision, which was intended to protect people from persecution by their governments, has been broadened to include a wide range of people who might be subjected to objectionable cultural and social practices.

[Since 1992] political asylum has been granted to people claiming to fear social customs, such as female circumcision, and even social ostracization based on sexual orientation or disability. In addition to these Democratic expansions, Republicans have pressed to include people who claim to oppose China's strict family planning policies. While all these practices are reprehensible, they hardly fit the definition of political persecution. The policies that have been promulgated over the past eight years have moved us from the murky area of rendering judgments about the actions of foreign governments to the even murkier area of judging social and cultural practices.

If the United States has sometimes been viewed as the world's policeman, these recent expansions of political asylum are moving us toward the role of the international nanny. Virtually everyone who is subjected to any injustice, whether perpetrated by a government, social group, or a relative, can seek protection by the United States.

## An Unworkable Definition

Even if we could absolutely guarantee all such claims were legitimate, such a broad definition of the asylum law is unworkable. We have a hard enough time providing shelter and services for American women who are abused by their spouses, much less assuming responsibility for battered women in other countries. It is difficult enough dealing with the real and imagined grievances of those who feel ostracized in our own society, much less taking on the aggrieved of the entire planet.

But, of course, we can't even guarantee that all the claims for social asylum will be legitimate. We have a foreign service and intelligence apparatus that can substantiate or refute claims of what foreign governments are doing. But how does the United States monitor what is taking place in every village square and in every bedroom around the world?

> *"We cannot maintain [an asylum] policy that attempts to right every wrong and rectify every misfortune, wherever it occurs, no matter who is responsible."*

Even as the Justice Department was announcing its plans to include battered spouses as a class of people eligible for asylum, it was uncovering evidence of just how difficult it is to prevent fraud. The *Washington Post* . . . reported that the INS [Immigration and Naturalization Service] had granted asylum to a woman who claimed to fear the abhorrent social custom of female circumcision to someone who had made up the story in order to take advantage of this new asylum category.

The same Clinton Administration that maturely understood that it was not possible to have a government program to cure every domestic problem, will leave as its legacy a naïve set of regulations that attempt to solve every social and cultural problem around the world by offering asylum in the United States. We cannot maintain a policy that attempts to right every wrong and rectify every misfortune, wherever it occurs, no matter who is responsible.

In a world of 6 billion people, most of whom live under political systems and cultures that leave a lot to be desired, we unfortunately must pick and choose who we will offer protection. Granting asylum to people who claim to be a member of one group that isn't liked or fairly treated by another group only morphs the political asylum process into a policy that is unmanageable since arguably millions of people on the planet [are] a member of one group that isn't liked by another. Political asylum must not become social asylum, or it will destroy our ability to help anyone.

# Asking Immigrants to Assimilate Is Fair

by Stephen Browne

**About the author:** *Stephen Browne, a teacher and writer, has lived in eastern Europe since 1991.*

A few years ago, when I was living and working in Belgrade, colleagues would sometimes joke with me, "Hey Steve, what are you really doing here? You're a spy, right?" I always got a kick out of the look on their faces when I answered, "No, I'm not a spy, I'm a Cultural Imperialist. I'm plotting to make the whole world American."

They didn't know it, but I was totally serious. I want everybody in the world to be free of the fear of arbitrary arrest and imprisonment and of getting the holy shit kicked out of them for speaking their minds. I don't care whether you eat at McDonald's or not, I make a better hamburger anyway.

I know the Red Chinese, among others, have learned enough PC [politically correct]-speak to tell us sternly that they have their own cultural and political traditions, different but not inferior from ours. Yeah, right. I bet some Chinese guy getting the eyeballs knocked out of his head for speaking out of turn gets warm fuzzies thinking, "Gosh. I'm participating in my people's ancient tradition of Getting the Shit Kicked Out of You for Speaking Freely. I feel so Chinese."

Historically, if by chance you did not care to participate in such ancient customs, there was an alternative. If you had the guts to leave what was familiar behind and risk everything on the unknown, you could become an American.

## Challenging Immigration Policy

In the January [2002] issue of *Liberty*, my friend [economics and political science professor] Ken Schoolland told why he believes we should leave the door open to anybody who makes that choice. In the February [2002] issue, [edito-

Stephen Browne, "Immigration and Culture," *Liberty*, vol. 16, August 2003, pp. 39–40. Copyright © 2003 by the Liberty Foundation. Reproduced by permission.

rial writer] Bruce Ramsey told why he believes we no longer have that luxury. Since then, almost all the responses from letter writers have been against Ken Schoolland's position, sometimes hysterically so.

It's interesting that both Schoolland and Ramsey are married to immigrants. I myself am an expatriate American living in Poland and married to a Pole. I must admit that I am a bit uncomfortable with the fact that I can easily come to Poland and stay for indefinite periods of time with little bureaucratic hassle, but Poles cannot do the same in my country. I also find disturbing that, to accompany me back to the States, my wife will have to go through a lot of official bother,

> *"Brawling, drinking, whoring, dope-smoking scoundrels . . . did assimilate and their descendants are now gravely debating about who is unassimilable."*

answering some nasty intrusive personal questions from immigration bureaucrats, while my son and I can breeze through after merely flashing our passports.

Furthermore, in the (highly unlikely) event of a return of communist despotism, or an invasion of the Tartar hordes (perhaps less unlikely than one might think), I want very much to be able to get my in-laws into America. I don't think any Americans would object to a few more computer experts or good-looking, well-educated ladies with pleasant personalities.

Or maybe some would. I remember meeting in Bulgaria a beautiful young opera singer, who had won international competitions in Europe and had earned a full scholarship to study in America. Her visa was denied by a woman at the American embassy who told her, "Oh you beautiful Bulgarian girls, you just want to go to America and find an American boy to marry, and then what will our poor girls do?" I dunno, maybe re-examine their attitudes? Dear gentlemen of this 80%-male movement, you would weep bitter tears if you could meet some of the ladies I have known who were denied visas to America.

But what about the hordes of unskilled laborers that pour across our southern border, and even through our ports? Well, I am not an economist, but I do grasp the notion that wealth comes from labor, and there is no economic sophistry that can convince me that a large labor pool willing to work for low wages, under conditions unacceptable to the native-born, can be bad for a country's economy.

What seems to be lacking in the immigration debate is imagination and sufficient tough-mindedness. Hordes of unskilled Chinese and Irish built the transcontinental railroad, and what an appalling lot they were! Brawling, drinking, whoring, dope-smoking scoundrels you wouldn't want near your daughters, many of whom you'd rather have hanged than had for neighbors—and yes that's great-granddad I'm talking about here. But they did assimilate and their descendants are now gravely debating about who is unassimilable and shouldn't be let in.

But we're talking about the worst of all possible immigrants! Not the cultured and well-educated, but the uneducated and unskilled. But often it has been precisely these kinds of people that have been the most willing to assimilate, eager to forget the customs, habits, and even the language of countries that offered them nothing but lives of grinding poverty and a place at the bottom of the "natural order of things." Their children grew up in America proud, cocky, even arrogant—and afraid of nothing under the sun.

Irish writer Walter Bryan spoke of the miraculous change of the feckless and irresponsible Irish immigrants into bold, self-confident Irish-Americans. "A change so total that it can only be ascribed to the action of something previously lacking in their diet. Probably food." The tragedy of our immigration rules is that they keep out people who would make fine Americans. Americans I'd swap for any number of the ones we've already got. As Eric Hoffer said, "Nobody hates America like native Americans. America needs immigrants to love and cherish it."

And yet, I am afraid.

## Supporting the American Way of Life

Some time ago, I saw on *60 Minutes* the story of an immigrant Palestinian family, that had a conflict between the father, who wanted his daughter to grow up in a proper Muslim way, and the daughter, who wanted to live like a normal American high-school kid. Because the father was suspected of ties to Hamas, the FBI was bugging the house and thus got it all on tape when the father stabbed his daughter to death. They got the daughter's screams and her mother comforting her, "Hush little one. Hush, and die."

I am afraid that we have lost our nerve. Afraid that as a society we no longer have the self-confidence to tell immigrants, "This is what we believe, this is the way we live and it works for us. You may bring something to offer from your culture, indeed we welcome it, but certain things you must leave behind. Your wars and ancient hatreds have no place here. You must abandon customs which are incompatible with our rights and freedoms. Your loyalty must be to America and your

> *"[The uneducated and unskilled] have been the most willing to assimilate, eager to forget the customs . . . of countries that offered them nothing."*

fellow Americans, even those who were hereditary enemies in your homelands. We know this is a great deal to ask, but a great deal is given in return."

Why can't we tell these people that if they try to practice that quaint custom in our country, we will stuff their mouths with pig flesh and hang them in its hide?

I have also heard about a Spanish-language radio station in California that advertises itself as "The Voice of Occupied Aztlan" and openly advocates the colonization and *reconquista* of the formerly Mexican lands in the West. I understand very well that no American remembers what no Mexican ever forgets—that the southwestern quarter of the continental United States was once the northern half of Mexico. American settlers were invited to settle in Texas and other parts of the Southwest because Mexico could not fill the land themselves. Eventually the immigrants preferred to live under the political institutions they were familiar with. Now that it's desirable real estate Mexicans want it back.

> *"Once our schools were the means of assimilating countless immigrants who were often amazed and grateful that this land would freely give them education."*

So why haven't we told these people that we respect their opinions so much that we have decided that if we catch them in arms against us, we will treat them, not as criminals subject to the rules of criminal justice, but as soldiers subject to the rules of war.

Hell, even a first-generation Mexican-American friend of mine admitted that if Mexico still owned the Southwest it would just mean that wetbacks would have another 1,500 miles to hike to sneak across the border.

Once our schools were the means of assimilating countless immigrants who were often amazed and grateful that this land would freely give them education, the privilege of aristocrats in their homelands. Nowadays, schoolchildren are taught that they should never consider anyone else's way of life to be in any way inferior and that we have no right to demand that anyone adopt our way of life, or even our language, when they come to live in our country.

Maybe travel to America has become just too damned easy. In times past, immigrants were to some degree self-selected by the expense and sheer physical difficulty of just getting here. This biased things in favor of the brave and resourceful and limited the number of people willing to risk the voyage. It has been estimated that to immigrate from Europe to America in the 17th and 18th centuries, or to migrate westward across America in the 19th century cost a family about seven years' income, not to mention the travel time and the dangers of the trip. It's easier these days.

## A Difficult Question

Deng Xiaoping famously remarked to Jimmy Carter that America is still at least a sea voyage or an air trip from the largest mass of population on earth. Where I live, it's an overland trip of a week on the Trans-Siberian railroad. When Chinese first started to come to Hungary in large numbers about ten years ago, the government reacted by making each family from China sign an agreement to have only one child while they are living in the country. Poland and other countries in the region have similarly limited entry from China.

Is this an unconscionable violation of their rights? Poland is the size of New

Mexico and has a population of about 38 million. How many people could China send here in a year? A decade? Is it wrong for Hungary or Poland to try to keep their country for themselves? Is it wrong for us? Are the questions equivalent?

The Kingdom of Hawaii allowed (or could not prevent) unlimited immigration of laborers to do the plantation work the native population was not willing to do. There is no Kingdom of Hawaii anymore. Good for us, but the native Hawaiians may not see it that way.

Some of our friends in Lithuania are concerned about the presence of a large Russian population in their newly independent country, and are not very comfortable with a fair-sized population of ethnic Poles either. After regaining their long-desired independence, they wonder whether their fate is to become a political appendage of a resurgent Russian Empire or a new dynamic Poland.

Sometimes I despair of the short-sightedness of the policy of keeping so many visitors out of our country. We have a chance to gain cultural hegemony over the world without firing a shot, by exposing as many foreigners as possible to our way of life. Yet, in this age of cheap mass transportation we could possibly be swamped by invaders too numerous to assimilate. And the fact is that any conceivable measures we could take may only slow down the process.

Experience has shown that people overwhelmingly prefer to live their lives in the environment they grew up in when the conditions are at least bearable. I have noticed over the past ten years that Poles are no longer anxious to leave Poland in large numbers now that the country has become a much more pleasant place to live. Those that do leave for professional reasons have a much greater likelihood of returning. Our future may be a race to Americanize the world before the world descends en masse on America.

Chapter 3

# How Should the United States Respond to Illegal Immigration?

# Chapter Preface

Illegal immigrants crossing the U.S.-Mexico border face a new danger in their harrowing trip across the vast Sonoran desert of America's Southwest. According to journalist R.M. Arrieta, "Overzealous U.S. citizens—often carrying high-powered rifles, sporting homemade badges and wearing camouflage fatigues—have forcefully detained thousands of migrants before turning them over to border patrol agents." Some U.S. citizens who live near America's southwestern border with Mexico are frustrated by what they see as an unrestricted flow of illegal immigrants. These Americans believe that they have the right to protect the U.S. border and have formed citizen militia groups to do just that. Immigrant rights advocates claim that these organizations put migrants at risk and hold these groups responsible for murders and attacks on migrants in the Arizona desert.

One of the most well-known civilian militias is Civil Homeland Defense (CHD), created by Cochise County, Arizona, resident Chris Simcox, editor and publisher of the weekly *Tombstone Tumbleweed*. Frustrated by what he sees as a seemingly unending flow of illegal immigrants crossing the border into his town, Simcox used his paper to call for federal help. When he failed to get a response, he founded CHD. "It is time we, the citizens, band together to show our inept Homeland Security Department a thing or two about how to protect national security and the sovereignty of our Democratic Republic," asserts Simcox in an October 24, 2003, editorial. "American citizens, under the Second Amendment to the Constitution, have the right to bear arms and to form a militia," he maintains, "and I dare the president of the United States to do anything about it."

While Border Patrol officials do not directly oppose civilian militias, they do not encourage them. According to Border Patrol spokesman Mario Villarreal, "The Border Patrol appreciates the efforts of non-governmental organizations and members of the general public, but we discourage private parties from taking matters into their own hands." Villarreal adds, "What's important is that any organization or group abide by the law and work within the parameters of the law."

Local leaders and human rights organizations, however, take an affirmative stand against what they call the militias' vigilante actions. Congressman Raul Grijalva, who represents Arizona's Seventh District, claims that groups "are talking about a containment policy based on race, they are talking about a policy that violates human rights, they are talking about a movement that takes the law into their own hands, ignoring due process, ignoring human rights, ignoring civil liberties, and taking it on themselves." Since 1999 human rights advocates in Arizona have been warning state officials about the threat these civilian militia groups pose. "There have been a number of documented instances where migrants have been intimidated and threatened by groups patrolling the border," claims Jennifer Allen of the Border Action Network, an organization formed in 1999 to protect human and civil rights in the Sonoran desert along the Arizona-Mexico border. "That in itself is enough to warrant the state to take action," she asserts.

One alleged example of violence against illegal immigrants occurred in October 2002 in Red Rock, Arizona. A thirty-two-year-old man told a sheriff's department investigator that he was standing in the desert with a group of twelve illegal immigrants when two men wearing camouflage fatigues pulled up in a vehicle and opened fire. The man escaped, but when the sheriff arrived, two men lay dead and the remaining nine had disappeared. Pima County sheriff's department spokesman Mike Minter claims that there was no evidence the crime was a result of civilian militia action, asserting instead that it looked more like the act of warring smugglers—called "coyotes." "We aren't ruling [civilian militia] out, but it looks like it was coyote vs. coyote," Minter maintains. "We believe the group was with a group of smugglers who were then kidnapped by another group of smugglers. It's a business."

Claims that smugglers alone are responsible for violence against illegal immigrants frustrate human rights groups. According to Cecile Lumer of Citizens for a Border Solution in Cochise County, "Law enforcement says, 'Oh, it's the coyotes,' but coyotes have never killed and shot their people." Such claims go against her understanding of smugglers. "They may abandon them, but I've never heard of that before," Lumer contends. Attorney Isabel Garcia of the Coalicion de Derechos Humanos [Arizona Border Rights Project] agrees. "It's a convenient thing to say it was coyotes," argues Garcia. "It's embarrassing for them to think it might be [civilian militias] because law enforcement has turned a blind eye to what's been going on over the past three years."

While local residents in the Southwest are frustrated with U.S. border policy, most do not support civilian militias. The boards of supervisors and city councils in the Arizona communities of Bisbee, Sierra Vista, Tombstone, and Douglas have passed resolutions that oppose the formation of civilian militias. Responding to discontent in their communities, political leaders have begun to ask for federal help. U.S. senator John McCain of Arizona has advised the Senate, "Vigilante groups have formed, taking up arms, and taking the law into their own hands because they do not believe the federal government is doing its job at preventing illegal immigration at the border. We simply cannot tolerate this type of violence at the border." He and Senator Jon Kyl, also of Arizona, support resolutions against civilian militias and ask that the federal government take responsibility for border problems.

Whether civilian militias are a threat to migrants or an effective tool in controlling the U.S.-Mexico border remains controversial. The authors in the following chapter debate other issues concerning how the United States should respond to illegal immigration.

# The United States Should Legalize Illegal Immigrants

**by Tamar Jacoby**

**About the author:** *Tamar Jacoby, a senior fellow at the Manhattan Institute, a conservative, free-market think tank, is editor of* Reinventing the Melting Pot: The New Immigrants and What It Means to Be American.

The five U.S. Border Patrol agents hovered around a desk in the hut at the 15-mile checkpoint on Interstate 35. All were strapping, blunt-faced men with revolvers on their hips, and there was no mistaking their seriousness of purpose. The Border Patrol's Laredo sector—one of nine along the southwest frontier—considers this Texas outpost, 15 miles from Mexico on the major artery from South and Central America into the U.S. heartland, its "major defense" against unauthorized alien penetrations. Closed-circuit TV screens bathed the room in a somber gray light; contraband-sniffing dogs yapped noisily at the traffic outside. And now the men were clustered intently around a computer terminal, apparently checking if a newly arrested suspect was linked to organized crime or terrorist activity. Clearly, they had caught someone—maybe even someone of interest.

It was hard to know what to make of the incongruity when the knot of men shifted and their prey came into view. There were three of them, and the young, shy-looking woman—it was impossible not to think "girl"—was doing the talking. Small, slender, in jeans and a sweater, she looked as if she had come straight from hanging out with friends at the mall. Her cousin and younger brother—who turned out to be only 13—were even less prepossessing.

The agents conducting the interrogation were pleased by the collar, but even they seemed nonplussed. They had nabbed the trio on a bus with what one officer called "50-yarders"—identity documents so poorly forged you could tell they were counterfeit from that far away. The teenagers had waded through the river several hundred miles downstream and were now making their way via Greyhound to Houston, where they said they had family. Their fresh-looking jeans and rucksacks, plainly purchased on this side of the borders, suggested that someone in Houston was paying handsomely for the trip. And not only one trip, it turned out. Running the kids' photos and fingerprints through the computer, agents found they had made the trip three previous times in the past two weeks—made the trip, been caught, had their papers confiscated, been deported back to Mexico, bought new papers, crossed again, and once again been caught, albeit each time on a different bus route. No wonder the agents were flummoxed. One of the best-equipped, most professional agencies of the U.S. government was playing cat-and-mouse with three teenagers—and it wasn't clear who was winning.

## A Futile Effort

Striking as it seemed, the episode was far from unusual. Despite a historic buildup of forces on America's southwest border—the number of agents has nearly tripled in a decade, and budgets have multiplied even faster—there has been no appreciable decrease in the number of illegal migrants entering the country. New strategies and new technologies have significantly raised the probability of getting caught, but this stops almost no one. Like these teenagers, migrants just try again—often in more remote border areas where the United States has fewer agents and less sophisticated defenses. In the Laredo sector alone, the Border Patrol catches between 100 and 200 people per day; the daily figure for the entire frontier is about 2,500—some 932,000 last year [2003], according to the Department of Homeland Security (DHS). And, in all but a handful of cases, after a few hours detainees are escorted back to the border and released—free to try again. It's impossible to calculate how many actually get through, but estimates run as high as half a million per year.

This failure has dire consequences for America's security, its economy, and the rule of law. Clearly, the immigration system is broken, and enforcement alone—whether on the border or in the heartland—isn't going to fix it. Which is why President [George W.] Bush's proposal to create a guest-worker program that would divert the illegal influx into legal channels and legalize up to eight million undocu-

> *"Despite a historic buildup of forces on America's southwest border . . . there has been no appreciable decrease in the number of illegal migrants entering the country."*

mented laborers already in the country is such an important development.[1] The initiative isn't perfect, but it is a bold step in the right direction, all the more significant coming from a Republican president. Not that its boldness has insulated the proposal from heavy criticism on both the left and the right. Hardly a Demo-

---

1. As of August 2004, no legislation has been introduced on behalf of the administration, and no bills in Congress have been approved.

crat has a good word for it, and the conservative blogosphere has gone ballistic. Presidential candidate Howard Dean claimed it would do nothing but "help big corporations," while paleocon Pat Buchanan denounced it as a "blanket amnesty." Some, like UPI [United Press International] columnist Steve Sailer, even suggested that the plan might justify "conservatives sitting out the November election, voting for a third-party candidate, or, in the ultimate extremity, voting for the Democratic nominee." Yet critics—particularly those in Congress, who now must choose whether or not to take up the president's proposal— would do well to recognize it as a key first step and an opportunity to be seized. After all, if something isn't done, the problems posed by illegal immigration are only going to get worse.

A visit to the border is a troubling experience, not least for security reasons. Although, according to an investigation by the Associated Press, not a single terrorist suspect has been apprehended on the U.S.-Mexican border in the years since [the terrorist attacks of] September 11, 2001, we plainly need to patrol our southern frontier. Even if we never catch a terrorist there—and most agents believe would-be terrorists have the savvy and resources to choose other routes—we need to know who is entering the country and to control the number of immigrants we admit. But border enforcement as we know it is an exercise in futility. In 1986, hoping to eliminate the underground population that had accumulated from decades of unsanctioned migra-

> *"A guest-worker program . . . would divert the illegal influx into legal channels and legalize up to eight million undocumented laborers."*

tion, Congress passed legislation legalizing nearly three million undocumented workers. Today, the number of immigrants without papers has crept back up to more than eight million—the highest in U.S. history. And our attempts to catch them once they have established themselves in the United States are even less effective than our efforts to control border-crossings. In October [2003], in a rare battery of workplace raids, the DHS made national news by arresting exactly 250 of the eight million: overworked janitors, mostly Mexican and Eastern European, employed by Wal-Marts. Authorities hope these arrests and the prosecutions to come will have a chilling effect, but, like the endless apprehensions on the border, they seem unlikely to make much of a dent.

## Prohibition Parallels

In fact, the more one looks at these futile enforcement efforts, the more they recall an earlier era in our history: Prohibition. The problem with Prohibition, as every schoolchild knows, was that it was so out of sync with reality, so remote from human behavior and established economic patterns, that it had no hope of succeeding. It's not that alcohol is beyond government control. Realistic regulations—liquor licensing, blue laws, import duties, and the like—work effectively to keep both sales and use in check. But, by overreaching, Prohibition did far more harm than good, producing a national black market, a many-tentacled web of international smuggling, widespread criminal activity by otherwise law-abiding citizens, and underworld violence of a kind not seen before or since.

> *"What kind of democracy depends for its livelihood on a vast pool of noncitizen nonpersons who cannot participate in civil society?"*

The parallels with our current immigration policy are already apparent. The failure to regulate our southern border has eroded the rule of law throughout the country. Hundreds of thousands of people migrate to the United States each year and join those living on the margins of American society with false identities and counterfeit documents. California alone is home to more than two million illegal residents; New York state to more than one million. Undocumented workers fear police and other authorities, thereby undermining law enforcement in their communities. They come to believe that U.S. laws, like the immigration code, are meant to be winked at. Their illegal status also hurts Americans economically: Because illegal immigrants can't bargain for better, they undercut wages and work conditions for native-born laborers. And the consequences of forcing millions of people underground are deeply corrosive to our political values. After all, what kind of democracy depends for its livelihood on a vast pool of noncitizen nonpersons who cannot participate in civil society?

## Modern Tactics Are Not Enough

The problem does not stem from a lack of will on the part of the Border Patrol. On the contrary, the agency has all the hallmarks of a dedicated, professional force, and it has shrewdly modernized both tactics and strategies in recent decades. Thirty years ago, enforcement in Laredo was a very different business: more Wild West than modern military efficiency. The entire Border Patrol had fewer than 2,000 men, a budget under $100 million, and its main task, at least in Laredo, was keeping the city free of vagrants, shoplifters, prostitutes, and the like who drifted over from the Mexican town of Nuevo Laredo. Then, in the mid-'70s, the illegal flow started growing and the border buildup began. Today, the Border Patrol boasts nearly 11,000 men, and—including expenditures by other, related DHS agencies—the total amount spent policing the southwest frontier exceeds $9 billion. The most important changes stem from a new strategy, introduced in the mid-'90s, based on the notion of "prevention through deterrence." Today, in Laredo, agents are stationed like sentries high on the bluffs overlooking the Rio Grande, where would-be immigrants are sure to see their SUVs. Stadium lighting, 24/7 remote video monitors, seismic motion detectors, and other high-tech devices guard the well-worn paths up along the riverbank. And, as soon as migrants are detected, officers swoop down to arrest them. The force's computer system is state-of-the-art; central authorities track trends carefully and allocate resources accordingly. Indeed, it's hard to see what else they could be doing to stem the tide.

These improvements seemed successful at first. In Laredo, apprehensions shot up, then declined significantly, suggesting that would-be immigrants were being deterred. (Lacking any other way of measuring the flow, researchers use apprehensions as a proxy for the number that get across.) But apprehensions along the entire border, from sea to sea, did not decline during the '90s. Migrants simply moved their operations to more remote desert terrain. And, while increasing numbers die at those new crossing points, no fewer ultimately seem to make it into the United States. On the contrary, the illegal population is growing faster than ever. Apprehensions did fall somewhat in 2001, but no one who studies the issue can confidently tell you why: It could have been better enforcement, but it could also have been the sagging economy or new habits among migrants who, though not deterred from coming, now seem to visit home less frequently. And, whatever the reason, according to the Border Patrol, in 2003 apprehensions were on the rise again. "The best we can do is manage the border, not control it," Laredo Assistant Chief George Gunnoe explained ruefully. "'Manage' means we can account for all the entries. But, even with all the resources in the world, you won't stop the flow. Even if we shut the southern border, they'd come across the northern border and up along the coasts."

The reason, of course, is economic. Mexicans have accounted for the lion's share of farmworkers in the United States for more than 60 years, since we first started recruiting them for that purpose during World War II. The only thing that has changed from decade to decade, depending on U.S. policy, is whether they come legally (as immigrants), illegally, or as temporary guest workers. In many regions of Mexico, migration has become a way of life: Many villages, now effectively bedroom communities for dependent families, sustain themselves by exporting their able-bodied men. Of course, the market for low-skilled labor has expanded, and Mexicans now fill many other dirty, low-wage jobs as well. But, as study after study has found, it is the economic climate—wage levels in the United States, wage levels in Mexico, unemployment, the exchange rate—that most affects the flow of Mexican workers, not border enforcement.

> *"The migrant flow is inevitable and . . . we should aim to manage and make the most of it, not try futilely to interdict it."*

## The Lure of U.S. Employment

I caught an unusual glimpse of the flow—and why it is so hard to control—in Laredo. The Border Patrol was experimenting with a new program for deporting people apprehended while attempting to cross the desert in Arizona, and the Mexican consul decided to interview them, one by one, as they stepped onto Mexican soil. I watched one sunny afternoon as a batch of 150 people filed across the international bridge—tired, hungry, dirty, almost all of them men in their twenties. And I couldn't help noticing the way they carried themselves: neither particularly surprised by how they were being treated nor, apparently, discouraged. Some 20 percent told the consul frankly that they were going to try again straightaway. Another 10 percent said they were going to stay in Nuevo Laredo—another way of saying they would try again, since there could be no other reason to hang around in the sleepy border town. And, according to consulate staff, even those who declared they were going back to their home villages said it was to regroup for another attempt. Almost every man I spoke to had been to the United States before; indeed, a number had lived here many years, and several were on their way back to regular jobs. But even those making the trip for the first time had a destination in mind and information, from a relative or fellow villager, about a likely job. And that was when it struck me: They were just people on their way to work. This trip was turning out to be somewhat longer and more frustrating than usual, but, in truth, it was much as they expected—simply part of the price they pay for employment in the United States.

> *"It's hard to exaggerate the difference even temporary legalization could make—for immigrants and for the rest of us."*

Meanwhile, although U.S. law enforcement is having no appreciable effect on the size of the flow, we are making it more and more necessary for migrants to avail themselves of "professional" help—effectively spurring the growth of a vicious criminal underworld. More and more migrants pay smugglers to bring them across: One estimate, by the Public Policy Institute of California, suggests that nine in ten now use a "coyote." Smuggling fees have increased dramatically, from a few hundred dollars a decade ago to as much as $2,000 today. And, as the business becomes more lucrative, it also becomes more organized: Big-time criminal gangs seek to get involved. According to local law enforcement, several international drug-smuggling rings are now beginning to dabble in the human trade. Much of this new criminal activity is in Arizona, because that's where border enforcement has shunted the traffic. Crime is soaring in Phoenix: not just document fraud, long endemic in the illegal community, but murders (up by 45 percent in the last ten months), money-laundering ($160 million was funneled through the city in one six-month period in 2003), kidnappings, and extortions. Smuggling cases have increased by 50 percent since 1998. The DHS's immigration- and customs-enforcement division has recently apprehended a bumper crop of illegal weapons: everything from assault rifles to automatic handguns. And, in early November [2003] a shoot-out on an Arizona highway—probably between two rival smuggling gangs—killed four people and caused a wreck involving three other vehicles that happened to be traveling on the interstate.

## Chapter 3

## The Politics of Immigration

Why hasn't anyone, Democrat or Republican, taken action before now to remedy our disastrous border policy and the Prohibition-like activity it is spawning? The failure of what critics call an "enforcement-only" approach came to the surface with a vengeance in the summer of 2001: That year, as intensified patrolling blocked the easiest paths in places like Laredo, some 336 Mexicans died trying to cross the border in remote desert regions. Prodded by the deaths and by the way newly elected Mexican President Vicente Fox was engaging the White House, pro-immigration Democrats and Republicans, business lobbies, labor unions, and immigrant advocates suddenly got serious about trying to work out a bipartisan solution. In July [2003], the Bush administration leaked to the press that it, too, was crafting a reform package.

Then, after the September 11 attacks, all talk of immigration reform came to an abrupt halt. For two years, the Bush administration sat on its hands rather than spend political capital opening a border that Americans, more than ever, wanted to close. It wasn't until [the summer of 2003] that more horrific deaths along the frontier prompted both Democrats and Republicans to introduce reform bills in Congress. Some of the more interesting were initiated by border-state Republicans—including Senator John McCain, Representative Jim Kolbe, and Representative Jeff Flake, all of Arizona—who saw the havoc that unrealistic efforts to stop the flow were wreaking in their jurisdictions. But, without a bipartisan proposal or backing from the president, it was all but impossible to make progress. Business wanted a reliable stream of workers but was less enthusiastic about labor protections. Unions and their Democratic allies wanted to legalize the undocumented workers already in the country but were wary of guest-worker programs. And the Republican Party was split down the middle— divided between a proimmigrant business wing and rank-and-file voters tempted by the siren song of restrictionism. The one promising bipartisan measure introduced [in the fall of 2003] was a compromise known as the Agricultural Job Opportunity Benefits and Security bill, which would create a new guest-worker program and a path to legalization for up to half a million Mexican farmhands. A balanced bill with some four dozen Senate sponsors, half Democrats and half Republicans, it stood an excellent chance of passing—until it was held up in subcommittee by Saxby Chambliss, a Georgia Republican with restrictionist leanings.

## A New Proposal

It was into this morass that the president waded [in January 2004]. Though he plainly has political motives, that doesn't mean he isn't serious, and his proposal—which would apply to all types of workers, not just farmhands—could form the basis of the kind of comprehensive, bipartisan reform that's needed. In many ways, it builds on the work going on behind the scenes since before September 11, 2001: most important, the recognition, widely shared among reformers, that the migrant flow is inevitable and that we should aim to manage and make the most of it, not try futilely to interdict it. The Bush administration aims to do this through a temporary-worker program open both to illegal laborers already in the United States and others, not yet arrived, who would like to find jobs here. There would be no limits on the number who could participate: Anyone with a job or a job offer—theoretically the entire illegal immigrant workforce of eight million or more. Participants would enjoy full labor rights, they could get driver's licenses and health insurance, those who wished could bring their families to the United States, and they could travel freely back and forth to their home countries—life-altering improvements to the way they live now.

*"Without immigration reform, it will be business as usual on our southern frontier: more futile law enforcement, more migrant deaths, and more crime."*

The proposal would provide a steady stream of reliable laborers for industries—from agriculture to the restaurant business—that now rely on an unpredictable, illegal workforce. With its realistic guidelines, instead of the current unworkable prohibitions, it would help restore respect for the rule of law in immigrant communities. And it would enhance national security, regularizing and regulating border-crossings and freeing up resources so law enforcement could zero in on more suspicious aliens. Altogether, it's hard to exaggerate the difference even temporary legalization could make—for immigrants and for the rest of us.

But the Bush proposal has a critical flaw: It makes no provision for these temporary workers to become citizens. On the contrary, administration officials have repeated over and over that they expect most participants in the program eventually to return to their home countries. In fact, President Bush has proposed an array of incentives to ensure that they do, including portable Social Security benefits that immigrants could not collect until they left the United States. This is no accident: The president is bowing to political pressure from the Republican right, which sees legalization as an immoral "amnesty" and—probably more important—dreads the prospect of any new citizens, let alone eight million or more, likely to vote Democratic. But, by failing to provide a better track to citizenship, Bush's proposal undercuts the gains it hopes to make. Imagine, for example, a Mexican short-order cook who has been in the United States for 15 years, working, paying taxes, and raising children born here, who are American citizens. Mexico is no longer his home country; the United States is. And yet, rather than reward him for working hard and assimilating, the president's proposal bars him from full membership in U.S. society. If the cook is smart, he won't sign up for the program or will simply skip out and return to the shadows before he and his American family are due to go "home." Without an adequate bridge from the temporary-work program to a full-fledged citizenship track, the president's proposal cannot hope to eliminate the underground economy and will only perpetuate a permanent foreign-born underclass.

The problem is not insurmountable—Bush has not ruled out creating a bridge between a temporary-work program and the existing citizenship track. Indeed, the administration seems willing to lift the barriers that now make it extremely difficult for undocumented workers to apply for green cards—the first step toward citizenship—and has suggested augmenting the number of cards issued each year. The increase required would be substantial. But, rather than dismiss the president's proposal, Democrats should jump at this opportunity to negotiate a better reform package. Although Bush is never going to accept a plan that puts all temporary workers automatically on the road to citizenship, as reform advocates once hoped, Democrats can widen the path—whether by adding green cards or creating some other mechanism. Admittedly, success would come with a heavy political cost, giving the president a big victory in what may be a close election year. But Democrats would be making a big mistake to allow this opportunity to pass. Without Bush's leadership, there is virtually no chance that a majority of Republicans will acknowledge the inevitability of the unskilled migrant flow, and they will not support reform. Conservatives who criticize the Bush proposal as an unprincipled "amnesty" assume that there are alternatives—that we can simply crack down harder on the border and enforce any quota we like, no matter how unrealistic. But we can't. Mexican workers want to fill jobs in the United States, and they will continue to find ways to enter the country. Without immigration reform, it will be business as usual on our southern frontier: more futile law enforcement, more migrant deaths, and more crime. Just ask the Border Patrol agents in Laredo.

# The United States Should Not Legalize Illegal Immigrants

by William Norman Grigg

**About the author:** *William Norman Grigg, a columnist and senior editor of the conservative magazine the* New American, *is author of* America's Engineered Decline.

Bill Clinton uttered countless deceptive words during his eight-year occupancy of the White House, but perhaps none captured the essence of his slippery dishonesty better than these: "It depends on what the meaning of the word 'is' is." In defending his proposed amnesty for millions of illegal aliens, George W. Bush is striving to set a new record for brazen presidential dishonesty.

"This plan is not amnesty, placing undocumented workers on the automatic path of citizenship," insisted Mr. Bush at a January 12 [2004] press conference in Monterrey, Mexico, as he stood alongside Mexican President Vicente Fox. "I oppose amnesty because it encourages the violation of our laws and perpetuates illegal immigration."

## The Temporary Worker Program

As has often been said, crime unpunished is crime rewarded. In his January 7 [2004] White House address calling for a "new temporary worker program," the president outlined a plan that would reward those who violated our immigration laws by jumping the queue and taking up residence here illegally:

- The president proposed "legal status, as temporary workers, to the millions of undocumented men and women now employed in the United States, and to those in foreign countries who seek to participate in the program and have been offered employment here";

- That temporary legal status, the president said, "will last three years and will be renewable";
- Mr. Bush claimed that "our current limits on legal immigration are too low." He added that his administration will work with Congress to "increase the annual number of green cards that can lead to citizenship" for illegal aliens currently residing here, as well as others arriving every day in anticipation of being legalized once the proposal goes into effect.

It's vitally important to recognize that the Bush plan would not be limited to the current illegal alien population, which is commonly estimated to be 6–12 million (but may be 20 million or more). As the president's own words demonstrate, it would also extend to "those in foreign countries who seek to participate in the program."

Supposedly, those coming from foreign countries would need a job offer in advance of their arrival. But the president's invitation had an immediate, and quite predictable, effect. "The U.S. Border Patrol marks January 7 as the day illegal crossing numbers surge," reported a January 10 *Arizona Star* dispatch from the Mexican border town of Hermosillo. "We're starting to see an increase already," commented Border Patrol spokesman Andy Adame. It's reasonable to expect that a similar "amnesty rush" is underway elsewhere as millions—or tens of millions—of others race to take advantage of the Bush plan.

Ah, but that plan isn't an amnesty, insists the president, clinging to his official fiction with Clintonian tenacity. Representative Ron Paul (R-Texas) has no use for such evasions. "Millions of people who broke the law by entering, staying, and working in our country will not be punished, but rather rewarded with a visa," comments Rep. Paul. "This is amnesty, plain and simple. Lawbreakers are given legal status, while those seeking to immigrate legally face years of paperwork and long waits for a visa."

More disturbing still is the fact that the Bush plan represents merely the first installment. The Mexican regime has already broadcast demands for further concessions. Mexican President Fox offered honeyed words of support for the Bush plan during his January 12 joint press conference with Bush. But prior to Bush's trip to Monterrey, Fox had told the Mexican press that the Bush plan "es mas pequenito de lo que buscamos" ("it's much smaller than what we're looking for"). And Mexico's *El Universal* had reported, "The secretary of Foreign Relations, Luis Ernesto Derbez, affirmed that [Fox] cannot be satisfied with George W.

> *"A 'new temporary worker program' . . . would reward those who violated our immigration laws by jumping the queue and taking up residence here illegally."*

Bush's proposal to grant temporary employment to immigrants. . . . The goal is a total and complete program that protects those [Mexicans] in the United States and *those who aspire to go there*." (Emphasis added.)

The Mexican regime will be satisfied with nothing less than the abolition of our southern border, and our absorption of as many people as that government sees fit to send north. Eventually, the process begun by the Bush plan would "solve" the illegal immigration problem by simply removing our borders altogether—and by effectively destroying the concept of U.S. citizenship as well.

## Anatomy of a Betrayal

Supposedly, the newly legalized "temporary workers" would return to their home countries after the permits expire.

"My proposal expects that most temporary workers will eventually return permanently to their home countries when the period of work that I will be negotiating with Congress has expired," explained the president in Monterrey. Toward that end, he continued, "I'll work with [Mexican] President Fox and other leaders on a plan to give temporary workers credit in their home countries' retirement systems for the time they work in the United States."

The administration's proposal would also "reduce the cost of sending money home to families and local communities," continued the president. Such remittances from Mexican workers in America are that nation's second-largest source of foreign income. Additionally, as the president pointed out, through the Inter-American Development Bank "we"—meaning American taxpayers—"are expanding

> *"[Amnesty] would 'solve' the illegal immigration problem by simply removing our borders altogether—and by effectively destroying the concept of U.S. citizenship as well."*

access to credit for small business entrepreneurs" in Mexico and elsewhere in Latin America.

All of this taxpayer-funded largesse is necessary, insists the president, in order to "reduce the pressures that create illegal immigration" by expanding economic opportunity south of our border. But the amnesty itself creates a powerful incentive for newly legalized immigrants to establish themselves here and begin the process of chain immigration, through which untold millions of new immigrants would be brought in. This is what happened with the most recent immigration amnesty in 1986.

In anticipation of George W. Bush's "compassionate conservative" rhetoric, former Senator Alan Simpson of Wyoming, the chief sponsor of the 1986 Immigration Reform and Control Act (IRCA), insisted that the earlier amnesty was "a humane approach to immigration reform." Simpson also admitted at the time, "I don't know what the impact will be." Eighteen years later, we now know the impact: 6–12 million, and possibly 20 million or more, illegal aliens. If amnesty is granted to that population, and it begins the process of chain immigration of relatives from abroad, and it is supplemented by millions of others who come here based on job offers extended through Bush's temporary worker program, we might as well disband the border patrol and discontinue the fiction of having immigration controls at all.

## A Global "Job Fair"

President Bush's concern for the economic plight of illegal aliens in our midst is as puzzling as his indifference to the economic circumstances of American workers.

"Over the past 10 years, more than 2 million low-skilled American workers have been displaced from their jobs," writes CNN financial analyst Lou Dobbs. "And each 10 percent increase in the immigrant workforce decreases U.S. wages by 3.5 percent." Mr. Bush and his political allies blithely assure the public that il-

> *"Each 10 percent increase in the immigrant workforce decreases U.S. wages by 3.5 percent."*

legal immigrants are doing jobs nobody wants. However, points out Steve Camarota of the Center for Immigration Studies, "what they really mean is that they are doing jobs that they as middle- and upper-class people don't want."

"Massive immigration is vastly more popular among the elites than among the public," Steve Sailer, president of the Human Biodiversity Institute, told *The New American*. "Lawyers, politicians, and business executives won't find their pay driven down much by increased competition. On the other hand, if I was, say, a carpenter, I'd be horrified by what the President of the United States is planning to do to me and my family. What's the global average wage made by carpenters? I'd be surprised if it were more than 33 percent of the average American carpenter's wage, and I wouldn't be shocked if it were only 10 percent as much."

"It's all a matter of supply and demand," explains Sailer. "As they teach you during the first week of Econ 101, when the supply of labor goes up its price [wage] goes down. . . . The only restriction the Bush people are talking about is that the job oilers to foreigners must meet the minimum wage. That's $5.15 per hour, or $10,712 for a full-time worker."

Sailer describes the Bush plan as "a globalist libertarian's fantasy. It's essentially identical to the *Wall Street Journal* editorial page's long campaign for a constitutional amendment reading 'There shall be open borders.'" This would mean not only a deluge of low-skilled, low-paid labor from Mexico, but from across the globe. According to Dobbs, "for all the world the president's [immigration proposal] . . . sounds like a national job fair for those businesses and farms that don't want to pay a living wage and for those foreigners who correctly think U.S. border security is a joke and are willing to break our laws to live here."

The immediate beneficiaries would be illegal workers from Mexico, and a Mexican government that uses illegal immigration to the U.S. as (in the words of former foreign minister Jorge Castaneda) a "safety valve." But there are literally billions of people willing to work for even less than Mexicans are. "In this age of cheap jet travel, poor Mexican immigrant job hunters might find themselves undercut by even poorer temporary workers from, say, Bangladesh who may be willing to work for even less," Sailer predicts. "According to UN figures, there are several billion people poorer than the average Mexican."

With hi-tech and manufacturing jobs fleeing the country, and millions of low-skill workers flooding in, what will America look like just a few years from now if Bush's amnesty proposal is enacted?

## Just the First Step

The January 8 [2004] *New York Times* editorially praised the Bush amnesty as a prelude to a larger effort to reform our immigration system: "For simply re-opening what has always been a torturous debate in this country, the president deserves applause. He has recognized that the nation's immigration system is, as he put it, 'broken.'" But the unspoken purpose of the process the Bush plan would inaugurate is to demolish, rather than repair, what remains of our immigration system.

The invited audience for President Bush's January 7 White House announcement included representatives from various "citizen groups," such as the Hispanic Alliance for Progress, the Association for the Advancement of Mexican Americans, the Latino Coalition, and the League of United Latin American Citizens. The address itself served as an overture for a hastily called "Summit of the Americas" in Monterrey, Mexico, the following week. These two facts underscore the real purpose of the amnesty proposal: It is a significant step toward the amalgamation of the U.S. with Mexico—as well as Canada, and eventually every other country in this hemisphere—into a regional political bloc.

> *"[Amnesty] is a significant step toward the amalgamation of the U.S. with Mexico—as well as . . . every other country in this hemisphere—into a regional political bloc."*

Shortly after taking office, Mr. Bush and Mexican President Vicente Fox signed a document called the "Guanajuato Proposal," pledging that their governments would "strive to consolidate a North American economic community whose benefits reach the lesser-developed areas of the region and extend to the most vulnerable social groups in our countries."

Within a few months of that declaration, the Mexican government had composed a five-point program to hasten "consolidation" with the U.S.:

- Legalization of "undocumented" workers (that is, illegal aliens from Mexico);
- An expanded permanent visas program;
- An enhanced guest workers visas program;
- Border control cooperation;

• Economic development in immigrant-sending regions of Mexico.

This list of demands, according to then–Mexican Foreign Minister Jorge Castaneda, were essentially non-negotiable: He insisted that the U.S. had to accept "the whole enchilada, or nothing." The Bush administration has dutifully worked to meet that nation's demands—without exacting anything from Mexico in return.

> *"[Amnesty is] part of a campaign that will—if successful—result in an end to our national independence and our constitutional order."*

During Fox's 2001 visit to the U.S., the groundwork was laid for the so-called "Partnership for Prosperity" (PfP)—an initiative designed to use American tax dollars to build Mexico's manufacturing sector. According to the U.S. State Department, PfP's action plan calls for U.S. assistance—meaning taxpayer subsidies—to Mexico to boost investment in housing and commercial infrastructure to boost Mexican productivity. This has the unavoidable effect of drawing manufacturing jobs south of the border—even as low-wage jobs are increasingly snapped up by illegal immigrants (pardon me—future temporary workers) surging northward.

## A North American Alliance

The Bush administration's indecent eagerness to eradicate our southern border and consolidate our nation with Mexico was noted by *Newsweek* political analyst Howard Fineman. "Whatever else George W. Bush does, or doesn't do, he has earned a place in history as the first American president to place Hispanic voters at the center of politics, and the first to view the land between Canada and Guatemala as one," noted Fineman. "It makes sense, if you think about it: Texas, long ago and far away, was part of Mexico. Now a Texan is trying to reassemble the Old Country, and then some."

"The ultimate goal of any White House policy ought to be a North American economic and political alliance similar in scope and ambition to the European Union," opined an *Atlanta Journal-Constitution* editorial on September 7, 2001. "Unlike the varied landscapes and cultures of European Union members, the United States, Canada and Mexico already share a great deal in common, and language is not as great a barrier. President Bush, for example, is quite comfortable with the blended Mexican-Anglo culture forged in the border states of Texas, California and Arizona."

President Bush has only offered oblique hints of the agenda that Fineman correctly described. Mexican President Fox has been more candid.

During a May 16, 2002 speech in Madrid, Fox boasted: "In the last few months we have managed to achieve an improvement in the situation of many Mexicans in [the United States], regardless of their migratory status, through schemes that have permitted them access to health and education systems, identity documents, as well as the full respect for their human rights." Here Fox referred to the incremental legalization illegal Mexican immigrants achieved when various state and local governments began to accept matricula consular cards as official ID. Those cards are issued by Mexican consulates without regard to the recipient's legal status. Easily counterfeited, the matricula cards give illegal aliens access to employment, health benefits, banking services and—in some states—driver's licenses.

In the Madrid speech, Fox explained that demolishing the distinction between legal and illegal Mexican immigrants is necessary in order to advance the merger of the U.S. and Mexico: "Eventually our long range objective is to establish with the United States, but also with Canada, our other regional partner, an ensemble of connections and institutions similar to those created by the European Union, with the goal of attending to future themes [such as] the future prosperity of North America, and the movement of capital, goods, services, and persons." Such movement of persons would no longer be "immigration" or "emigration"—terms referring to the crossing of international borders—but merely "migration" within one vast political entity. In other words: goodbye to U.S. citizenship.

Significantly, in his remarks at the January 12 press conference in Monterrey, Fox pointedly, and repeatedly, used the term "migration" to refer to the Bush plan, referring variously to "that migration topic," "the migration matters," "this migration proposal," the "migration flow," and so on. Tellingly, he also referred to "the leaders of the countries of America"—rather than to national leaders of separate and independent nations.

## Patient Persistence

Amnesty for illegal aliens, a central piece in the agenda for hemispheric consolidation, would almost certainly have been announced long ago were it not for [the terrorist attacks of September 11, 2001]—an event that demonstrated, in a tragic and lethal fashion, the mortal danger resulting from the failure to secure our borders.

However, merger-minded elites in both the U.S. and Mexico regrouped and continued their campaign for amnesty. [In the fall of 2003], a coalition of radical groups—including the Communist Party—organized the "Immigrant Workers Freedom Ride." In that campaign, busloads of illegal aliens were brought to Washington to lobby on behalf of amnesty.

Vicente Fox did his part by visiting three southwestern states—Texas, Arizona and New Mexico—to lobby state legislatures to support the amnesty drive. "We share nation and language," Fox told the New Mexico legislature. "In addition to our geographical vicinity, we are [united] by inseparable bonds, history, values and interests. . . . We must join together. . . . You need Mexico and Mexicans, and we need you."

Acting as the supposed leader of "Mexicans living abroad" (a group that, according to the Mexican government, includes Americans of Mexican ancestry born in this country), Fox demanded that lawmakers in this country "facilitate access to health care and education services for all those who share our border. . . . Without this, it is impossible to think about the path to greater integration and shared prosperity."

Open borders, amnesty for illegals, subsidies for Mexico's economy, exporting manufacturing capacity south of the border, expanded welfare benefits for foreigners who entered our nation illegally—these are all part of the same seamless design. As Fox himself put it, that design is the "integration" of the U.S. and Mexico into a hemisphere-wide political unit.

Many observers believe that the Bush amnesty plan is part of a political strategy aimed at courting the Hispanic vote—which would be a shockingly cynical and opportunistic venture. But the truth is even worse: President Bush is consciously betraying our nation by undermining our borders, our sovereignty, and the integrity of our laws. And he is doing this as part of a campaign that will—if successful—result in an end to our national independence and our constitutional order.

Every American worthy of the name must not accept this incredible betrayal—and must not allow it to be consummated.

# States Should Issue Driver's Licenses to Undocumented Immigrants

by the American Immigration Lawyers Association

**About the author:** *The American Immigration Lawyers Association is a national association of attorneys and law professors who practice and teach immigration law and whose goal is to convince the American people and elected leaders that immigration brings many benefits to U.S. society.*

The U.S. Congress and state legislatures have begun considering measures to restrict immigrants' access to driver's licenses.[1] These proposals go well beyond denying undocumented immigrants access to driver's licenses and are likely to effect legal immigrants and even U.S. citizens. While intended to increase national security, these measures will not enhance our security but will interfere with effective law enforcement.

The September 11 [2001] terrorist attacks have led to renewed calls for a national identification (ID) system. However, since national ID proposals have been defeated in the past, proponents are seeking to develop such a national system indirectly, through existing forms of ID such as state driver's licenses. The American Association of Motor Vehicle Administrators (AAMVA) is urging the federal government to fund and authorize a proposal to standardize state driver's licenses. The AAMVA . . . announced that it supports uniform standards for driver's licenses across all fifty states. If implemented, uniform driver's licenses would result in a de facto national ID card.

Representative Jeff Flake (R-AZ) introduced H.R. 4043 in March of 2002.

---

1. Of forty-four restrictive proposals, four passed in Colorado, Kentucky, New Jersey, and Virginia, and fourteen have been defeated. No vote has been taken on the remaining twenty-four as of August 2004. Campaigns to expand access to driver's licenses are moving forward. One law passed in New Mexico, and at least four states—California, Missouri, New York, and South Carolina—are considering proposals, but no vote has yet been taken as of August 2004.

This measure would bar federal agencies from accepting for any identification-related purpose any state-issued driver's license, or other comparable identification document, unless the state requires that such licenses or documents issued to nonimmigrant aliens expire upon the expiration of the aliens' nonimmigrant visa. [As of July 2004, this bill remains in the House Judiciary Committee.]

At the same time, some state officials have linked the denial of driver's licenses to undocumented immigrants to efforts to combat terrorism, alleging that the driver's licenses that several of the terrorists obtained facilitated their activities. (However, the terrorists did not need U.S.-issued driver's licenses to board planes on September 11 because they had foreign passports that would have enabled them to board.) Since September 11, many states are considering proposals to tighten the rules regarding driver's license eligibility and to further restrict immigrants' access to driver's licenses.

## Arguments Against Restricting Licenses

AILA [American Immigration Lawyers Association] opposes limiting immigrants' access to driver's licenses based on immigration status. Denying driver's licenses to large segments of the population is an inefficient way to enforce immigration laws and prevent terrorism and would make everyone in the community less safe.

*Restrictive Licensing Will Impede Law Enforcement and National Security.* Many local law enforcement officials oppose restrictive licensing proposals because driver's license databases play an important role in enforcement. Restrictive proposals will undermine law enforcement because:

- Licensing noncitizens enriches our domestic intelligence by allowing law enforcement authorities to verify and obtain the identities, residences, and addresses of millions of foreign nationals. Restrictive licensing will deprive authorities of this information.
- The proliferation of fraudulent documents that will result from restrictive licensing will impede law enforcement efforts by contaminating intelligence regarding who is present in the United States.

*State Driver's License Agencies Have Neither the Authorization nor Knowledge to Interpret Immigration Laws and Documents.* Restrictive licensing will require state motor vehicle administrators to become INS [Immigration and Naturalization Service] law and document experts in order to evaluate properly an applicant's immigration status and determine when such status expires. Immigration law creates approximately 60 ever-changing nonimmigrant visa categories in addition to classifications for asylees, refugees, parolees, persons in immigration proceedings, persons under orders of supervision, and applicants for many of these categories, as well as applicants for extension, change, or adjustment of status, to name a few. The scheme of documents issued by the INS, the State Department, and other agencies as evidence of these classifications is even more perplexing and includes visa stamps, laminated cards, unlaminated handwritten cards, forms, letters, and many other documents, either in combination or alone, which, even to the trained eye, often do not clearly show an applicant's status or duration of lawful admission. Additionally, due to extensive INS delays in application processing, many immigrants and lawful nonimmigrants will be unable to present documentation of their status. It is highly unlikely that motor vehicle administrators will be able to determine correctly whether a particular document or combination of documents establishes lawful status. This task requires the interpretation and application of a complex body of law. Requiring DMV personnel to understand and enforce immigration laws will most likely result in legal United States residents facing wrongful license denials and revocations for reasons that are wholly unrelated to driver competence.

> *"Licensing noncitizens enriches our domestic intelligence by allowing law enforcement authorities to verify and obtain the identities . . . of foreign nationals."*

*Restrictive Licensing Will Severely Jeopardize Highway Safety.* Proposals to restrict immigrants' access to driver's licenses will result in more unlicensed drivers operating vehicles on U.S. roads. Whether licensed or not, many individuals will have no choice but to drive—to work, to schools, to doctors, and to many other destinations—to meet basic everyday needs. Thus, restrictive licensing has the potential to reduce the safety of Americans and all drivers on our roads because it will:

- Remove an entire segment of the driving population from the reach of administrators charged with testing and certifying driver competence, which will contribute to the national highway mortality rate of 40,000 persons each year;
- Deprive motor vehicle administrators of the driving records of millions of drivers;
- Discourage or prevent millions of drivers from registering their vehicles;
- Eliminate incentives for foreign nationals to attend driver education schools;
- Increase the rate of minor traffic violations for unlicensed driving, which will divert law enforcement and judicial resources from truly serious offenses; and
- Create incentives for unlicensed drivers to flee accident scenes.

Denying driver's licenses based on immigration status also will prevent millions of drivers from obtaining insurance, which will increase uninsured motorist pools, contribute to current uninsured motorist losses of $4.1 billion, and increase insurance rates.

*Production and Sale of Falsified Documents Is Likely to Increase if Larger Numbers of Noncitizens Are Denied Drivers Licenses.* Restrictive licensing will encourage the fraudulent production and use of the many documents that are available to establish lawful immigration status by transforming the driver's license into a de facto INS document that will become necessary to establish lawful status. These fraudulent documents will further complicate the task of motor vehicle administrators by requiring them to detect fraudulent INS documents. Additionally, restrictive licensing will increase the market for easily obtained fraudulent documents, such as birth certificates and social security numbers, to establish identity. According to the Department of Health and Human Services, there are 14,000 different versions of birth certificates currently in circulation.

# States Should Not Issue Driver's Licenses to Illegal Immigrants

by Michael W. Cutler

**About the author:** *Michael W. Cutler, an immigration and naturalization agent for thirty years, is a fellow at the Center for Immigration Studies, a think tank that studies the economic, social, demographic, fiscal, and other impacts of immigration on the United States. The center favors proimmigrant policies but fewer admissions.*

*Editor's Note: This viewpoint was originally given as testimony before the State of Maryland House of Delegates on February 18, 2004.*

I welcome this opportunity to address you [State of Maryland House of Delegates] today about the critical issue of the issuance of driver's licenses to illegal aliens. I think it would be appropriate to begin by telling you about my background. I retired from the Immigration and Naturalization Service (INS) as a Senior Special Agent in New York in February 2002, having served that agency in various capacities during the course of my career which spanned some 30 years. I began as an Immigration Inspector assigned to John F. Kennedy International Airport in October 1971. For one year I was assigned as an examiner to the unit that adjudicates petitions filed by spouses to accord resident alien status to the husband or wife of resident aliens or United States citizens.

In 1975, I became a criminal investigator, or special agent as that position is now referred to. I rotated through every squad within the investigations branch, and in 1988 I was assigned to the Unified Intelligence Division of the Drug Enforcement Administration's New York office. In 1991, I was promoted to the position of Senior Special Agent and assigned to the Organized Crime Drug Enforcement Task Force, where I worked with a wide variety of law enforce-

Michael W. Cutler, testimony before the State of Maryland House of Delegates, Judiciary Committee, February 18, 2004.

ment officers from various federal, state, local, and foreign law enforcement organizations, including the FBI, DEA [Drug Enforcement Administration], IRS, U.S. Customs, ATF [Bureau of Alcohol, Tobacco, Firearms and Explosives], New York State Police, New Jersey State Police, New York City Police and various county police departments, as well as with representatives of the Royal Canadian Mounted Police, New Scotland Yard, British Customs, Japanese National Police, and the Israeli National Police. Finally, I have testified at several congressional hearings as an expert witness at hearings that dealt with immigration issues.

I am currently a fellow at the Center for Immigration Studies.

My professional experiences have provided me with a unique insight that I hope will be helpful to you as you grapple with this issue.

## Blurring the Lines

We currently live in a nation in which being politically correct permeates our society. In some ways this is a good thing, as it causes us to be careful to not offend any groups of people and show respect for everyone. On the other hand, it may also cloud issues and perceptions. George Orwell, the author of the book "1984" devised the concept of "Newspeak" in which words were regularly eliminated from the vernacular to alter perceptions and thought processes. An example of this Orwellian approach to immigration is the use of the politically correct term, "Undocumented worker" which has supplanted the legally correct term, "Illegal alien." The term alien is not a pejorative term but rather is a legal term. According to Section 1101 of Title 8 of the United States Code, the body of law that focuses on immigration issues, the term alien is defined as, ". . . any person who is not a citizen or national of the United States." When citizens of the United States travel outside the United States, they become aliens in the countries to which they travel. I respectfully suggest that by failing to properly recognize the fact that when aliens, especially illegal aliens, enter this country, they are not automatically entitled to every right and privilege enjoyed by United States citizens or by Lawfully Admitted Permanent Resident Aliens. We have sovereign borders that we must enforce if our country's continued existence is to be ensured. A country without borders can no more stand than can a house without walls. By blurring the distinction between what is legal and what is illegal, we encourage the rampant entry of illegal aliens into the United States, and we also encourage other criminal activi-

> *"The issuance of driver's licenses to illegal aliens aids and abets illegal aliens in living and working illegally in the United States."*

ties. While it is true that the responsibility to enforce the Immigration and Nationality Act falls to the federal government, individual states must do their part in creating an environment that is not conducive to illegal immigration.

We are often told that the immigration laws are not enforceable. Those who take this position will point to the 8 to 14 million illegal aliens currently estimated to be living in the United States today and draw the conclusion that these massive numbers illustrate how unenforceable the laws governing the presence of aliens in the United States are. I would respond by telling you that the immigration laws are no more, nor no less enforceable than any other laws. Motor vehicle laws, drug laws, firearms laws, and others are not more inherently enforceable than the immigration laws, yet no one would seriously suggest we give up attempting to enforce those other laws. The only laws which enjoy a 100 percent compliance rate are the laws of nature. The scientists and engineers at NASA might like to find a way of violating the law of gravity but have thus far been unable to do so.

Man's laws, on the other hand, are imperfect, and so the best we can do, in addition to our limited efforts at enforcing our laws, is to offer deterrence to discourage people from violating our laws. We set up sobriety checkpoints and impose severe penalties for drivers who are caught driving while intoxicated. We seize the assets of criminals who amass money and material property through criminal activities both as a way of generating funds for the government as well as a way of punishing and deterring criminals.

> *"Access to driver's licenses in an assumed identity will go a long way in [illegal aliens'] quest to create new identities for themselves."*

We understand that the way to increase the rate of compliance in which law violators are concerned is to devise strategies that discourage the violations of law and to impose penalties on those who break the law nevertheless.

## Aiding and Abetting Illegal Aliens

We are here today to discuss whether or not the state of Maryland should issue driver's licenses to illegal aliens. I believe that the issuance of driver's licenses to illegal aliens is the wrong thing to do. The issuance of driver's licenses to illegal aliens aids and abets illegal aliens in living and working illegally in the United States. My understanding of Maryland's motor vehicle law is that the state of Maryland accepts foreign driver's licenses for a period of one year if the license is accompanied by a passport and other such documentation.

It is clear that the desire by aliens who are illegally in the United States to obtain a driver's license goes beyond the need to drive a car in the United States. In the [aftermath of the terrorist attacks of September 11, 2001] we have come to use a driver's license as an identity document that can facilitate the bearer's boarding an airplane or train. It can also be used to gain entry into various government buildings. Additionally, the driver's license is one of several documents that are enumerated on the form I-9 which an employer must maintain on file

for each employee and may therefore facilitate an illegal alien seeking employment in the United States. Additionally, the driver's license can be used as a so-
called "breeder document" in which the bearer of the license obtains other identity documents based on the driver's
license.

> *"The issuance of driver's licenses to illegal aliens will make it easier for aliens who are living and working illegally in the United States to circumvent our laws."*

What I find disturbing about the
use of driver's licenses is that there
are no guarantees that the bearer of
the license is who he or she claims to
be. This is a flaw in the system that
goes beyond the reach of this hearing, but it is worth considering. The
only thing worse than no security is false security. The way we currently use
driver's licenses as an identity document provides us with a false sense of security, but it is the method by which we currently do business today. In my career
as an immigration officer I have encountered many individuals who had several
different driver's licenses in different names that they had procured in an effort
to conceal their true identity. This is why we often hear that the illegal aliens
who live in our country inhabit the "shadows."

According to recently published statistics, some 400,000 illegal aliens who
have been ordered deported from the United States are currently being sought,
having failed to turn themselves in. In my experience, many of them will have
succeeded in creating false identities for themselves as they seek to evade the
immigration authorities. Access to driver's licenses in an assumed identity will
go a long way in their quest to create new identities for themselves.

## Circumventing U.S. Laws

Consider this: aliens who are illegally in the United States became illegal
aliens in one of two ways; they either entered the United States by crossing the
border without being properly inspected—this includes stowaways who hide in
boats or airplanes—or they enter the United States through a port of entry.
Some of the aliens who enter through ports of entry do so under assumed identities, concealing their true identities and, perhaps, criminal backgrounds or
other issues that if known by the inspector at the time of entry would have
served as a basis for denial of admission. Other aliens enter with valid visas or
under the Visa Waiver Program which permits aliens from some 28 countries to
enter the United States without first obtaining a visa and then, in one way or another, violate their respective immigration status in the United States. That
means that they overstay the allotted period of time for which they were admitted, they accept employment without proper authorization, or they get arrested
and are subsequently convicted of committing a felony.

According to . . . published estimates, perhaps half of all illegal aliens did not
enter without inspection but rather entered the United States through a port of

entry and then violated the law. This was the case with each and every one of the 19 hijackers who attacked our nation on September 11.

In most cases, the goal of illegal aliens is to obtain employment in the United States, but this is not the only motivation for illegal aliens. While it is only a relatively small proportion of illegal aliens who become involved in serious criminal activity, a disproportionately large percentage of our criminal population is comprised of aliens. In 1988 I was assigned to the DEA Unified Intelligence Division in New York. I conducted an analysis of DEA arrest records and determined that some 60 percent of individuals who were arrested by DEA in the New York City area were identified as being "foreign born," while nationwide, some 30 percent were identified as being "foreign born."

As you may know, the two reasons that law enforcement officials fingerprint defendants when they are arrested is to properly identify the suspect in custody and to document the fact that the suspect was indeed arrested. This is essential because criminals often have multiple identities. They conceal their true identities in order to evade detection and when caught, they hope to thwart efforts by law enforcement officers from learning their true identities and their criminal backgrounds. In many cases, illegal aliens who were arrested attempted to conceal the fact that they were aliens and falsely claimed to be United States citizens to avoid being deported after they completed their prison sentences. In my experience, numerous drug suspects, in whose arrest I participated, were found to be in possession of multiple identity documents that they used to attempt to conceal their true identities. The most common identity documents that they carried were false Social Security cards and driver's licenses in different names.

Finally, I would like to remind you that a driver's license is a privilege and not a right. The issuance of driver's licenses to illegal aliens will make it easier for aliens who are living and working illegally in the United States to circumvent our laws. It will also aid criminal aliens and terrorists in concealing themselves within our country. The only reasonable course of action is to not issue driver's licenses to aliens who are illegally in the United States.

# Undocumented Workers Should Receive Social Security Benefits

**by O. Ricardo Pimentel**

**About the author:** *O. Ricardo Pimentel is a member of the editorial board of and a columnist for the* Arizona Republic.

It's an imperfect comparison, but let's say that your company offers a pension. You hired on with that knowledge. Let's get real here: This pension, while it is accruing, is really just deferred compensation.

It's your money, but you won't get it to pay the rent until way down the road.

Now suppose, well before retirement, your company arbitrarily says that this money isn't yours anymore. It's the company's.

The company has just stolen your money, though I suspect there are all kinds of ways that companies get to do this legally in real life. The central concept here, though, is that whether the company takes it legally or not, it really was your money—emphasis on *was*.

In much the same way, we steal money from undocumented immigrants all the time. We call it Social Security.

This is where the analogy is imprecise. The immigrants know they are paying into a system in which they aren't allowed to participate. They, in fact, expect to be robbed when they use fake Social Security numbers and their employers withhold payroll taxes.

This, however, doesn't make the robbery right, no more than serfs "electing" fealty to a feudal lord represents pure free choice, much less just governance.

A couple of years ago, the Arizona-Mexico Commission released a report titled "Labor Shortages and Illegal Immigration: Arizona's Three-pronged Strategy."

When payroll taxes are collected from folks without valid Social Security numbers—which is to say, fake numbers—the money goes into a pot that totaled $265 billion when the report came out. It had grown about $17 billion a year since 1990, according to the report.

This, too, is just deferred compensation, but the folks who are entitled to it will never see it. Unless, of course, we fix things. My guess, however, is that we would rather keep the money.

## A Common-Sense Proposal

How else to view the reaction to the common-sense proposal[1] to enter into an agreement with Mexico for the same kind of totalization agreement that we already have with 20 countries?

This kind of pact would allow Mexicans working here to collect the Social Security benefits that they've accrued here, once they return to Mexico. And it would allow Americans working in Mexico to be eligible for Social Security benefits accrued while they were there.

By and large, the Mexicans we're talking about in these cases are *legal* U.S. residents.

> *"[The Social Security] system has been predicated on the notion that if you pay in, you're entitled to get something out."*

However, Sergio Bustos of Gannett News Service notes in a story about the proposed agreement that the Social Security Act would allow even undocumented immigrants to get their benefits if a totalization agreement is negotiated. This if they can prove that they paid into the U.S. system.

This wouldn't be difficult to do for a lot of undocumented immigrants.

A . . . story by *Arizona Republic* reporter Daniel Gonzalez demonstrated that it is extremely easy to get a fake Social Security card. It costs, according to the peddler quoted in the story, $20 or $25.

Some of you have cited this story as an example of just how unscrupulous and nefarious this black market is.

I agree.

It exists, however, because we apparently like it this way. I mean, if we admitted that we needed this labor, we might have to do something as drastic as legitimizing its presence. And we couldn't possibly do that, according to many of you.

It's difficult to tell which is more unscrupulous and nefarious, the black market or the hypocrisy that created it.

Many of you will now call and e-mail to tell me how, even with their contributions to Social Security, undocumented immigrants consume more in taxes than they pay.

---

1. Commissioner of U.S. Social Security Jo Ann Barnhart and Dr. Santiago Levy Algazi, director general of the Mexican Social Security Institute, signed a U.S.-Mexican Social Security agreement on June 29, 2004. The agreement, which must be submitted to the U.S. Congress and the Mexican Senate for review, is not expected to enter into force before autumn 2005.

*Chapter 3*

We can argue this until the *vacas* [cows] come home, but the fact would remain that all those proposals for guest-worker programs are really just tacit recognition that we can't live without these immigrants. It really matters little whether they are net users or payers in taxes.

Though we have decreed that immigrants without documents are here illegally, we have also made it illegal, as a matter of justice, conscience and principle, to rip them off.

In other words, though we don't make near the effort needed to find thieving employers, we have said that those who cheat undocumented workers are also "illegal," the anti-immigrant crowd's favorite word.

Except, of course, when it comes to Social Security and when all of us, collectively, are holding the purse strings.

Yes, I know, Social Security might not even be there when I retire. But the system has been predicated on the notion that if you pay in, you're entitled to get something out.

Except when the folks who have paid in are undocumented. But if this is true, then it follows that none of us who pay in are any more entitled.

# Illegal Immigrants Should Not Receive Social Security Benefits

**by Paul M. Weyrich**

**About the author:** *Paul M. Weyrich is chairman and CEO of the Free Congress Foundation, a conservative think tank that promotes a return to a traditional, Judeo-Christian culture.*

U.S. and Mexican government officials are engaged in talks about a plan[1] that would allow Mexicans who have been illegal immigrants to collect Social Security for the work that they did during the time they were breaking our nation's laws.

I have had many good things to say about President [George W.] Bush, and I still do. However, there are some areas on which I harbor concerns about administration policy, and one of those has been the courting of Muslims by the White House.

Ditto for this attempt that is being fervently promoted by the Mexican government, aided and abetted by federal bureaucrats at [the Department of] State and the Social Security Administration, to mesh our Social Security system with their own retirement system. The end result may end up encouraging more illegal immigration.

## The Problem with Totalization

"Totalization" is the name for this idea, and it would permit a Mexican worker to combine their years spent working in the United States and Mexico when applying for Social Security benefits.

1. Commissioner of U.S. Social Security Jo Ann Barnhart and Dr. Santiago Levy Algazi, director general of the Mexican Social Security Institute, signed a U.S.-Mexican Social Security agreement on June 29, 2004. The agreement, which must be submitted to the U.S. Congress and the Mexican senate for review, is not expected to enter into force before autumn 2005.

There is very good reason for Americans to be concerned about "totalization" because we could end up sending hundreds of millions of dollars a year to Mexico, further straining our Social Security system. We could add as many as 162,000 Mexicans to our Social Security rolls during the agreement's first five years.

We already have totalization agreements with other countries. But a Social Security Administration memo predicts that "the application workloads generated by an agreement with Mexico will be much larger than those resulting from any of the 20 existing agreements."

And implementation of a totalization program may start much sooner than you would think. [In 2002] it was predicted that this scheme could take effect as early as October [2003]

> *"We could end up sending hundreds of millions of dollars a year to Mexico, further straining our Social Security system."*

because "informal" negotiations about totalization were going so well.

Even more shocking, an anonymous House Republican aide, quoted in *The Washington Post*, worried that, if the Mexican government got its way, legal Mexican workers who had also worked illegally in the United States and used a false Social Security number would be able to claim higher Social Security benefits than that to which they are legally entitled.

The rationale is that the payments made by the workers at the time they were illegal would have been to false Social Security numbers.

Give credit to Rep. Ron Paul (R-TX) for his willingness to take on totalization by introducing the "Social Security for American Citizens Only Act."[2] Paul is a congressman with Libertarian views whom I respect for his willingness to stand on principle even though, over the years, there have been times we have been at odds over one thing or another.

Paul argues that the enactment of totalization would mean Mexican immigrants would have little incentive to assimilate and to become American citizens.

As he put it, . . . "The Federal government may actually allow someone who actually came to the United States illegally, worked less than the required number of years to qualify for Social Security, and then returned to Mexico for the rest of his working years, to collect full U.S. Social Security benefits while living in Mexico. That is an insult to the millions of Americans who pay their entire working lives into the system and now face the possibility that there may be nothing left when it is their turn to retire."

"We should protect Social Security dollars by putting an end to congressional spending raids, not threaten the system even more by essentially sending foreign aid welfare to noncitizens."

2. As of August 2004, the act, H.R. 489, has been referred to the House Committee on Ways and Means and the Subcommittee on Social Security, where it remains.

Mexico's government sees this as a way to intertwine our two countries' relationship even further. But totalization is no tree planting ceremony at the border but an agreement that, if it comes to fruition, threatens to endanger the solvency of our Social Security system and to encourage illegal immigration.

Now is the time for grassroots conservatives to sound the alarm about this plan, when pressure can still be applied to stop it. It will take time to bring Americans up to speed as to what's really going on. But the more they learn about this plan and what it means, the more they will come to dislike it and want to have it stopped.

President Bush and the GOP have no idea what the political environment will be like in 2004. But his administration's support of a measure like this one is likely to make things more difficult than they would otherwise be.

Let us hope that good old American common sense prevails on totalization.

# Alternatives to Mandatory Detention Will Protect the Rights of Illegal Immigrants

**by George M. Anderson**

**About the author:** *George M. Anderson is associate editor of* America, *a national Catholic weekly magazine.*

The U.S. [Catholic] bishops issued a statement at their November [2001] meeting in Washington, D.C., called Welcoming the Stranger Among Us. Although largely intended as guidelines for parishes with many new members who come from other countries and cultures, the document also makes brief but pointed reference to the destructive effects of the 1996 immigration laws that have, to use its own words, "undermined some basic human rights for immigrants." In a resolution they passed at the same meeting, the bishops consequently called for the reform of these two laws: the Illegal Immigration Reform and Immigrant Responsibility Act and the Anti-Terrorism and Death Penalty Act.

## The Problem of Mandatory Detention

Among other punitive provisions, these laws call for the mandatory detention of immigrants—including bona fide asylum seekers—who lack adequate documentation. Over 20,000 people are now being held on any given day in facilities around the country. Among them are children, or unaccompanied minors, as they are officially known. The Immigration and Naturalization Service [I.N.S.] apprehends approximately 5,000 minors annually. They come here for a variety of reasons: to join family members, or because they have been neglected or abused, or to earn money to send home. The more fortunate ones are held in privately run shelter facilities, where they receive adequate care and visits from legal representatives. But a quarter are placed in state-run secure facilities with juveniles who are being held on criminal charges. Not surprisingly, the detention of unaccompanied minors has come under sharp criticism from groups like Human Rights Watch, which argue that alternatives like foster care should be far more widely used in such situations instead of detention, which can result in seriously damaging experiences.

Whether for children or adults, the bishops are thus calling for the repeal of the laws' mandatory detention provisions and the development of alternatives to detention. A few months before the bishops met, in fact, the Catholic Legal Immigration Network Inc. (Clinic)—a subsidiary of the

> *"Alternatives . . . would both safeguard the public and prevent immigrants from absconding while awaiting the outcome of their immigration court cases."*

U.S. Catholic Conference—issued a report that addressed the issue. Called The Needless Detention of Immigrants in the United States, it takes the I.N.S. to task for what it terms its "unconscionable failure" to develop alternatives that would both safeguard the public and prevent immigrants from absconding while awaiting the outcome of their immigration court cases. And models for such alternatives do exist. The I.N.S., however, has been reluctant to employ them on the scale needed in view of the ever-rising numbers of detainees.

Because of the 1996 laws, the number of detained immigrants has tripled. So rapidly have their numbers risen that the I.N.S. is unable to house them all in its own facilities or even in contract detention centers operated by for-profit companies like the Corrections Corporation of America and the Wackenhut Corporation. As a result, 60 percent are locked up in city and county jails where they are frequently subjected to poor living conditions, overseen by guards who may speak only English, and far from family members and attorneys who might be able to help them. For many, therefore—as the bishops observe—basic rights are indeed undermined.

## Exploring Successful Alternatives

The pressing need to make greater use of alternatives to detention was one of the themes explored at the fourth annual conference of the Detention Watch Network, a coalition of immigration lawyers, religious and other advocates that met in suburban Washington soon after the bishops' meeting concluded. One focus centered around lifers, or indefinite detainees. These are immigrants who, having committed crimes here and having served their sentences in American prisons, are neither deported nor granted their freedom. Instead, they are transferred to detention centers where they exist in a limbo-like situation. They cannot be deported either because the United States does not have diplomatic relations with their governments or because their governments will not accept them back. Cuba, Iraq and Iran are examples of such countries.

Although it has done reviews of the status of "Mariel" Cubans for years, only recently has the I.N.S. begun a six-monthly review process for other indefinite detainees, and a few have been released into programs. One, operated by Catholic Charities in New Orleans, has accepted two dozen lifers since it began in 1999. There they receive various forms of assistance, including housing, help in finding jobs and English lessons. The program's director, Kathleen Harrison, said at the conference that only one of the lifers accepted into the program had to be re-incarcerated for a subsequent offense.

Another successful model aimed not at lifers, but at asylum seekers, was developed by the Lutheran Immigration and Refugee Service. During the spring of 1999, the I.N.S. contacted the Lutheran agency in what Matthew Wilch, director there of asylum and immigration concerns, described at the same conference as a surprise telephone call. The I.N.S. was about to bring nine Chinese asylum seekers from detention on Guam to an isolated location in Ullin, Ill. The good news, as Mr. Wilch put it, was that the I.N.S. contacted them at all. The bad news was that the I.N.S. merely wanted the agency's help in assisting the Chinese with the asylum applications process—holding them all the while in a locked facility.

"We told the I.N.S.," Mr. Wilch said, "that our assistance would have to lead to their agreeing to an alternative to detention for the Chinese in their custody." A group of attorneys from Clinic, with which the Lutheran agency has a working relationship in immigration matters, provided legal representation for the Chinese who lacked it. Then it was discovered that some of the asylum seekers were already being represented—but by lawyers employed by so-called snake heads who work with

> *"Half [in the Appearance Assistance Program] eventually won the right to remain in the country, a circumstance suggesting that they need not have been detained."*

crime syndicates that smuggle Chinese into the United States. "At that point," Mr. Wilch said, "the I.N.S. denied all our requests" on the grounds that it wanted to keep the immigrants in detention in order to protect them from the snake heads. For him and other advocates, this denial amounted to punishing the immigrants because they were victims of the snake heads. It was only after media coverage— an article in *The Washington Post*, together with a letter to the editor by the president of the Lutheran agency—that the I.N.S. relented and agreed to release the detained Chinese to shelters, where they received a variety of supportive services. For Mr. Wilch, the I.N.S.'s barriers to achieving this reasonable goal were a reflection of what he referred to as the "4 D's" of I.N.S. policy: detect, detain, deter, and deport. These 4 D's, he observed, are rooted deep in I.N.S. culture.

## Community Supervision

A third example of alternatives to detention is a pilot program that was initiated by the I.N.S. itself in 1997 as a three-year demonstration project involving three groups: asylum seekers, lifers and undocumented workers arrested at work sites. Developed in conjunction with the non-profit Vera Institute of Justice in New York City, it was given the name Appearance Assistance Program; the goal, as the name suggests, was to test the viability of community supervision for noncitizens in removal proceedings, to see whether they would appear for their immigration court hearings while awaiting resolution of their cases. The project provided intensive supervision for people detained in local for-profit contract facilities who were released into the program.

A Vera staff member present at the conference spoke of the program's impressive success rate: over 90 percent of participants did attend their required immigration hearings. Half eventually won the right to remain in the country, a circumstance suggesting that they need not have been detained in the first place. Given its success, the I.N.S. plans to establish three more sites for the Appearance Assistance Program in other parts of the country. In its final evaluation report, the Vera institute goes so far as to recommend that the I.N.S. "move toward a nationwide supervision program." But in view of the service's longstanding reluctance to consider alternatives to detention on any but the smallest scale, one doubts that a nationwide endeavor will be undertaken any time in the foreseeable future.

The Vera program, moreover, was cost effective: $12 a day in contrast to $61 a day for detention. Advocates accordingly wonder why other programs of proven effectiveness, like the one conducted by Catholic Charities in New Orleans, could not receive federal funding. But far from moving that way, the dynamic seems to be in the opposite direction. As the Clinic report notes, a successful federally funded program to resettle "Mariel" Cubans who had been released from detention into a program run by the Migration and Refugee Service of the U.S. Catholic Conference, was actually de-funded in 1999 after being in operation for a dozen years.

## Factors Working Against Alternatives

A principal author of the Clinic report, Donald Kerwin—an attorney who is Clinic's chief operating officer—believes that besides the need for far greater utilization of alternatives, there is an even greater need to roll back the number of beds currently in use for immigrants in detention. "Once beds exist," he said, "they're going to be filled by I.N.S. directors who know they have them." Reducing the number of beds, though, will be all the more difficult because the federal administration has requested $79 million in funds for a thousand more. "And yet," Mr. Kerwin observed, "if just a fifth of that amount were used for alternatives to detention, many immigrants could be released from secure facilities who don't need to be there." He made particular reference to asylum seekers who have passed the credible fear test regarding the likelihood of persecution were they to be returned to their own countries. "But often," he added, "the I.N.S. won't release them until they are actually granted asylum, at the end of the very day they receive it."

Also working against alternatives is the fact that the creation of more bed space means financial windfalls for the numerous vested interests that stand to profit from the increased use of detention facilities and county jails with which the I.N.S. enters into contractual agreements. Within the facilities themselves, Mr. Kerwin noted that sweetheart deals with phone companies and other service providers are common. Members of Congress, too, tend to look favorably on new facilities because these can provide more jobs in their districts.

## Issuing New Standards

One of the few bright spots in the overall detention picture emerged [in] November [2000]. At that time, responding to pressure over a period of five years from the American Bar Association and other groups, the I.N.S. agreed to implement a set of three dozen standards pertaining to the treatment of detained immigrants. Among the most important are access to legal counsel—a matter of great significance, because 90 percent of detainees have no legal representation at all. And attorneys for the relatively few that do have representation frequently encounter difficulties meeting with their clients—sometimes even being barred from visits.

> *"Immigration detention is, after all, just another term for imprisonment."*

Writing in a recent issue of *The National Law Journal*, for example, Elizabeth Amon noted that although the American Bar Association has created a program to encourage and train attorneys to donate their time to immigration cases, lawyers have encountered daunting obstacles in making contact with clients. She cites the example of an attorney at a Texas firm who volunteered to represent two Cubans held at a federal prison. Although he had arranged for an interview in advance, he was refused entry when he arrived. The Cubans, as a result, never had representation. Under the new standards, however, attorneys are to be granted access seven days a week, in a private room where conversations cannot be overheard. Other significant standards include permission for nongovernmental agencies to make presentations to groups of detainees concerning their rights—a subject about which many immigrants are largely ignorant.

Also important is the standard regarding access to pastoral services. Previously, chaplains have entered detention centers as volunteers only, with no authority. Now, however, the I.N.S. is to appoint chaplains who, as fully accredited staff members, will be able to enter all parts of a facility—including administrative segregation where (very inappropriately) people at risk for suicide are placed. Space for private counseling must also be provided, along with a designated area for religious observances. The right of immigrants to practice their religion can be the basis of significant spiritual support during long periods of uncertainty and fear.

In announcing the standards, the I.N.S. commissioner, Doris Meissner, said that their purpose is to ensure "safe, secure and humane conditions . . . for all aliens in I.N.S. custody," wherever they are—in facilities run by the I.N.S. itself, in for-profit facilities or in county jails. But while the standards do represent a step forward in terms of providing uniform rules governing the treatment of immigrants in detention, they are not federal regulations. This means that they are not enforceable. Even if they are observed with a reasonable degree of probity, moreover, the central issue still remains: too many immigrants are held in detention who should not be there. And immigration detention is, after all, just another term for imprisonment.

# Immigration Laws Should Be Enforced to Reduce Crimes Committed by Illegal Immigrants

by Heather MacDonald

**About the author:** *Heather MacDonald, a fellow at the Manhattan Institute, a conservative, free-market think tank, is a contributing editor to* City Journal, *the institute's quarterly magazine.*

Some of the most violent criminals at large today are illegal aliens. Yet in cities where crime from these lawbreakers is highest, the police cannot use the most obvious tool to apprehend them: their immigration status. In Los Angeles, for example, dozens of gang members from a ruthless Salvadoran prison gang have snuck back into town after having been deported for such crimes as murder, shootings, and drug trafficking. Police officers know who they are and know that their mere presence in the country is a felony. Yet should an LAPD [Los Angeles Police Department] officer arrest an illegal gangbanger for felonious reentry, it is the officer who will be treated as a criminal by his own department—for violating the LAPD's rule against enforcing immigration law.

## The Ban on Immigration Enforcement

The LAPD'S ban on immigration enforcement is replicated in immigrant-heavy localities across the country—in New York, Chicago, Austin, San Diego, and Houston, for example. These so-called "sanctuary policies" generally prohibit a city's employees, including the police, from reporting immigration violations to federal authorities.

Sanctuary laws are a testament to the political power of immigrant lobbies. So powerful is this demographic clout that police officials shrink from even mentioning the illegal alien crime wave. "We can't even talk about it," says a frustrated LAPD captain. "People are afraid of a backlash from Hispanics." Another LAPD commander in a predominantly Hispanic, gang-infested district sighs: "I would get a firestorm of criticism if I talked about [enforcing the immigration law against illegals]." Neither captain would speak for attribution.

But however pernicious in themselves, sanctuary rules are a symptom of a much broader disease: the near total loss of control over immigration policy. Fifty years ago, immigration policy may have driven immigration numbers, but today the numbers drive policy. The non-stop increase of legal and illegal aliens is reshaping

> *"These so-called 'sanctuary policies' generally prohibit a city's employees, including the police, from reporting immigration violations to federal authorities."*

the language and the law to dissolve any distinction between legal and illegal immigration and, ultimately, the very idea of national borders.

It is a measure of how topsy-turvy the immigration environment has become that to ask police officials about the illegal crime problem feels like a gross social faux pas, something simply not done in polite company. And a police official, asked to violate this powerful taboo against discussing criminal aliens, will respond with a strangled response—sometimes, as in the case of a New York deputy commissioner with whom I spoke, disappearing from communication altogether. At the same time, millions of illegal aliens work, shop, travel, and commit crimes in plain view, utterly confident in their de facto immunity from the immigration law.

I asked the Miami Police Department's spokesman, Detective Delrish Moss, about his employer's policy on illegal law-breakers. In September 2003, the force had arrested a Honduran visa violator for seven terrifying rapes. The previous year, Miami officers had had the suspect, Reynaldo Elias Rapalo, in custody for lewd and lascivious molestation, without checking his immigration status. Had they done so, they would have discovered his visa overstay, a deportable offense. "We have shied away from unnecessary involvement dealing with immigration issues," explains Detective Moss, choosing his words carefully, "because of our large immigration population."

Police commanders may not want to discuss, much less respond to, the illegal alien crisis, but its magnitude for law enforcement is startling. Some examples:

• In Los Angeles, 95 percent of all outstanding warrants for homicide (which total 1,200 to 1,500) target illegal aliens. Up to two-thirds of all fugitive felony warrants (17,000) are for illegal aliens.

• A confidential California Department of Justice study reported in 1995 that 60 percent of the bloody 18th Street Gang in California is illegal (estimated membership: 20,000); police officers say the proportion is undoubtedly much greater. The gang collaborates with the Mexican Mafia, the dominant force in

California prisons, on complicated drug distribution schemes, extortion, and drive-by assassinations, and is responsible for an assault or robbery every day in Los Angeles County. The gang has dramatically expanded its numbers over the last two decades by recruiting recently arrived youngsters, a vast proportion illegal, from Central America and Mexico.

• The leadership of the Columbia Li'l Cycos gang, which uses murder and racketeering to control the drug market around L.A.'s MacArthur Park, was about 60 percent illegal in 2002, says former Assistant U.S. Attorney Luis Li. Frank "Pancho Villa" Martinez, a Mexican Mafia member and illegal alien, controlled the gang from prison, while serving time for felonious reentry following deportation.

Good luck finding any reference to such facts in official crime analysis. The LAPD and the Los Angeles City Attorney recently requested a judicial injunction against drug trafficking in Hollywood. The injunction targets the 18th Street Gang and, as the press release puts it, the "non-gang members" who sell drugs in Hollywood on behalf of the gang. Those "non-gang members" are virtually all illegal Mexicans, smuggled into the country by a trafficking ring organized by 18th Street bigs. The illegal Mexicans pay off their transportation debt to the gang by selling drugs; many soon realize how lucrative that line of work is and stay in the business.

The immigration status of these non-gang "Hollywood dealers," as the City Attorney calls them, is universally known among officers and gang prosecutors. But the gang injunction is silent on the matter. And if a Hollywood officer were to arrest an illegal

> *"Sanctuary rules are a symptom of a much broader disease: the near total loss of control over immigration policy."*

dealer (known on the street as a "border brother") for his immigration status, or even notify Immigration and Customs Enforcement (ICE),[1] he would be severely disciplined for violation of Special Order 40, the city's sanctuary policy.

## A Safe Haven

The ordinarily tough-as-nails former LAPD Chief Daryl Gates enacted Special Order 40 in 1979—in response to the city's burgeoning population of illegal aliens—showing that even the most unapologetic law-and-order cop is no match for immigration demographics. The order prohibits officers from "initiating police action where the objective is to discover the alien status of a person." In practice, this means that the police may not even ask someone they have arrested about his immigration status until after criminal charges have been en-

---

1. In 2003, the Immigration and Naturalization Service (INS) was broken up into three bureaus in the Department of Homeland Security (DHS): the Bureau of Immigration and Customs Enforcement (ICE); the Bureau of Customs and Border Protection (CBP); and U.S. Citizenship and Immigration Services (USCIS).

tered. They may not arrest someone for immigration violations. Officers certainly may not check a suspect's immigration status prior to arrest, nor may they notify ICE about an illegal alien picked up for minor violations. Only if an illegal alien has already been booked for a felony or multiple misdemeanors may they inquire into his status or report him to immigration authorities. The bottom line: a *cordon sanitaire* between local law enforcement and federal immigration authorities that creates a safe haven for illegal criminals.

Los Angeles' sanctuary law, and all others like it, contradicts everything that has been learned about public safety in the 1990s. A key policing discovery of the last decade was the "great chain of being" in criminal be-

> *"Millions of illegal aliens work, shop, travel, and commit crimes in plain view, utterly confident in their de facto immunity from the immigration law."*

havior [also known as "broken windows" policing]. Pick up a law-violator for a "minor" crime, and you'll likely prevent a major crime. Enforcing graffiti and turnstile-jumping laws nabs you murderers and robbers. Enforcing known immigration violations, such as reentry following deportation, against known felons would be even more productive. LAPD officers recognize illegal deported gang members all the time—flashing gang signs at court hearings for rival gangbangers, hanging out on the corner, or casing a target. These illegal returnees are, simply by being in the country after deportation, committing a felony. "But if I see a deportee from the Mara Salvatrucha [Salvadoran prison] gang crossing the street, I know I can't touch him," laments a Los Angeles gang officer. Only if the deported felon has given the officer some other reason to stop him—such as an observed narcotics sale—can the officer accost him, and only for that non-immigration-related reason. The officer cannot arrest him for the immigration felony.

Such a policy is extraordinarily inefficient and puts the community at risk for as long as these vicious immigration-law-breakers remain free. The department's top brass brush off such concerns. No big deal if you're seeing deported gangbangers back on the streets, they say. Just put them under surveillance for "real" crimes and arrest them for those. But surveillance is very manpower-intensive. Where there is an immediate ground for arresting a violent felon, it is absurd to demand that the woefully understaffed LAPD ignore it.

## The Impact of Sanctuary Policies

The stated reason for sanctuary policies is to encourage illegal alien crime victims and witnesses to cooperate with the police without fear of deportation and to encourage all illegal aliens to take advantage of city services like health care and education (to whose maintenance illegals contribute little). There has never been any empirical verification whether sanctuary laws actually increase cooperation with the police or other city agencies. And no one has ever suggested not enforcing drug laws, say, for fear of intimidating drug-using crime victims. But in any case, the official rationale for sanctuary rules could be honored by limiting police utilization of immigration laws to some subset of immigration violators: deported felons, say, or repeat criminal offenders whose immigration status is already known to the police.

The real reason why cities prohibit their police officers and other employees from immigration reporting and enforcement is, like nearly everything else in immigration policy, the numbers. The population of illegal aliens and their legal brethren has grown so large that public officials are terrified of alienating them, even at the expense of annulling the law and tolerating avoidable violence. In 1996, a breathtaking *Los Angeles Times* expose on the 18th Street Gang, which included descriptions of innocent bystanders being murdered by laughing *cholos* [gang members], disclosed for the first time the rate of illegal alien membership in the gang. In response to the public outcry, the Los Angeles City Council ordered the police to reexamine Special Order 40. You would have thought they had suggested violating some shocking social taboo. A police commander warned the council: "This is going to open a significant, heated debate." City councilwoman Laura Chick put on a brave front: "We mustn't be afraid," she said firmly.

But immigrant pandering, of course, trumped public safety. Law-abiding residents of gang-infested neighborhoods may live in terror of the tattooed gangbangers dealing drugs, spraying graffiti, and shooting up rivals outside their homes, but such distress cannot compare to a politician's fear of offending Hispanics. At the start of the reexamination process, LAPD Deputy Chief John White had argued that allowing the department to work more closely with the INS would give officers another means to get gang members off the streets. Trying to build a case for homicide, say, against an illegal gang member is often futile, he explained, since witnesses fear deadly retaliation if they cooperate with the police. Enforcing an immigration violation would allow the cops to lock up the murderer right now, without putting a witness' life at risk.

> *"The population of illegal aliens and their legal brethren has grown so large that public officials are terrified of alienating them."*

Six months later Deputy Chief White had changed his tune: "Any broadening of the policy gets us into the immigration business. It's a federal law enforcement issue, not a local law enforcement issue." Interim Police Chief Bayan Lewis told the Los Angeles Police Commission: "It is not the time. It is not the day to look at Special Order 40."

Nor will it ever be the time to reexamine sanctuary policies, as long as immigration numbers continue to grow. After the brief window of opportunity in 1996 to strengthen the department's weapons against gangs, Los Angeles politicians have only grown more adamant in their defense of Special Order 40. After learning that police officers in the scandal-plagued Rampart Division had cooperated with the INS to try to remove murderous gangbangers from the community, local politicians threw a fit. They criticized district commanders for even allowing INS agents into their station houses. The offending officers were seriously disciplined by the department.

Immigration politics have had the same deleterious effect in New York. Former New York Mayor Rudolph Giuliani sued all the way up to the Supreme Court to defend the city's sanctuary policy against Congressional override. A 1996 federal law declared that cities could not prohibit their employees from cooperating with the INS. Oh yeah? said Giuliani; just watch me. He sued to declare the 1996 federal ban on sanctuary policies unconstitutional, and though he lost in court, he remained defiant to the end. On September 5, 2001, his hand-picked charter revision committee ruled that New York may still require that its employees keep immigration information confidential to preserve trust between immigrants and government. Six days later, several former visa-overstayers conducted the most devastating attack on the city and the country in history [in the terrorist attacks of September 11, 2001].

The 1996 federal ban on sanctuary laws was conveniently forgotten in New York until a gang of five Mexicans—four of them illegal—abducted and brutally raped a 42-year-old mother of two near some railroad tracks in Queens. Three of the illegal aliens had already been arrested numerous times by the NYPD for such crimes as assault, attempted robbery in the second degree, criminal trespass, illegal gun possession, and drug offenses. The department had never notified the INS.

Unfortunately, big city police chiefs are by now just as determined to defend sanctuary policies as the politicians who appoint them. They repudiate any interest in access to immigration law, even though doing so contradicts the universally respected theory of broken windows policing. (Sentiment is quite otherwise among the rank-and-file, who see daily the benefit that an immigration tool would bring.)

## Overwhelmed by Numbers

But the same reality that drives cities to enact sanctuary policies—the growing numbers of legal and illegal immigrants—also cripples federal authorities' own ability to enforce the immigration law against criminals. Even if immigrant-saturated cities were to discard their sanctuary policies and start enforcing immigration violations where public safety demands it, it is hard to believe that ICE could handle the additional workload. Perennially starved for resources by Congress and the executive branch, ICE lacks the detention space to house the massive criminal alien population and the manpower to manage it. In fact, little the INS and its successors have done over the last 30 years—above all its numerous displays of managerial incompetence—can be understood outside of the sheer overmatch between the agency and the size of the population it theoretically oversees.

In theory, ICE is supposed to find and deport all aliens who have entered the country illegally through stealth or fraudulent documents. (Illegal entry could in theory also be prosecuted as a misdemeanor by a U.S. Attorney prior to the alien's deportation, but such low-level prosecutions virtually never occur.) In fact, immigration authorities have not gone after mere status violators for years. The chronic shortage of manpower to oversee, and detention space to house, aliens as they await their deportation hearings (or, following an order of removal from an immigration judge, their actual deportation) has forced the agency to practice a constant triage. The bar for persuading managers to detain someone has risen ever higher.

Even in the days when the INS and the police could cooperate, the lack of detention space defeated their efforts. Former INS criminal investigator Mike Cutler worked with the NYPD catching Brooklyn drug dealers in the 1970s. "If you arrested someone who you wanted to detain, you'd go to your boss and start a bidding war," Cutler recalls. "He'd say: 'Whaddya got?' You'd say: 'My guy ran three blocks, threw a couple of punches, and had six pieces of ID.' The boss would turn to another agent: 'Next! Whaddid your guy do?' 'He ran 18 blocks, pushed over an old lady, and had a gun.'" But such one-upmanship was usually unavailing. "Without the jail space," explains Cutler, "it was like the Fish and Wildlife Service—you'd tag their ear and let them go."

*Triage.* Currently, the only types of aliens who run any risk of catching the attention of immigration authorities are, in ascending order of interest: illegal aliens who have been convicted of a crime; illegal aliens who have reentered the country following deportation without explicit approval of the attorney general (a felony punishable by up to two years in jail); illegal aliens who have been convicted of an "aggravated felony"—a term of art to refer to particularly egregious crimes; and illegal aliens who have been deported following conviction for an aggravated felony and who have reentered. (Aggravated felons become inadmissible for life, whereas mere deported aliens may apply for a visa after 10 years.) A deported aggravated felon who has reentered may be sentenced for up to 20 years. The deported Mara Salvatrucha gang members that LAPD officers are seeing back on the streets fall into the latter category: they are aggravated felons who have reentered, and hence are punishable with 20 years in jail.

> *"Enforcing an immigration violation would allow the cops to lock up the murderer right now, without putting a witness' life at risk."*

To other law enforcement agencies, triage by immigration authorities often looks like complete indifference to immigration violations. An illegal alien who has merely been arrested 14 times for robbery, say, without a conviction will draw only a yawn from an ICE district director. In practice, the only real sources of interest for immigration authorities are aggravated felons and returned deported aggravated felons.

## Derailing Deportation

*"Run Letters."* Lack of resources also derails the conclusion of the deportation process. If a judge has issued a final order of deportation (usually after years of litigation and appeals), ICE in theory can put the alien right on a bus or plane and take him across the border. It rarely has the manpower to do so, however. Second alternative: put the alien in detention pending actual removal. Again, no space and no staff in proportion to demand. In the early 1990s, for example, 15 INS officers were responsible for the deportation of approximately 85,000 aliens (not all of them criminals) in New York City. The agency's actual response to final orders of removal is what is known in the business as a "run letter"—a notice that immigration authorities send to a deportable alien requesting that he kindly show up in a month or two to be deported, when maybe the agency would have some officers and equipment to take custody of him. The results are foreordained: in 2001, 87 percent of deportable aliens who received "run letters" disappeared, a number that was even higher—94 percent—if the alien was from a terror-sponsoring country.

John Mullaly, a former homicide detective with the NYPD, shakes his head remembering the INS's futile task in Manhattan's Washington Heights, where Mullaly estimates that 70 percent of the drug dealers and other criminals were illegal. "It's so overwhelming, you can't believe it," he explains. "The INS's workload was astronomical, beyond belief. Usually, they could do nothing." Were Mullaly to threaten a thug in custody that his

> *"The message sent to the drug lord and to the community could not be more clear: this is a culture that can't enforce its most basic law of entry."*

next stop would be El Salvador unless he cooperated, the criminal just laughed, knowing that immigration authorities would never show up. The message sent to the drug lord and to the community could not be more clear: this is a culture that can't enforce its most basic law of entry. And if policing's broken windows theory is correct, the suspension of one set of rules breeds more universal contempt for the law.

ICE's capacity deficit gives an easy out to police departments when a known immigration violator commits a terrible crime. Testifying before Congress about the Queens rape by the illegal Mexicans, New York's criminal justice coordinator, John Feinblatt, peevishly defended the city's failure to notify the INS after the rapists' previous arrests on the ground that the agency wouldn't have responded anyway. "We have time and time again been unable to reach INS on the phone," Feinblatt told the House immigration subcommittee in February 2003. "When we reach them on the phone, they require that we write a letter. When we write a letter, they require that it be by a superior."

*No Answer.* However inadmirable his failure to take responsibility, Feinblatt nevertheless was describing a sad fact of life: Even when police agencies do contact immigration authorities about illegal aliens, they rarely get a response. Federal probation authorities in Brooklyn, who currently have 148 illegal alien felons on their active caseload, have given up trying to coordinate with ICE on deportation. "Our thinking is: these guys should be removed ASAP," says a probation supervisor. "Should the taxpayer be paying for our services to monitor, investigate, and provide services for individuals who are not citizens and should not be here at all?" But the supervisors' sense of urgency is not answered at the other end of the line. "You send the paperwork over to the INS, and you never hear back," explains the federal probation official. "We used to have a person assigned to us from the agency, who told us to not even bother sending over forms."

> *"The police should be given the option of reporting and acting on immigration violations, where doing so would contribute to public safety."*

Immigration numbers stymied a program to ensure that criminal aliens were in fact deported after serving time in federal and state prisons. The Institutional Hearing Program, begun in 1988, was supposed to allow the INS to complete deportation hearings while a criminal was still in state or federal prison, so that upon his release, he could be immediately deported without taking up precious detention space. But the process immediately bogged down due to the magnitude of the problem—in 2000, for example, nearly 30 percent of federal prisoners were foreign-born. The agency couldn't find enough pro bono attorneys to represent criminal aliens (who have extensive due process rights in contesting deportation), and so would have to request continuance after continuance for the deportation hearings. Securing immigration judges was a difficulty as well. In 1997, the INS simply had no record of a whopping 36 percent of foreign-born inmates who had been released from federal and four state prisons without any review of their deportability. They included 1,198 aggravated felons, 80 of whom were rearrested for new crimes in short order. . . .

## Taking Immigration Law Seriously

The most striking political constant in the last four decades of immigration policy is the overwhelming popular desire to rein in immigration, and the utter pulverization of that desire by special interests. No poll has ever shown that Americans want ever-more open borders, yet that is exactly what the elites deliver year after year. If the idea of giving voting rights to non-citizen majorities catches on—and don't be surprised if it does—Americans could be faced with the ultimate absurdity of people outside the social compact making rules for those inside it.

But the push to annul the laws of immigration does not even help its purported beneficiaries. Sanctuary policies contribute to the terrorization of immigrant communities. By stripping the police of what on occasion may be their only immediate tool to remove a psychopathic gangster from the streets, sanctuary policies leave law-abiding immigrants defenseless against the social and financial devastation of crime and handicapped in the march up the economic ladder. Anyone who cares about their future success should want every possible law enforcement means deployed to protect them. And immigration optimists, who argue that assimilation into American ideals is proceeding just fine and dandily, should take another look: In many immigrant communities, assimilation into gangs seems to be outstripping assimilation into civic culture. Toddlers are being taught to flash gang signals and to hate the police, reports the *Los Angeles Times*. In New York City, "every high school has its Mexican gang," and most 12- to 14-year-olds have already joined, claims Ernesto Vega, an illegal 18-year-old Mexican who works at a New York association for Mexican empowerment. Such pathologies are only exacerbated when the first lesson of American law learned by immigrants is that Americans don't bother to enforce it. "Institutionalizing illegal immigration creates a mindset in people that anything goes in the U.S.," observes Patrick Ortega, the News and Public Affairs Director of "Radio Nueva Vida" in Southern California. "It creates a new subculture, with a sequelae of social ills."

Taking immigration law seriously may make a start in combating these worrisome trends. The police should be given the option of reporting and acting on immigration violations, where doing so would contribute to public safety. The decision about when to use immigration rules will be a matter of discretion, but discretion is at the heart of all wise policing. The CLEAR [Clear Law Enforcement for Criminal Alien Removal] Act, now before Congress, would help by clarifying the authority of local law enforcement to cooperate with immigration authorities. The police should have access to federal databases of immigration violators, an idea that the administration is slowly acting upon, against great opposition from the usual suspects.

And then the successor agencies of the INS should be given the resources they need. More detention space should be built, or contracted through private providers, so that deportable aliens are not released back to the streets. The missing link in workforce law—a fraud-proof work ID—must be created, and then employers must be held responsible for demanding it.

Advocates for amnesty argue that it is the only solution to the illegal alien crisis, because enforcement clearly has not worked. They are wrong in their key assumption: Enforcement has never been tried. Amnesty, however, *has* been tried—in both an industrial-strength version in 1986, and in more limited doses ever since—and it was a clear failure. Before we proceed again to the ultimate suspension of the nation's self-definition, it is long past time to make immigration law a reality, not a charade.

# Chapter 4

# How Should Immigration Be Controlled?

# The Immigration Control Debate: An Overview

**by David Masci**

**About the author:** *David Masci, a staff writer for the* CQ Researcher, *specializes in social policy, religion, and foreign affairs.*

Hail a taxi, drop off dry cleaning, buy a lottery ticket at the local 7-Eleven. Chances are good that an immigrant from Ghana, South Korea, Mexico or some other faraway nation served you. Indeed, there's a good chance programmers from India or China wrote some of the software in your computer.

Across the country, in towns and cities alike, the United States, more than ever before, is a nation of immigrants.

"It's amazing how things have changed since the 1970s, how many people there now are in this country who were not born here," says Steven Moore, an economist at the Cato Institute, a libertarian think tank.

In the last 30 years the United States has absorbed the biggest wave of immigrants since the turn of the century, when millions arrived at Ellis Island in search of a better life. Today, more than 25 million Americans are foreign born—nearly 10 percent of the population.

## An Economic Gain

And that's good for the economy, according to Federal Reserve Chairman Alan Greenspan, who says the pools of skilled and unskilled workers created by high levels of immigration have greatly contributed to the nation's prosperity.

"As we are creating an ever more complex, sophisticated, accelerating economy, the necessity to have the ability to bring in . . . people from abroad to keep it functioning in the most effective manner increasingly strikes me as [sound] policy," he told lawmakers on Capitol Hill in February [2000].

Greenspan's comments were just the latest salvo in the continuing debate over immigration, a debate that is older than the country itself. More than 200 years ago, for instance, Benjamin Franklin pronounced recent arrivals from Germany as "the most stupid in the nation. Few of their children speak English, and through their indiscretion or ours, or both, great disorders may one day arise among us."

But to immigration boosters like Greenspan, immigrants' work ethic and motivation make them cornerstones of America's economic prosperity.

"We're getting a lot of the best and brightest from other countries, and of course these people benefit the U.S. economy because they are driven to improve their lots," says Bronwyn Lance, a senior fellow at the Alexis de Tocqueville Institution, which works to increase understanding of the cultural and economic benefits of legal immigration. Lance and others say immigrants are more likely to start businesses—from corner grocery stores to giant computer companies—than native-born Americans are. Even newcomers with little education aid the economy, immigration boosters say, taking undesirable jobs that employers can't fill with native-born Americans.

## An Economic Drain

Opponents of expanded immigration counter that the United States doesn't need a million newcomers each year to ensure a strong economy. Most immigrants aren't well-educated entrepreneurs but "poorly educated people who take low-skilled jobs for little money," says Dan Stein, executive director of the Federation for American Immigration Reform (FAIR), which opposes high immigration levels. In Stein's view, immigration largely benefits employers by providing a cheap and plentiful labor force. Moreover, he says, the newcomers take Americans' jobs and suppress wage levels.

Immigration opponents also reject the argument that immigrants are willing to do the jobs that most Americans won't do. In parts of the country with few immigrants, low-wage jobs still get done, and by native-born people, says Mark Krikorian, executive director of the Center for Immigration Studies.

"Employers could find Americans to do these jobs if they wanted to, but they'd have to provide training and raise wages to do so," Krikorian says. Immigrants are simply an easier and cheaper alternative for businesses, he and others maintain.

Finally, opponents point out, high immigration levels are overcrowding the United States, especially in urban areas, and preventing immigrants already here from assimilating into American society.

> *"Immigrants' work ethic and motivation make them cornerstones of America's economic prosperity."*

"The way we're going now we won't turn these people into Americans, and without assimilation we will increasingly be beset by ethnic conflicts," says John O'Sullivan, editor-at-large at the conservative *National Review* magazine and a noted expert on immigration.

Still, immigration supporters argue, today's newcomers, like those who sailed into New York Harbor in the past, come because they want to be Americans.

"We've always been afraid that new immigrants aren't assimilating and becoming American," Moore says. But immigrants are attracted to the United States for more than job opportunities. "America is more than a country, it's an idea with concepts like freedom," he says. "Most new immigrants buy into this idea. That's one of the reasons they want to be here."

## The Problem of Illegal Immigration

Not all immigrants, of course, are here legally. While there is wide disagreement about how many newcomers the nation should admit, most experts favor taking at least some steps to block the estimated 300,000 or more illegal immigrants who come to the United States annually. Many support beefing up the U.S. Border Patrol, the enforcement arm of the Immigration and Naturalization Service (INS), and some call for greater use of a rarely enforced provision of the 1986 immigration law that punishes employers who knowingly hire illegal immigrants.

Proponents of employer sanctions argue that some form of "internal enforcement" is necessary to catch the thousands who slip by border police. "The way things are right now we're sending a message to illegal aliens that once they get into the country they don't have to worry about getting caught," Krikorian says. This encourages more people to try to enter the U.S. illegally, he says.

*"The United States doesn't need a million newcomers each year to ensure a strong economy."*

Opponents of employer sanctions argue, however, that instead of discouraging illegal aliens, sanctions merely force them to take jobs with employers who are more likely to exploit them.

"In many cases, all we do is push people to take jobs for less pay and with unsafe working conditions," says Cecilia Muñoz, vice president for policy at the National Council of La Raza, the nation's largest Latino advocacy group. Moreover, Muñoz adds, if employer sanctions did work, many businesses, especially in the service sector, would find themselves without workers.

"Many industries rely on [undocumented] labor," she says, pointing out that illegal aliens are ubiquitous on farms and construction sites and other sectors of the economy that depend on low-skilled workers willing to do grimy, often back-breaking labor.

## The Highly Skilled Immigrant

But immigrants are not just an important source of low-skill, low-wage labor. Skilled workers from abroad are also in demand, mainly in the high-technology sector, and controversy is raging over how many should be issued so-called H-1B visas and admitted on a temporary basis. Current laws permit up to 115,000 H-1B workers, which employers say is not enough.

Those who favor expanding the H-1B program argue that it is needed to offset the drastic labor shortage facing high-tech companies. They see the importation of highly educated and skilled workers from overseas as an unfortunate but necessary step in their efforts to stay competitive in a fast-changing and cutthroat industry. "Our colleges and universities are

*"Most experts favor taking at least some steps to block the estimated 300,000 or more illegal immigrants who come to the United States annually."*

gearing up to turn out more people qualified to do this kind of work, and so we don't see [H-1B visas] as a long-term solution," says Harris Miller, president of the Information Technology Association of America (ITAA). "But right now, we simply don't have enough people to fill all of the jobs available."

Norman Matloff, a professor of computer science at the University of California at Davis, challenges that claim. "There are plenty of people right here for these jobs," he says, contending that high-tech firms would rather import well-educated workers from overseas at lower salaries than go to the trouble of recruiting and training Americans.

As the United States enters a new millennium, here are some of the questions being asked in the debate over how many newcomers the United States should admit.

## Does the United States Admit Too Many Immigrants?

During the 1990s, the United States took in nearly 10 million foreigners, almost double the number that came during the 1980s and more than in any previous decade.

For many Americans the large number of newcomers and the prospect of millions more is disquieting. "We've already got gridlock from sea to shining sea," says FAIR's Stein. "So, of course, people are asking themselves how many new people does this country really need?"

But for the Cato Institute's Moore, the surge in immigration has largely been a blessing, one he hopes will continue, "Over the last 20 years, we've let in more than 15 million people, and it's been a stunning success story," he says.

In fact, Moore and other immigration proponents credit immigrants with playing a key role in the American economy's stellar performance in the past decade. "If we want to keep this phenomenal economic growth rate up," the de Tocqueville Institution's Lance says, "then we'd better keep letting in immigrants because they are helping this economy."

Immigrants aid the economy, Lance and other experts say, because they tend, almost by definition, to be highly motivated and hard working. "This is a self-selected group of people," Moore says, "because the very act of leaving your home country and taking a risk to come here means that you're probably ambitious and likely to succeed."

Indeed, proponents say, studies show that immigrants start more small businesses than the native population. And while many are modest "mom and pop" operations, others are at the leading edge of the new economy. For instance, one out of every four new businesses in Silicon Valley is founded by an entrepreneur of Indian or Chinese origin.

In addition, immigration proponents argue, immigrants are stoking the economic flames by taking hard-to-fill jobs. "Immigrants offer us a ready supply of hard-working people to fill niches in the labor market in vital ways, be it picking crops or making our food, driving taxis, caring for our children or building our buildings," Moore says.

La Raza's Muñoz agrees, adding: "I don't think people realize how many important jobs are done by immigrants and what would happen if they all went away."

What would happen, Muñoz, Moore and others contend, is that many industries, especially in the growing service sector, would grind to a halt as the people who washed the dishes or cleaned the offices disappeared. "So many important parts of the economy have become very dependent on immigrants," Moore says.

## The Risks of Mass Immigration

But Stein says there is a downside to importing workers who are mainly poorly educated with few or no skills. "All we're doing is importing a huge pool of cheap labor, which helps employers but keeps wages low for Americans," he says

The great need, Stein notes, is for people with a lot of education and skills. "Our future lies in improving productivity by providing our own people with training and education, not importing low-wage labor," he says.

Moreover, says the Center for Immigration Studies' Krikorian, immigrants are not irreplaceable in certain segments of the economy. "Anyone who imagines that the fruit won't get picked or that the dishes won't get washed without immigrants has a fundamental misunderstanding of market economics," he says. "All of this service work gets done in the parts of the country where there are few immigrants," he says, "and it's done by Americans. The question isn't whether the work is going to be done, but who's going to do it?"

*"For many Americans the large number of newcomers and the prospect of millions more is disquieting."*

Krikorian and others say that instead of importing workers to fill vacancies, the United States should be focusing on training the unemployed here. "If we lost immigration as a source of workers, employers would seek to increase the labor pool by increasing wages," he says. "They would also look to communities with higher unemployment rates—more marginal elements of the population—like those on public assistance, ex-convicts or the handicapped."

But opposition to immigration extends beyond its economic impact. Many argue that the nation's population is already too high and that admitting close to a million people annually is going to cause intolerable crowding in some areas. Indeed, the Census Bureau predicts the nation's population will rise from the current level of 270 million to more than 400 million by 2050.

"More than 70 percent of this growth is going to come from immigration," says Tom McKenna, president of Population-Environment Balance, a grassroots organization that advocates population stabilization to protect the environment. "Think about how crowded our cities are now, and then think about what it will be like with twice the number of people."

Immigration opponents also claim that the nation needs to reduce current immigration levels to allow the nation to absorb the tens of millions of newcomers who are already here. In particular, they say, a steady stream of immigrants will overwhelm efforts to turn recent arrivals into Americans. "When you have these high numbers of people coming in year after year, you can't assimilate them so easily," says the *National Review*'s O'Sullivan.

> *"The nation needs to reduce current immigration levels to allow the nation to absorb the tens of millions of newcomers who are already here."*

O'Sullivan contends that a lull in immigration would allow schools and governing institutions to teach immigrants English and give them an appreciation for American history and values. "We are a transnational society, and in order to work together effectively we must maximize our common cultural sympathies," he says. "If every ethnic group retains its own cultural sympathies, it will be hard for us to work together as one people."

But immigration supporters say that concerns about assimilation are as old as the Republic and just as overblown now as they were in the 18th century. "People who come here want to be American," Lance says. "Very few would run the gauntlet to get here unless they wanted to become part of this country."

Lance and others point out that—just as with previous groups—today's immigrants are quickly integrating into American society and losing their ties to their country of origin. "Look at the Hispanic kids who grow up here," she says. "They don't speak Spanish or don't speak it well. They're American now."

In addition, proponents doubt that continued immigration is going to turn the United States into an overcrowded country like China or India. "The numbers [McKenna] uses assume that the birth rate among immigrants will stay constant for succeeding generations," Muñoz says, noting that recent arrivals have more children than native-born Americans. "But data show that the children of immigrants have far fewer children than their parents."

## Cracking Down on Employers Who
## Knowingly Hire Illegal Immigrants

Not long ago, the INS conducted a series of raids against undocumented aliens working in the onion fields of Vidalia, Ga. Within days of the action, five members of the state's congressional delegation—including both U.S. senators—had fired off a letter to Attorney General Janet Reno complaining that the agency she supervises had shown a "lack of regard for the farmers." The letter had the desired effect. The INS stopped arresting undocumented pickers, and the onion crop made it to market.

Similarly, in other parts of the country complaints from local and national politicians have prompted the INS to back off. "This is very ironic," Krikorian says. "Congress passed [the Immigration Reform and Control Act of 1986] making it illegal to employ illegal aliens and then basically told the INS not to enforce it."

The law, which made it a crime to knowingly employ undocumented workers, imposed fines on employers caught using illegal aliens and even authorized jail time for repeat offenders.

But the employment-related provisions of the 1986 act have not worked. According to the INS, there are 5 million illegal aliens in the United States, an estimate that many immigration experts believe to be low. In addition, at least 300,000 are believed to enter the country each year. Many industries in the United States rely heavily upon undocumented workers, from the meatpacking plants of the Midwest to the restaurants and garment factories of New York City. "It's very clear to me that we're not sufficiently enforcing the law at all," says Rep. Lamar Smith, R-Texas, chairman of the House Judiciary Subcommittee on Immigration.

In some places, the local economy is largely supported by the labor of illegal aliens. Thomas Fischer, who until recently headed the INS in Georgia and three other Southeastern states, estimates that one out of every three businesses in Atlanta employs undocumented workers. "I'm talking about everything from your *Fortune* 500 companies down to your mom-and-pop businesses," he says.

For supporters of tough controls on illegal immigration, the presence of so many undocumented workers in so many industries represents a major failure in immigration policy. "The INS is making no effort whatsoever

> *"Giving employers a green light to bring in undocumented workers has a snowball effect that leads to even more illegal immigration."*

to fight the ever-increasing presence of illegal immigrants in this country," says Peter Brimelow, author of *Alien Nation*, a best-selling 1995 book that argues for stricter controls on immigration. According to Brimelow, a senior editor at *Forbes* and *National Review*, the INS' abrogation of duty has led to "the development of a huge illegal economy that is growing."

The solution, Brimelow and others say, is stricter enforcement of the sanctions already on the books. "They're absolutely necessary, because without them many employers feel free to hire illegal immigrants," Krikorian says.

Giving employers a green light to bring in undocumented workers has a snowball effect that leads to even more illegal immigration, Krikorian claims. "As long as people in other countries know that they can get jobs easily here, regardless of their status, they will keep coming," he argues.

> *"Sanctions only drive immigrants further into the underground economy."*

"Once they get in, there is little to fear since employment laws are basically ignored."

Moreover, Stein says, "Once someone hires illegal aliens they have a competitive advantage because their labor costs have dropped." That forces competitors to follow suit, leading to an even greater demand for illegal immigrants and fewer jobs for citizens or legal residents. "It's a vicious cycle."

## Questioning Employer Sanctions

But opponents of employer sanctions argue that they are not being enforced for a good reason: They don't work. "When they've tried to enforce employer sanctions in one area or another, they haven't reduced illegal immigration," says Frank Sharry, executive director of the National Immigration Forum, a think tank that favors increased immigration.

Sharry argues that sanctions only drive immigrants further into the underground economy. "The only thing employer sanctions do is push illegal immigrants from decent employers into the hands of unscrupulous employers," he says. "They push them down into the shadier parts of the economy, but not out of it."

Opponents of sanctions also argue that sanctions are unfair to employers, many of whom don't know they've hired illegal aliens. "Many illegal immigrants are hired unwittingly, because they forged the right documents," says Lance of the de Tocqueville Institution. "Only a minority of employers knowingly hire illegal immigrants, so imposing sanctions would get many of them in trouble for a good-faith mistake."

Cato's Moore agrees, adding: "Businesses should not be responsible for being immigration policemen." Such a system "would lead to great discrimination against foreigners—regardless of their status—because businesses would automatically wonder whether a foreign worker was illegal and worth the risk of hiring."

Moore and Muñoz are among those who say that illegal immigration should be controlled at the border, not at the office or factory. "We need to put more people and resources at the border," Muñoz says. "It can work if we put our minds to it."

But supporters of sanctions say that relying on the Border Patrol to stem the flow of illegal immigration is close to meaningless without "internal enforcement" since, by its own estimate, the patrol only catches one in three people trying to cross into the United States.

Moreover, 40 percent of all illegal immigrants initially enter the United States legally, but stay longer than the time allowed on their visa. "There's no way to stop visa overstays because they came in a perfectly legal manner," Krikorian says.

## Should the Number of H-1B Visas Be Increased?

Michael Worry has a problem. The CEO of Nuvation Labs, a 30-person Silicon Valley software-engineering firm, said he is constantly grappling with a shortage of employees. "We've had positions go unfilled for months at a time," he said.

So Worry has done what many others in similar positions have done—hired workers from abroad, many admitted only on a temporary basis. In fact, one-third of his workers are temporary foreign employees.

For years, Worry and others in the information-technology industry have complained of an almost crippling shortage of skilled workers. "The number of jobs in our industry has grown so fast that our colleges and universities just can't keep up with demand," says ITAA's Miller. "We have no choice but to look abroad."

Miller says there is already a huge gap between the number of jobs and qualified workers in the information-technology industry. Industry estimates of the shortage run as high as 800,000. In addition, according to a . . . Cato report, the demand for skilled high-tech jobs is expected to grow 150,000 per year over the next five years.

Like many high-tech companies, Nuvation tries to bring in qualified workers from abroad using H-1B visas, which require applicants to have a bachelor's degree and allow a stay of up to six years.

But firms that fill vacancies with H-1B visa holders complain that the program is much too limited to fill their needs. "The demand for high-tech workers is clearly outpacing the number of people that can currently be brought in" under the H-1B program, says Rep. Smith.

*"Firms that fill vacancies with H-1B visa holders complain that the program is much too limited to fill their needs."*

In the . . . fiscal year, which ends Sept. 30 [2000], the INS can issue up to 115,000 H-1B visas. But pro-business groups point out that demand is so great that the agency already has issued its quota for the year. Moreover, under existing law, the number of H-1B visas issued will drop to 107,500 next year and 65,000 the year after that.

High-tech companies and others have vigorously lobbied Congress to substantially increase the number of H-1B visas, and several bills are under consideration, including one sponsored by Smith that would lift the cap on H-1Bs for the next three years. The House Judiciary Committee approved that measure on May 18. Another measure sponsored by Sen. Spencer Abraham, R-Mich., that would increase the number of available visas to 195,000 for the next three years won the approval of the Senate Judiciary Committee on March 9.

Supporters of expanding the H-1B program are confident that an increase will become law [in 2000], especially since the idea has the backing of the White House and numerous members of Congress from both parties. "The time is right for this, and I'm fairly optimistic that we'll be able to work something out," Miller says.

But opponents of an increase—including many labor unions and some Democrats in Congress—argue that they are unnecessary and harmful to American workers. They say that companies clamoring for more temporary foreign workers are not taking advantage of the domestic labor force.

"Just call any employer of programmers in any city—large or small—and they'll tell you that they reject the overwhelming majority of job applicants without even giving them an interview," the University of California's Matloff says. For instance, he says, Microsoft rejects all but 2 percent of the applicants for technology jobs. "Now, how can they do this when they claim they're so desperate for workers?" he asks.

## Refusing to Train U.S. Workers

The real reason employers want more H-1Bs is they don't want to find and train skilled U.S. workers, Matloff says, although there are many highly qualified Americans who only need to have their skills updated. "These companies don't want to take the time and spend the money it takes to hire and train domestic workers," he says. "I think many of them are afraid that they'll lose someone after they've trained them."

In addition, opponents say, temporary visas allow companies to keep industry wages low. "If there were a labor shortage in one industry or another, wages would naturally rise and workers would shift into this area," says David A. Smith, director of public policy at the AFL-CIO. "But H-1B visas distort the market by bringing in outside workers, and that holds down wages."

Matloff points out that 79 percent of H-1B visa holders make less than $50,000 per year. While such a pay level is above the national average, it is considered low for skilled high-technology workers. "This is the kind of industry where if you're any good, you make at least $100,000 a year," he says.

Finally, opponents argue, H-1B visas give employers too much leverage over these temporary workers, because many are desperate to get permanent work status and need the company's assistance to do so. According to the *National Review*'s O'Sullivan, "employers say that they will help them get a green card, but in the meantime, 'you belong to us.'" Since the process can take up to five years, O'Sullivan and others argue, an H-1B visa can often lead to a form of indentured servitude. "This whole aspect of the system is open to terrible abuse," he claims.

Instead of expanding the H-1B program, critics say business and the government should focus on training and hiring domestic workers for high-tech jobs. "H-1B visas prevent us from doing what we need to generate a long-term supply of skilled labor that we're eventually going to need in this industry," the AFL-CIO's Smith says.

But H-1B supporters counter that high-tech companies really are facing a skilled labor shortage. They note that the unemployment rate within the information-technology industry is generally much lower than the already low national rate of 4 percent. "Look, our colleges and universities simply can't keep up with demand," Miller says.

Moore agrees. "It's vital that we have access to these highly skilled workers in order to maintain our competitive edge," he says. "We're getting the cream of the crop from developing countries like India. It's sort of a form of reverse foreign aid, a gift from the rest of the world to the U.S."

In addition, supporters say, the information-technology industry is already doing much to train new and existing employees to keep up with industry changes. "We're already the leader in spending on worker training," Miller says. "We spend 60 percent more than the financial-services industry or more than $1,000 per year, per employee."

H-1B supporters also dispute the notion that they are trying to bring in temporary workers to permanently replace domestic talent in order to drive down wages. "The law requires that we pay these people the prevailing wage, so they are well compensated for what they do," Miller says.

# Immigration Controls Are Necessary

## by Mark Krikorian

**About the author:** *Mark Krikorian is executive director of the Center for Immigration Studies, a think tank devoted to research and policy analysis of the economic, social, demographic, fiscal, and other impacts of immigration on the United States.*

To the casual observer, it might seem that the federal government has made real progress on immigration since [the terrorist attacks of September 11, 2001]. And, in fact, some of the measures we've seen . . . are encouraging signs that immigration is again being taken seriously, after decades of malign neglect: the shift of the immigration function to the new Homeland Security Department [of the U.S. government], progress toward developing a tracking system for foreign visitors, and registration of aliens from certain Middle Eastern countries.

But these are scattered moves lacking an overall strategy; the discussion of immigration policy in the political realm remains mired in the "nation of immigrants" cliches. This drift in immigration policy has allowed the illegal-alien population to balloon to 9 million, with two consequences: First, irresponsible proposals for vast amnesties (usually tarted up as guest-worker programs) have been put forward by, among others, the White House and Sens. John McCain and Edward Kennedy. Second, the policy vacuum has enabled immigration policy to be set, by default, by state and local authorities, under the direction of the Mexican foreign ministry. Jurisdictions across the country are progressively enacting a series of measures that amount to a de facto illegal-alien amnesty—California's decision to issue driver's licenses to illegal aliens being only the most recent example.

## A Meta-Immigration Policy

There are many things the federal government should leave to lower levels of government or the private sector, but management of immigration isn't one of

Mark Krikorian, "A Stern Face and a Warm Welcome," *National Review*, vol. 55, October 27, 2003, p. 42. Copyright © 2003 by National Review, Inc. Reproduced by permission.

them. It's time Congress filled this vacuum, and with something other than the vacuities emanating from McCain, Kennedy, et al.

Many public-spirited lawmakers have introduced bills to address specific problems, no doubt calculating correctly that piecemeal measures have a better chance of passage. But what is the overall framework such measures should fit into? What should our immigration "meta-policy" be, the policy that determines our other policies?

We needn't go far to discover it. The popular wisdom on immigration, inchoate and incomplete as it is, should be our guide. The American people, in every survey taken, say they prefer less immigration and tighter controls—and with good reason, given the economic, fiscal, social, and political problems caused by mass immigration. At the same time, we can be proud of the fact that we are the least xenophobic society in human history, making Americans out of people from every corner of the earth. This recognizes the two parts of any approach to this issue: immigration policy and immigrant policy. The first governs the conditions we place on admission of newcomers, the second governs how we treat them once they're here. Thus the answer: a meta-policy that combines low immigration and no-nonsense enforcement with an enthusiastic embrace of lawfully admitted newcomers. In other words, a pro-immigrant policy of low immigration—fewer immigrants but a warmer welcome.

## What Is to Be Done?

The starting point of immigration policy must be adequate capacity, and willingness, actually to enforce the law, whatever the content of the law happens to be. Lack of enforcement has been the central problem of immigration policy. Congress can design the most elegant legal and administrative framework imaginable, but it won't matter if the immigration authorities are not permitted to use it to enforce the law. Let me be clear: The chief reason for the lack of enforcement of our immigration laws is not incompetence or malfeasance on the part of the immigration bureaucracy, though there is surely plenty of that to go around. The real problem is the firm determination in Congress and successive administrations that the law not be enforced. For instance, when the INS [Immigration and Naturalization Service] conducted raids during Georgia's Vidalia onion harvest in 1998, thousands of illegal aliens—knowingly hired by the farmers—abandoned the fields to avoid arrest. By the end of the week, both of the

> *"The American people, in every survey taken, say they prefer less immigration and tighter controls."*

state's senators and three congressmen had sent an outraged letter to Washington complaining that the INS "does not understand the needs of America's farmers," and that was the end of that.

After an attempt at devising a "kinder, gentler" means of enforcing the immigration law was similarly slapped down, the INS got the message. It developed a new interior enforcement policy that gave up on trying to reassert control over immigration and focused almost entirely on the important, but narrow, issues of criminal aliens and smugglers. The title of a *New York Times* story in 2000 sums it up: "I.N.S. Is Looking the Other Way as Illegal Immigrants Fill Jobs."

Assuming we can actually muster the political will to act, what can we do with the 9 million illegals and how can we prevent more from coming? The issue is usually presented as a stark choice: arrest them all or give them amnesty. Since no one thinks

> *"The relationships that give rise to special immigration rights should be limited to the nuclear family."*

we can, or even should, deport 9 million people en masse, the only remaining choice would seem to be amnesty, whatever fig leaves are used to mask the truth. But amnesty and overnight mass deportation are not the only choices. There is a third way: squeezing the illegal population so that it declines through attrition. The government estimates that each year, some 400,000 people leave the settled illegal-alien population, by returning home voluntarily, being deported, or getting a green card. The problem is that 800,000 new illegal aliens settle here each year, more than replacing the outflow.

## An Effective Enforcement Policy

The enforcement approach we must adopt, then, is clear. If we put pressure on illegal immigrants so that more of them leave and fewer new ones come, we will see the illegal population start to decline, allowing the problem, over time, to take care of itself. Nor is this mere speculation; we've actually seen it work on a small scale already. The immigration authorities . . . concluded a "Special Registration" program for visitors from Islamic countries. The affected nation with the largest illegal-alien population was Pakistan, with an estimated 26,000 illegals here in 2000. Once it became clear that the government was actually serious about enforcing the immigration law—at least with regard to Middle Easterners—Pakistani illegals started leaving in droves on their own. The Pakistani embassy estimated that more than 15,000 of its illegal aliens have left the U.S., and the *Washington Post* reported in May [2003] the "disquieting" fact that in Brooklyn's Little Pakistan the mosque is one-third empty, business is down, there are fewer want ads in the local Urdu-language paper, and "For Rent" signs are sprouting everywhere.

This example highlights the applicability of "broken windows" policing to immigration. As Michelle Malkin has pointed out, citing the famous *Atlantic Monthly* article by James Q. Wilson and George Kelling, ignoring "minor" immigration violations creates the same atmosphere of disorder as leaving broken windows unrepaired does in a run-down neighborhood. And, as Mayor Giuliani demonstrated in New York, the reassertion of control by the government over seemingly minor matters reestablishes a sense of order, leading to decreased lawbreaking in general.

The enforcement initiative that would yield the most bang for the buck in restoring a sense of order would be enforcement of employer sanctions (the shorthand term for the ban on hiring illegal aliens). Ideally, we need a national system to enable employers to determine whether new hires have the right to work in the United States. In fact, several pilot verification programs developed by the INS continue to operate, and participating employers are generally pleased with them. But developing a nationwide system will take time, and face political opposition. In the meantime, rather than letting the perfect be the enemy of the good, we should implement less comprehensive measures that can be achieved more easily and still have a very significant effect. For instance, an initiative to notify employers of Social Security numbers that didn't match the accompanying names has met with great success.

This principle underlying employer sanctions—requiring proof of legal status—should be extended to other activities that most people engage in, but do so infrequently: getting a driver's license, registering an automobile, opening a bank account, applying for a mortgage, enrolling in higher education, getting a business license.

## Who Should Be Let In?

Once an infrastructure is in place to enforce our immigration policy, what should the content of that policy be? Most immigration, regardless of the source or destination, is permitted for one of three reasons: family connections, employment needs, and pure humanitarian concern. Family-based immigration now accounts for nearly two-thirds of green-card recipients. The relationships that give rise to special immigration rights should be limited to the nuclear family: husbands, wives, and small children of U.S. citizens. That would reduce immigration based on blood or marriage by about half, to some 300,000 per year.

In addition to a handful of Einsteins, employment-based immigration admits a wide array of ordinary people who should not receive special immigration

> *"Temporary visas, technically known as 'nonimmigrant' visas, need to be capped at much lower levels."*

rights. A cap of 25,000 would be more than adequate for a highly targeted subset of the current categories, but if such a reduction proved difficult for political reasons, a good starting point would be to cut this stream by at least half, from the 1999–2002 average of 129,000 per year. Humanitarian immigration has three subparts: refugee resettlement (bringing refugees from overseas), grants of asylum (reclassifying as a refugee someone who is already here illegally or on a temporary visa), and cancellation of removal (a grant of amnesty to an illegal alien whose deportation would cause "exceptional and extremely unusual hardship"). The solution here is to depoliticize the determination of who should qualify and establish an overall cap, just as a family might set a target for the coming year's charitable giving.

In addition to these three main components of legal immigration, there are several other issues. The visa lottery, which gives 50,000 green cards a year to people from countries that send relatively few immigrants (mainly the Middle East and Africa), has no national-interest rationale and no real political support, and should be discontinued immediately. Also, temporary visas, technically known as "nonimmigrant" visas, need to be

> *"Lower levels of immigration would make less pressing the tough measures that have been proposed to deal with immigration-related problems."*

capped at much lower levels, especially those visas for foreign students, workers, and exchange visitors. These programs have become little more than side doors to permanent immigration. And guest-worker programs should never be instituted. Whether intended for tomato pickers or computer programmers, such schemes are inherently dishonest and have failed everywhere: They inevitably lead to permanent settlement and actually promote more illegal immigration.

## How Should Immigrants Be Treated?

So much for immigration policy; what of the second component of the metapolicy—the "warmer welcome"? The place to start fixing immigrant policy is the immigration office. The service side of the former INS, now called U.S. Citizenship and Immigration Services, has an abysmal record of dealing with applicants. There are long lines, surly staff, and applications lost in bureaucratic black holes. This should sound familiar to most Americans, because that's exactly the way most state motor-vehicle departments used to operate. But even as DMVs have gotten better over the past decade, the immigration service has not. This is wrong; one expects immigration enforcement to present a stern face to illegal aliens, but why are legal immigrants subjected to such caprice and discourtesy, especially when they're paying for the privilege through fees?

The analogy is not frivolous. Just as the DMV is the one government agency that virtually all adult citizens are sure to have business with, the immigration service is, necessarily, the one agency that all immigrants have to deal with at one time or another. As a recent article in *Governing* magazine pointed out, DMVs have made significant strides in technology and customer service. But the immigration authorities have just begun inching in this direction. Only this spring did they begin to permit electronic filing, and only of two specific forms, which account for about 30 percent of the total number of applications received in a year. Electronic filing, however, doesn't mean electronic processing. Employees still have to print out the applications at their end and file them with millions of others, filling row after row after row of bookshelves in service centers around the nation.

The first step, then, is to streamline the bureaucratic process; the second is to help newcomers integrate into our society more swiftly. To begin with, all newcomers we admit for long-term residence should be admitted as Americans-in-training, and not as servants whose labor we rent at our pleasure and discard when convenient. That means no guest-worker programs and no winking at illegal immigration, both of which allow foreigners to live here, but only on a contingent basis, at our sufferance.

Proactive efforts at assimilation have been sorely lacking during this latest wave of immigration. Nonetheless, there is much that can be done. The U.S. Commission on Immigration Reform recommended that orientation materials be presented to new legal immigrants upon admission, almost like an instruction manual for life in America. This would include a welcoming statement on behalf of the American people, a brief overview of American history and civics, and "tools for settlement," including basic information on paying your taxes, U.S. holidays, the importance of credit reports and paying bills on time, how to use the postal and telephone systems, etc. We take much of this for granted, but for a newcomer, having all this in one place can be a godsend. Political psychologist Stanley Renshon, in his upcoming book *The 50 Percent American*, recommends that governments go further and work with businesses and civic groups to set up welcome centers to help immigrants adjust to the U.S. Expanded English-language instruction is also vital.

The final component of the warmer welcome is counterintuitive, but very powerful: Immigrants will be helped by reductions in future immigration. The first beneficiaries of lower levels of admissions would be the immigrants already here, since they would experience less competition for jobs. More difficult to quantify, but perhaps as important, is that lower levels of immigration would make less pressing the tough measures that have been proposed to deal with immigration-related problems—sweeping restrictions on access to welfare, for instance. With a smaller flow of new immigrants, and a gradually shrinking immigrant population, we will have much more flexibility.

Our current immigration mess is politically unsustainable. Too many lawmakers from both parties have decided that amnesty and basically open borders are the only way to solve this problem, despite overwhelming public opposition. This disconnect between the public and the elite represents an enormous opportunity for a political figure championing a pro-immigrant/low-immigration approach to reform.

# Immigration Controls Should Be Abolished

**by Teresa Hayter**

**About the author:** *Teresa Hayter, an immigration activist, is author of* Open Borders: The Case Against Immigration Controls.

Immigration controls are a cruel 20th-century aberration. Although they may seem like common sense, an unavoidable reality, in fact, in most countries they are less than 100 years old.

International migration, on the other hand, has always existed. Twice as many people migrated from Europe to the rest of the world as have come in the opposite direction. And since the current theory is that human beings originated in East Africa, every other part of the world is the product of immigration. All of us, the racists and the rest of us, are either immigrants or descended from immigrants.

Freedom of movement should be the new common sense. It is hard to see why people should not be allowed to move around the world in search of work or safety or both.

Within the European Union there are growing attempts to secure the principle of freedom for its citizens to live and work in any member country. Between the states of the US federation there are no restrictions on the movement of people. It would be considered an outrage if the inhabitants of a country were not free to travel to another part of that country to get a job there, or if they were not allowed to leave it. Indeed, it was considered an outrage when this happened in the former USSR.

The 1948 Universal Declaration of Human Rights asserts these rights. Yet the Universal Declaration is strangely silent on the question of the right to enter another country. Governments cling to what seems to be one of their last remaining prerogatives: their right to keep people out of their territories. Few people question the morality, legality or practicality of this right.

## Nation-States in Decline

Nation-states are the agents and enforcers of immigration controls and country boundaries. Most were themselves not fully established until the 19th century.

Now nation-states are supposed to be on the decline. International institutions such as the United Nations, the International Monetary Fund [IMF], the World Bank and the World Trade Organization attempt to control the actions of national governments. Economic power is concentrated in fewer and bigger corporations. These put pressure on governments to allow goods and capital to move freely around the world, unaffected by considerations of national sovereignty. Sometimes they also press governments to allow the free movement of people, in order to secure the labour they need for expansion. Yet by the 1970s many countries, especially in Europe but not in North America, had more or less ended the right of people to enter and work.

In theory, the right to gain asylum under the United Nations 1951 Geneva convention, within certain restrictive conditions, remains. But during the past 15 years or so, governments have increasingly failed to observe the spirit of this undertaking.

Governments claim—unjustly—that most asylum seekers are in fact 'economic migrants', migrating to better their economic situation. Incorrectly labelling them as 'illegal immigrants', they build a vast edifice of repression.

## Immigration Boosts Wealth

Even if it were morally acceptable for the rich nations of the world to use immigration controls to preserve their disproportionate wealth, as the South African whites tried to use apartheid to preserve theirs, it is doubtful whether they achieve this purpose.

There is a mass of evidence to show that immigrants actually make a big contribution to the wealth and prosperity of the countries they go to. When asked after the IMF/World Bank meetings in Washington why he had raised upwards the estimates of his country's economic growth, British [finance] minister Gordon Brown said this was because net immigration was higher than expected. Economists have also suggested that the abolition of immigration controls would cause a doubling of world incomes.

Immigration is not just good for the capitalists. It also improves both the job prospects and the wages and conditions of workers. Without immigration, sectors of industry would collapse or move abroad, with knock-on

> *"Economists have . . . suggested that the abolition of immigration controls would cause a doubling of world incomes."*

effects on other jobs. The US economy, especially its agriculture, building trades and services, is heavily dependent on immigrants, including those who have no legal permission to work.

Many industrialized countries—especially in Europe—have declining and ageing populations. Unless immigration is increased, there will not be enough young workers to pay taxes, keep the public sector and industry functioning and look after the old people.

On average immigrants contribute more in taxes than they receive in public services, studies in the US have shown. In Britain too the Home Office estimates that immigrants make a net contribution of $3.75 billion a year to public finances. The cost of immigration controls, on the other hand, is at least $1.5 billion a year, and rising.

## Questioning National Identity

Immigration controls are explicable only by racism. Those who defend them often refer to the need to 'preserve national identity'. National identity is hard to define. More or less every country in the world is the product of successive waves of immigration. Each new group of arrivals has tended to be vilified as unable to assimilate, prone to disease, crime and so on.

It is sometimes argued that the numbers migrating from poor countries to the rich countries of Europe, North America and Australasia would be larger and might 'swamp' local populations and cause severe social disruption.

Yet the few migrants and refugees who make it to the rich countries are exceptional people who have to have some money and a great deal of courage and enterprise. They come

*"The abolition of immigration controls would mean a vast increase in freedom and prosperity for all of us."*

because there are jobs, or because they are in desperate danger. Few people want to uproot themselves and leave their families, friends and cultures and most of those who do so wish to return; immigration controls have the perverse effect of making this harder.

Contrary to predictions, the introduction of free internal movement within Europe did not lead to mass migration from the poor South to the richer North; on the contrary the authorities would like to have more rather than less labour mobility in the European Union. They also predict that the planned opening to the East will have a similarly limited effect on migration.

The existence of extreme world poverty and inequality does not cause mass migration, but rather the opposite. Most people in the Third World do not have a remote possibility of migrating. Economic development, where it occurs and especially of the skewed type which results from Western intervention, is more likely to cause an increase in migration than extreme poverty.

If the governments of the rich West really do wish to reduce the number of refugees in the world, including the tiny proportion who try to make it into their territories, there are things they should stop doing. For example they should not create refugees by selling arms in conflict zones or to repressive regimes.

As in apartheid, the apparatus of repression required to enforce immigration controls is becoming increasingly unsustainable.

The costs, the suffering, and the racism they engender are escalating. Sooner or later, immigration controls will be abandoned. The main issue is how much longer is the suffering to continue before they can be consigned to the dustbin of history?

Clearly it would not make much sense to campaign for immigration controls to be ended only in one country. Their abolition would need to be by agreement between the rich governments of the world.

A precedent for the opening of borders exists in the European Union. Those who worked for the abolition of European internal frontiers were animated not only by the interests of big business and free trade, but by an idealistic view of the future of Europe.

North American Free Trade Area (NAFTA) agreements provide only for the free movement of goods and capital. But president [Vicente] Fox of Mexico, who is a strong supporter of neo-liberal policies and also a friend of [U.S. president] George Bush, is pressing for the free movement of labour to be included in the agreements, as the *Wall Street Journal* and sections of US capital have done for some time.

Abolition of borders implies complete freedom of movement for all, and the right to settle and work in a place of the person's choice, just as people can now do within countries. This in turn implies the abandonment not just of immigration controls, but of the whole apparatus of determining whether or not a person is entitled to refugee status.

Little would be gained by expanding quotas or agreements on 'burden sharing' and dispersal of those who some agency decided were 'genuine' refugees. Refugees themselves are best able to decide whether or not they need to flee; the presumption that this can be determined by immigration officials operating quotas is absurd. Those whose claims were refused would have to be kept out, which would mean the continuation of repression.

Some argue that the way ahead is to increase the number of work permits issued to employers to employ immigrants and that this would get rid of 'people smuggling'. However, either the number of permits issued would meet demand in which case controls would be unnecessary, or those who failed to migrate legally would continue to try to do so illegally.

In a more just world order, movements of capital would be democratically controlled to meet people's needs and to reduce inequalities. But people are not goods or capital—and they should be free to move. The attempt to limit this basic freedom leads to some of the worst abuses of human rights which exist in the world today. The abolition of immigration controls would mean a vast increase in freedom and prosperity for all of us.

# Dual Citizenship Should Be Discouraged

**by Phyllis Schlafly**

**About the author:** *Phyllis Schlafly, editor of the monthly newsletter the* Phyllis Schlafly Report, *is a conservative columnist and representative of the pro-family movement.*

One of the goals of the globalists is to make everyone believe we are citizens of the world, not citizens of a particular country. This concept, widely taught in the schools, tends to diminish patriotism and allegiance to one's country while promoting open borders subject only to a network of international bureaucracies.

## Dual Citizenship Is an Oxymoron

We are also beginning to hear more frequently about "dual citizenship," but that phrase is an oxymoron. One cannot truly be a citizen of two different countries because ultimately loyalty cannot be divided. If the two countries went to war against each other, the so-called dual citizens would have to pick sides. No man can serve two masters: for either he will hate the one, and love the other; or else he will hold to the one and despise the other.

Dual citizenship is not the same as holding two active passports from different countries, because a passport alone does not prove citizenship.

The issue of dual citizenship arises because countries have different requirements for citizenship and it is possible to satisfy the requirements of two or more countries. U.S. citizenship is based on U.S. law, which is that one must be born in the United States or naturalized according to our naturalization law.

Thus, in order to become a U.S. citizen, immigrants are required by law to transfer their allegiance from their native country to the United States of America. *You cannot be a dual citizen with the country you emigrated from.* But our country is now confronted with the problem of immigrants who have been falsely led to believe that they are or can be dual citizens, and this dangerous

Phyllis Schlafly, "The Many Assaults on U.S. Sovereignty," *Phyllis Schlafly Report*, vol. 35, June 2002, p. 42. Copyright © 2002 by Phyllis Schlafly. Reproduced by permission.

notion is diluting our national identity and culture.

Mexico passed a law in 1998 that extends citizenship to Mexicans who are naturalized in other countries and to their children. This is an invitation to new U.S. citizens either to betray their oath of allegiance to the United States or to cross their fingers behind their backs when they take it.

Many statements by President Vicente Fox and other Mexican officials show that their plan is to export a segment of their population to the United States, let them become U.S. citizens, but retain them as Mexican citizens. Mexico wants these new American citizens to consider themselves "binationals," and to vote in both the U.S. and Mexico, with Mexican politicians campaigning for their votes and allegiance.

Mexico is also trying to legitimize Mexican aliens illegally living in the United States by giving them special ID cards called "matricula consulare." These Mexican ID cards are being used to pretend to validate their illegal residence, prevent deportation, and help them to get U.S. driver's licenses, jobs, taxpayer benefits, and in-state university tuition.

U.S. officials from San Francisco to Anaheim [California], Albuquerque [New Mexico] to Austin to Houston [Texas], have announced that they will accept these Mexican-issued ID cards. Some police, some banks, and some airlines have said they will accept them.

> *"It is unacceptable for a naturalized American to retain or reinstate allegiance to any other country."*

U.S. law allows U.S. citizenship to be removed if a person behaves like a citizen of another country or manifests an intent to give up U.S. citizenship as shown by statements or conduct. But a series of post–World War II U.S. Supreme Court 5-4 decisions have made it difficult to revoke U.S. citizenship.

Current law specifies at least seven reasons for revoking U.S. citizenship, such as obtaining naturalization in a foreign state or taking an oath to a foreign state. Voting is not one of the listed reasons.

We are told that millions of U.S. residents now claim dual citizenship. Congress should put an end to this dangerous notion and tighten up the law on what constitutes evidence that a naturalized U.S. citizen intends to retain or to reinstate his loyalty to a foreign country. Congress should legislate that voting in a foreign country is evidence of intent to relinquish U.S. citizenship. Congress should also authorize our government to revoke citizenship based on the preponderance of evidence standard.

It is unacceptable for a naturalized American to retain or reinstate allegiance to any other country. We only welcome immigrants who want to be Americans.

# Dual Citizenship Should Be Encouraged

**by David A. Martin and T. Alexander Aleinikoff**

**About the authors:** *David A. Martin, a law professor at the University of Virginia, is coauthor with Kay Hailbronner of* Rights and Duties of Dual Nationals: Evolution and Prospects. *T. Alexander Aleinikoff, a law professor at Georgetown University, is coauthor with Douglas Klusmeyer of* Citizenship Policies for an Age of Migration. *Both served as general counsel to the Immigration and Naturalization Service.*

Dual nationality was once likened to bigamy. U.S. President Theodore Roosevelt called it a "self-evident absurdity." In some nations, notably Germany and Austria, resistance to the idea endures. And terrorist threats have further raised sensitivities about national loyalty. Nevertheless, a revolution is occurring in citizenship law and policies. Spurred by increasing migration and a global economy, many nations now accept and even promote dual status.

Both host and home nations have changed their tune for several good reasons. Many countries of origin, wishing to improve ties with their diaspora—in part because these emigrants send home remittances—have abandoned rules that dictated loss of nationality for citizens who naturalize elsewhere. Some receiving countries, like Australia, have also changed their rules to encourage naturalization and now permit naturalizing citizens to retain their former nationalities.

Migrants generally welcome the change. With cheaper communication and travel, emigration rarely requires a decisive break with their countries of origin. Dual nationality better reflects a migrant's mix of affections and loyalties.

Critics of dual nationality usually target policies that allow newcomers to naturalize without giving up their home-country citizenship, wholly missing the primary cause of the increase in dual nationality: the growing number of people who automatically obtain that status at birth. The move toward gender equality has dictated a break with the traditional rule that a father's citizenship determines his child's.

Children now born to parents of different nationalities inherit both. Further, to promote the integration of immigrant communities, more countries are adopting rules that bestow citizenship on children born to immigrants. These children thus acquire both citizenship from their birth country and the nationality of their parents.

U.S. law and practice reflect the trend toward acceptance of dual citizenship. Since the 1960s, the U.S. Supreme Court has held that Americans taking citizenship abroad cannot be stripped of their U.S. nationality. And despite laws going back to the early days of the republic requiring people seeking citizenship in the United States to renounce foreign allegiances, federal authorities now make no attempt to enforce this pledge. The result is that natives of Mexico who become U.S.

> *"The growth in dual nationality presents more opportunities than dangers, freeing individuals from irreconcilable choices and fostering connections."*

citizens are not asked to surrender their Mexican passports, and since 1998, Mexico has permitted them to maintain their Mexican nationality. Moreover, under the U.S. Constitution's 14th Amendment, all children born in the United States are U.S. citizens, so if they are born to immigrant parents, they are likely to have more than one citizenship. The numbers of such cases are not trivial. Drawing on census data, we estimate that 500,000 children are born in the United States each year with more than one nationality.

## Answering the Skeptics

For skeptics, these developments provoke alarm. But dual nationality poses few risks. Through thoughtful management, governments can address the concerns that typically feed resistance, including fears that dual citizens will shop for justice, vote, or hold elected office in two nations and thus divide their loyalties between their original and adopted countries.

Critics seize on the case of Samuel Sheinbein, a U.S. citizen who murdered a fellow teenager in Maryland and then fled to Israel. Sheinbein had never lived in Israel, but courts there ruled that he held Israeli citizenship through his father. Because Israel followed the European rule forbidding extradition of nationals, he escaped U.S. prosecution (though he was eventually tried and sentenced in Israel). But this undesirable outcome can't be blamed on Sheinbein's dual citizenship. The fault lay with an obsolete extradition rule; Israel changed it after his trial. In general, whenever laws, entitlements, or obligations (such as military service) conflict, states should give primacy to the country of primary residence.

Dual nationals, it is sometimes argued, may vote in elections in two nations and if the economy turns sour in one can pick up and move to the other. Dual nationality thus allows individuals to manipulate their ties to states to their own advantage. But shifting national residences at will is more a function of wealth or determination than of dual nationality. Many countries also prevent nonresidents from voting, and in others, few nonresidents exercise their franchise anyway. In the unlikely event such votes become a significant problem, states can regulate voting; they need not outlaw dual nationality. Worries about supposed unfair advantages would also fade, albeit more gradually, if a state did not extend citizenship to future generations abroad when a family loses all connection with the country of origin.

After the fall of the Soviet Union, a number of naturalized U.S. citizens returned to Eastern Europe to take up high-level positions in new governments. One, Valdas Adamkus, a former regional administrator of the U.S. Environmental Protection Agency, became president of his native Lithuania in 1998. The possibilities for conflicts or entanglements involving dual citizens who hold high office are real, but political considerations will normally lead officials to give up their citizenship to the other country, as Adamkus did before taking office. If not, both states concerned could properly bar dual nationals from holding such posts.

Doubters maintain that residents with dual nationalities may be reluctant to give the newly adopted nations their undivided loyalty. States are right to promote robust citizenship. But complex loyalties are a feature of the modern world. Liberal democracies generally tolerate, or even encourage, a host of affiliations and loyalties on the part of their inhabitants—to family, religious group, college, hometown—and don't regard these as incompatible with national allegiance. The increasing convergence of state interests, built around commitments to democracy and the free market, along with the decline of conscription and interstate war, also minimizes real conflict.

The growth in dual nationality presents more opportunities than dangers, freeing individuals from irreconcilable choices and fostering connections that can further travel, trade, and peaceful relations. The claim that dual nationality is bigamy adopts the wrong family analogy. Marriage makes a person a member of two families: one's own and one's spouse's. To give love or loyalty to the second does not require subtracting it from the first.

# Illegal Immigration Controls Are Necessary to Reduce Terrorism

by Mark Krikorian

**About the author:** *Mark Krikorian is the director of the Center for Immigration Studies, a think tank that studies the effects of immigration on the United States.*

In 2002, there were more than 33,000,000 foreign-born residents living in the United States, approximately one-fifth of all the people worldwide living outside the country of their birth. But that's only one part of the phenomenon of population mobility. In 2001, in addition to granting permanent residence (green cards) to more than one million people, the United States also performed approximately thirty-three million inspections of foreign visitors (not immigrants) entering the United States legally through ports of entry—some of those inspections being of people who had entered more than once during that year. Add to that figure the cross-border commuters and Americans returning from abroad, and the number of border inspections conducted in 2001 surpassed 400,000,000.

American policymakers should take this amount of human traffic seriously as the security threat it is. Granted, the vast majority of this traffic is perfectly benign, but there are indeed terrorists and criminals overseas who would use this flow of people as cover to harm us. And although better technology, better intelligence, and better international cooperation are necessary, they are insufficient to make America secure from such threats. They will not do the job unless combined with reductions in the total number of people admitted to the country and changes in the criteria for the selection of those people.

There are two reasons for this, one administrative and one social. The administrative reason is that such an enormous flow of people makes it impossible for the government to devote adequate resources to keeping the bad guys out and removing those that get in. The Immigration and Naturalization Service (INS)—

and the State Department, which issues visas—have been notoriously ineffective at immigration control, and it is simply not credible to claim that we can significantly reform these tools in the midst of today's very high level of arrivals from overseas. Even the move of most immigration functions to the new Department of Homeland Security, and the division of those functions between enforcement (such as border patrol and airport inspections) and services (granting green cards, citizenship status, and so forth) will not be of much help without reductions in the workload.

## Globalization Is a Security Threat

But let us suspend our disbelief for a moment and ask the deeper question, namely whether there are factors inherent in globalization that make the mass movement of people a security threat? Here we come to the social reason for reducing the movement of people into the United States.

Globalization—understood as the unfolding implications of advanced communications and transportation technologies—fosters the creation of transnational communities, which impede the kind of deep assimilation that undergirds national cohesion and fosters genuine loyalty. These poorly assimilated communities (within the United States and other countries), which globalization both creates and keeps connected to their overseas counterparts, serve as the sea within which terrorists and criminals can swim as fish, to borrow an image from [Chinese leader Mao Zedong].

Of course, this is nothing new: immigrant communities have always been home to gangs of bad guys (though, interestingly, some research suggests that individual immigrants may be less likely than natives to be criminals). The Italian criminal organizations that cropped up in the United States early in the last century are the best-known examples, but there were prominent Jewish and Irish gangs as well. During the great wave of immigration near the turn of the twentieth century, and for more than a generation after it was stopped in the 1920s, the Mafia flourished and law enforcement had very little success penetrating it. This was because immigrants had little stake in the larger society, lived in enclaves with limited knowledge of English, were suspicious of government institutions, and clung to Old World prejudices and attitudes like "omerta" (the code of silence).

Thus it should be no surprise that similar problems exist today, with immigrant communities exhibiting characteristics that shield or even promote criminality. For instance, as criminologist Ko-lin Chin has written, "The isolation of the Chinese community, the inability of American law enforcement authorities to penetrate the Chinese criminal underworld, and the reluctance of Chinese victims to come forward for help all conspire to enable Chinese gangs to endure." In addition to the Chinese, William Kleinknecht, author of *The New Ethnic Mobs* (1996), documents Russian, Latin American, and other criminal organizations using immigrant communities for cover and sustenance.

The greatest threat was alluded to by President [George W.] Bush in his address to the joint session of Congress after the [September 11, 2001, terrorist attacks]: "Al Qaeda is to terror what the Mafia is to crime." The role—however unwilling in most cases—of today's immigrant communities as hosts for terrorists is clear. A *New York Times* story observed about Paterson, N.J., "The hijackers' stay here also shows how, in an area that speaks many languages and keeps absorbing immigrants, a few young men with no apparent means of support and no furniture can settle in for months without drawing attention." ("A Hub for Hijackers Found in New Jersey," *New York Times*, September 27, 2001).

## Sheltering Terrorists

Nor is the role of the immigrant community always merely passive. Two of the September 11 hijackers—Nawaf Alhamzi and Khalid Almihdhar—had been embraced by the Muslim immigrant community in San Diego. As the *Washington Post* noted, "From their arrival here in late 1999 until they departed a few months before the September 11 attacks, Alhazmi and Almihdhar repeatedly enlisted help from San Diego's mosques and established members of its Islamic community. The terrorists leaned on them to find housing, open a bank account, obtain car insurance—even, at one point, get a job." ("Hijackers Found Welcome Mat on West Coast; San Diego Islamic Community Unwittingly Aided Two Who Crashed into Pentagon," *Washington Post*, December 29, 2001).

Even more threatening than the role immigrant enclaves play in simply shielding terrorists is their role in recruiting new ones. The *San Francisco Chronicle* described naturalized U.S. citizen Khalid Abu al Dahab as "a one-man communications hub" for al Qaeda, shuttling money and fake passports to terrorists around the world from his Silicon Valley apartment. According to the *Chronicle*, "Dahab said [terrorist leader Osama] bin Laden was eager to recruit American citizens of Middle Eastern descent." When Dahab and fellow terrorist and naturalized citizen Ali Mohammed (a U.S. army veteran and author of al Qaeda's terrorist handbook) traveled to Afghanistan in the mid-1990s to report on their efforts to recruit American citizens, "bin Laden praised their efforts and emphasized the necessity of recruiting as many Muslims with American citizenship as possible into the organization."

> *"Immigrant communities have always been home to gangs of bad guys."*

Perhaps the most disturbing example so far of such recruitment in immigrant communities comes from Lackawanna, New York, where six Yemeni Americans—five of them born and raised in the United States to immigrant parents—were arrested in September 2002 for operating an al Qaeda terrorist sleeper cell. The alleged ringleader of the cell, also born in the United States, is believed to be hiding in Yemen. The six arrested men are accused of traveling to Pakistan . . . , ostensibly for religious training, and then going to an al Qaeda terrorist training camp in Afghanistan. The community that bred this cell is made up largely of immigrants and is intimately connected to its home country. As the *Buffalo News* put it: "This is a piece of ethnic America where the Arabic-speaking Al-Jazeera television station is beamed in from Qatar through satellite dishes to Yemenite-American homes; where young children answer 'Salaam' when the cell phone rings, while older children travel to the Middle East to meet their future husband or wife; where soccer moms don't seem to exist, and where girls don't get to play soccer or, as some would say, "football."

Nor is this likely to be the last such cell uncovered. As another story in the *Buffalo News* reported, "Federal officials say privately that there could be dozens of similar cells across the country, together posing a grave danger to national security. They believe that such cells tend to be concentrated in communities with large Arab populations, such as Detroit."

## Many Immigrants No Longer Assimilate

In considering what to do about all this, the lessons of the past aren't entirely applicable. With the end of mass immigration, and in the absence of cheap and easy trans-Atlantic links, the assimilation of Italian immigrants in the early twentieth century accelerated, and immigrants' offspring developed a sense of genuine membership and ownership in America—what John Fonte has called "patriotic assimilation." It was this process that drained the waters within which the Mafia had been able to swim, allowing law enforcement to do its job more effectively, and eventually cripple the organizations.

Thirty years ago, anthropologist Francis Ianni described this process: "An era of Italo-American crime seems to be passing in large measure due to the changing character of the Italo-American community," including "the disappearance of the kinship model on which such [Mafia] families are based." Ianni continued, "After three generations of acculturation," Ianni continued, "this powerful pattern of organization is finally losing its hold on Italo-Americans generally—and on the crime families as well." Kleinknecht, in *The New Ethnic Mobs*, argues that the same could happen today in other immigrant communities: "If the mass immigration of Chinese should come to a halt, the Chinese gangster may disappear in a blaze of assimilation after a couple of decades."

> *"Even more threatening than the role immigrant enclaves play in simply shielding terrorists is their role in recruiting new ones."*

Maybe, but globalization has changed the terms of assimilation, making such an outcome much more difficult. In the past, it was all but impossible to live in two countries simultaneously, which forced most newcomers to put down permanent roots. Of course, immigrants in the past tried to maintain ties with the old country, but the cost and difficulties involved were such that the ties tended to atrophy fairly quickly. As Princeton sociologist Alejandro Portes observes, "Earlier in the twentieth century, the expense and difficulty of long-distance communication and travel simply made it impossible to lead a dual existence in two countries. Polish peasants couldn't just hop a plane or make a phone call, for that matter, to check out how things were going at home over the weekend."

But now, with low-cost long-distance rates and air fares, a transnational life is available to the masses. Wellesley sociologist Peggy Levitt has even described what she calls a "transnational village," a community split between the original village in the Dominican Republic and its doppelganger in Boston. Political parties operate in both places, people watch the same soap operas, telephone contacts become ever more frequent as rates fall, gossip travels instantly between the two halves of the village, parents in one half try to raise children in the other.

Another notable example is Jesus R. Galvis, a Colombian immigrant who started a business in New Jersey, became an American citizen, and eventually got elected to the Hackensack City Council (he's still there). In 1998, he ran for the Senate—the Colombian Senate. Had he won, he would have held elective office in two nations simultaneously, a first in American history. In 2000, at least three Mexican immigrants living in the United States ran for local political offices in Mexico, a phenomenon likely to proliferate wildly in the wake of Mexico's passage of a law permitting dual nationality and the fact that within the next few years immigrants living in the U.S. will be able to vote in Mexican elections.

## Disunity

This process, repeated all across America by immigrants from many different countries, is blurring the distinction between immigrants and sojourners. As such, it is aiding the transformation of the United States from a unified nation, which admitted immigrants in order to make them full members of the national community, into merely "one node in a post-national network of diasporas," in the words of University of Chicago anthropologist Arjun Appadurai.

The effects of this "network of diasporas" trend in globalization is evident in recent research done on national self-identification. The aforementioned Professor Portes, with Ruben Rumbaut of Michigan State, recently published *Legacies: The Story of the Immigrant Second Generation* (2001), the product of a multi-year longitudinal study of thousands of children of immigrants in San Diego and South Florida. Most interesting for our purposes was their analysis of how these young people identified their nationality, something they were asked when they started high school and again when they were finishing.

When first surveyed, the majority of the students identified themselves as Americans in some form, either as simply "American" or as a hyphenated American (Cuban-American, for instance, or Filipino-American). After four years of American high school, barely one-third still identified themselves in this way; the majority choosing an identification with no American component at all, opting for either a foreign national-origin identity (Cuban, Filipino) or a racial identity (Hispanic, Asian).

A rare study of the identifications of Muslim immigrants wasn't any more reassuring. Kambiz Ghanea Bassiri, an Iranian doctoral student at Harvard, found that the Muslim immigrants he surveyed were at least more likely to feel "closer ties or loyalties" to Islamic countries than to the United States. Similarly, the 2002 (U.S.) National Survey of Latinos, released in December [2002] by the Pew Hispanic Center, found that even among the grandchildren of Hispanic immigrants, only 57 percent thought of themselves as primarily American.

What to do? The solutions already undertaken, though insufficient, are a first step. Better identification systems, greater scrutiny of money transfers, more attention by intelligence and law-enforcement agencies to penetrating terrorist and criminal groups are all necessary measures. In addition, there are steps we can take to better ensure that those who move to our society learn to love America, comfort her, honor and keep her, in sickness and in health, forsaking all others, as long as they live. Improved American history education, as championed by President Bush, is a must, as are efforts to raise the standards for naturalization and curb radical multiculturalism.

Ultimately, however, America's security in a globalized world depends on the curtailment of the mass admission of people, especially from less-developed societies where terrorist and criminal organizations are more likely to flourish.

# Tough Illegal Immigration Controls Will Not Stop Terrorism

by Cathy Young

**About the author:** *Cathy Young, a writer whose work has appeared in the* Washington Post, Newsday, Wall Street Journal, New Republic, Reason, *and* Salon *is author of* Growing Up in Moscow: Memories of a Soviet Girlhood *and* Ceasefire: Why Women and Men Must Join Forces to Achieve True Equality.

Shortly after two men were arrested in [the October 2002] sniper shootings, ending a crime spree that had terrorized the [Washington] D.C.-Baltimore area and left 10 people dead, a detail emerged that galvanized a large segment of the American punditry. One of the suspects, 17-year-old John Lee Malvo, was an illegal alien—a Jamaican who had entered Florida as a stowaway. Moreover, in December 2001 the U.S. Border Patrol had taken him and his mother into custody. A month later, despite their admission that they were here illegally, the Seattle office of the Immigration and Naturalization Service [INS] released them on bond instead of deporting them.

## Creating an Immigration Connection

Writing in *National Review*, the syndicated columnist Michelle Malkin—author of the book *Invasion: How America Still Welcomes Terrorists, Criminals, and Other Foreign Menaces to Our Shores* and the first to break the story of Malvo's brush with the INS—charged that such "catch and release" decisions have "cost scores of American lives," now including the victims of the snipers. [Conservative public figure] Pat Buchanan put it even more bluntly on Fox News: "Whoever turned him loose in the INS has got blood on his hands."

Never mind that, at the time of Malvo's detention, no one could have predicted that he would engage in homicidal violence. True, he lived in a homeless shelter with his Svengali-like "stepfather," John Allen Muhammad. But he was a clean-cut boy who attended school and had never been in trouble with the law. Blaming the INS for the sniper deaths makes no more sense than blaming a highway patrol officer who lets a motorist with an expired car registration get back behind the wheel if, five miles down the road, that motorist holds up a convenience store and kills the salesclerk.

Never mind, too, that while Malvo may have been the actual triggerman in most of the shootings, the U.S.-born Muhammad was clearly the mastermind. There is little doubt that Malvo, who apparently had a troubled relationship with his mother, wanted only to please the surrogate father he idolized. "There is a large pool of messed-up teenagers in the United States," points out Daniel Griswold, a trade and immigration analyst at the Cato Institute. "John Muhammad did not need to recruit an illegal immigrant to do what he did."

One could easily turn around and argue that the shootings could have been prevented if Malvo's mother, Uma James, had been free to seek the authorities' help in extricating her son from Muhammad's clutches. (In fact, it was her attempt to do so that led to the pair's arrest by the Border Patrol.)

Alas, the attempt to exploit Malvo's crime to advance an anti-immigrant agenda is all too typical of many conservatives' rhetoric since, [the terrorist attacks of] September 11 [2001] on immigration and terrorism.

## The Wrong Solution

It's understandable, of course, that a terrorist act committed by foreign nationals should raise concerns about national security and border control. But that doesn't mean the problem of terrorism should be conflated with that of illegal immigration.

The 19 hijackers who struck on September 11 all entered the U.S. legally as tourists or business travelers, although three of them had overstayed their visas. At the same time, not one of the millions of illegals who cross the border from Mexico or get smuggled in on cargo vessels from China has been implicated in terrorism. The most Malkin can muster for a terrorist connection is that two illegal immigrants, along with one legal permanent resident from El Salvador, helped four of the hijackers get the phony driver's licenses they used to get on the airplanes.

"It's true that the system is broken," says Tamar Jacoby, a senior fellow at the Manhattan Institute. "But the

> *"A wholesale crackdown on illegal immigration could . . . hinder rather than help the effort to keep potential terrorists out of this country."*

people who are exploiting these legitimate fears to cut back on immigration are going in the wrong direction. It sounds logical at first, but it's not realistic, it's not going to be enforceable, and ultimately it's not going to give us better security."

Indeed, a wholesale crackdown on illegal immigration could, by consuming scarce resources, hinder rather than help the effort to keep potential terrorists out of this country. "By some estimates," says Griswold, "we spend $3 billion a year trying to keep Mexican workers out of the United States. I'd much rather spend that money trying to keep out Middle Eastern terrorists."

Given the realities of the global economy and the U.S. labor market, the flow of migrants into this country will be a fact for the foreseeable future. Making legal entry easier for people who want to better their lot in life is a much more feasible solution

> *"An amnesty for illegal immigrants would bring people out of the shadows in which terror cells can lurk."*

than making entry "a fiercely guarded privilege," as Malkin suggests in *Invasion*. It is also, of course, far more feasible than the fantasy of deporting the 9 million to 11 million illegal immigrants who are already here.

Besides freeing up resources to target terrorists, such legalization would severely diminish the document fraud and smuggling that can in fact assist terrorists. An amnesty for illegal immigrants would bring people out of the shadows in which terror cells can lurk and make it safe for people with useful information about possible terrorists to cooperate with law enforcement. (Oddly, for all her concern about threats to national security, Malkin deplores Attorney General John Ashcroft's offer to grant U.S. citizenship to any alien, legal or illegal, who comes forward with tips that aid the investigation into the 9/11 attacks.)

Immigration hard-liners lament that businesses and local politicians oppose tough measures against illegal aliens, but they rarely stop to wonder if there are good reasons for this opposition. "Polls show that the public opinion is squeamish about immigration," says Jacoby, "but people are squeamish in the abstract. When it comes to their own lives and their local economy, they're not so squeamish."

## Weeding Out Potential Terrorists

None of this is to say that we shouldn't try to weed out potential terrorists who come to our shores, or that political correctness never gets in the way of border control. Both Griswold and Jacoby favor targeted scrutiny of immigrants and visitors from countries with special links to terrorism—including the new Justice Department rules requiring visa holders from 20 countries, nearly all of them Arab and/or Muslim, to register with the INS.

Such profiling may smack of ethnic and religious prejudice, but unfortunately it also reflects reality. Forty-five of the 48 foreigners known to have committed or plotted terrorist acts in the U.S. since the first World Trade Center bombing in 1993 have been Middle Eastern Arabs.

Even so, profiling should be tempered with discretion. In December [2002] about 400 men who showed up for registration in Southern California were arrested for minor violations of immigration law. Many of these violations were unintended, due to slow INS paperwork on their applications for permanent residency or visa extensions.

All but 20 (whose names showed up in law enforcement records) were released within three days—but not until after considerable humiliation and discomfort. Such measures can only make aliens less likely to cooperate with the authorities.

It may be a cliché to say that radically altering our life in response to terrorism means letting the terrorists win. But it's also true, perhaps especially with regard to immigration—and not just because fully implementing the anti-immigrant agenda would cause our economy to collapse.

The openness, freedom, and plenitude that lead radical Islamists to hate America are precisely what draw so many people from around the world to live here. Among them, do not forget, were the hundreds of foreign nationals who were among those killed in the World Trade Center.

# The United States Must Control Immigration from the Middle East

by Steven A. Camarota

About the author: *Steven A. Camarota is director of research at the Center for Immigration Studies, a think tank devoted to research and policy analysis of the economic, social, demographic, fiscal, and other impacts of immigration on the United States.*

When most people think of immigrants today, they think chiefly of those from Latin America or East Asia. But while most immigrants still come from those regions, an increasing number are coming from a less traditional source: the Middle East. The number of Middle Eastern immigrants in the U.S. has grown nearly eightfold from 1970 to 2000, and is expected to double again by 2010. This growth could have significant repercussions for our homeland security—and our support for Israel.

The Center for Immigration Studies has . . . issued a study of this group of immigrants, based on new Census Bureau data. (We defined the Middle East broadly, as running roughly from Morocco to Pakistan.) While the overall size of the foreign-born population has tripled since 1970 and now stands at 31 million, the number of immigrants from the Middle East has grown more than twice as fast—from fewer than 200,000 in 1970 to nearly 1.5 million in 2000. Of this population roughly 10 percent or about 150,000, are illegal aliens (based on INS [Immigration and Naturalization Service] estimates).

## An Increase in Muslim Immigrants

The new Middle Eastern immigration is not just more numerous than the old, but also very different in religion. While the Mideast itself is overwhelmingly Muslim, historically this has not been true of the region's immigrants to the

Steven A. Camarota, "The Muslim Wave: Dealing with Immigration from the Middle East," *National Review*, vol. 54, September 16, 2003. Copyright © 2003 by National Review, Inc. Reproduced by permission.

U.S. Up until the 1960s, Middle Eastern immigrants were mostly Christian Arabs from Lebanon, or Armenians, Assyrians, Greeks, and other Christian minorities fleeing predominantly Muslim countries. In 1970, roughly 15 percent of Middle Eastern immigrants were Muslim; by 2000, almost 73 percent were.

Muslim immigrants and their progeny now number some 2 million. Add in today's perhaps 1 million American converts to Islam—mostly blacks—and you have a total Muslim population of about 3 million. The estimates put out by Muslim advocacy groups of 6 or even 12 million Muslims are almost certainly too high, but it is important to note that—absent a change in U.S. immigration policy—they almost certainly will become true.

We know that interest in emigrating to the U.S. remains very strong in the Middle East. Even after the terror attacks [of September 11, 2001] the State Department in October 2001 received some 1.5 million entries from the region for the visa lottery, which awards 50,000 green cards worldwide to those who win a random drawing. Assuming no change in immigration policy, we project that in just the next decade 1.1 million new immigrants (legal and illegal) from the Middle East will settle in the U.S. Looking forward a little further, within less than 20 years the number of Muslim immigrants and their progeny will grow to perhaps 6 million.

## The Meaning of Middle Eastern Immigrants

What does this immigration mean for the U.S.? To begin with, immigrants from the Middle East are one of the most highly educated groups in America, with almost half having a bachelor's degree, compared with 28 percent of natives; these education levels should make it easier for them to assimilate. Their average income is higher than that of natives. Another positive sign is their high rates of citizenship: Half are U.S. citizens, compared with 38 percent of immigrants overall. One would think that radicalism would have relatively little appeal for this group, but there are troubling indicators as well. In 2000, nearly one in five Middle Eastern immigrants lived in poverty, compared with about one in ten natives, and 23 percent used at least one major welfare program, compared with only 15 percent of natives. Immigration from the Middle East is no longer an entirely elite phenomenon.

> *"A large Middle Eastern immigrant population makes it easier for Islamic extremists to operate within the U.S."*

Opinion polls indicate that Middle Eastern immigrants are highly dissatisfied with U.S. policy toward the Arab-Israeli conflict and wish to see a tilt away from support for Israel. Given this, continued Mideast immigration appears likely to lead to changes in U.S. policy, as elected officials respond to Muslim Americans' growing electoral importance. Their increasing political influence was evident [in 2002] when three Democratic House members from Michigan, whose districts contain fast-growing Arab immigrant communities, were among only 21 members voting against a resolution expressing solidarity with Israel against terrorism.

## Areas of Concern

On the domestic level, there are three general areas of concern about this influx into the U.S. First, large-scale Mideast immigration is a cause of overworked American consulates overseas. The State Department, by its own admission, is completely overwhelmed by the numbers. In such an environment, it is much more likely that the wrong person will get a visa. Less immigration, of course, would mean that each applicant could be more carefully scrutinized.

Second, a large Middle Eastern immigrant population makes it easier for Islamic extremists to operate within the U.S. The September 11 hijackers used Middle Eastern immigrant communities for cover. The *Washington Post* has reported that two 9/11 hijackers who lived in San Diego got help from "mosques and established members of [the city's] Islamic community" to "find housing, open a bank account, obtain car insurance—even, at one point, get a job." The *New York Times* has observed that one of the many reasons Islamic terrorists prefer Germany as a base is that it's easier to "blend into a society with a large Muslim population."

Third, and perhaps most important, cultural adaptation poses a special problem for Middle Eastern Muslim immigrants. There has been and continues to be a debate within Islam about whether someone can be a good Muslim while living in the land of unbelievers. There is also a debate among Muslims about whether a good Muslim can give his political allegiance to a secular government, such as ours, that is composed of non-Muslims. Many Muslims can and do become loyal Americans; they have served with distinction in the U.S. military. But for some share of Muslims, coming to identify fully with America will be difficult.

> *"Reducing legal immigration from the Mideast [would require] . . . the enactment of an immigration cap that would apply across the board."*

And this problem could become more pronounced over time. [As of 2002] the way Middle Eastern immigrants have navigated life in the U.S. reflects the group's relatively small size. A modestly sized group has to accommodate itself to American society, because there is not the critical mass necessary in most cities to support institutions that preserve group customs and identity—such as ethnic-based media outlets, schools, or political and social organizations. But this dynamic is changing as the group grows very rapidly as a result of immigration.

## The Impact of Immigration Policy

The settlement of 1 million new Mideast immigrants by 2010 will overwhelmingly be the result of legal immigration—but levels of legal immigration can be changed by statute. For example, . . . proposed legislation [which as of July 2004 had not been passed] to eliminate the visa lottery would reduce Middle Eastern immigration, because many Mideast immigrants have been using this process to obtain their green cards. Alternatively, an amnesty for illegal aliens would increase Mideast immigration, by creating more legal immigrants who could then sponsor their relatives.

Some conservatives have suggested doing away altogether with immigration from the region, at least until the war on terrorism is over. But such proposals are not really worth debating: Even after September 11, not a single member of Congress proposed cutting off Middle Eastern immigration. Congress would never single out one region of the world for exclusion from green cards. Consider Iraq: Although the U.S. was engaged in open hostilities with that country throughout the 1990s, census data show that 68,000 Iraqi immigrants were allowed into the U.S. during that decade. Moreover, all the countries on the State Department's list of sponsors of terrorism are eligible to send immigrants to the U.S. and have in fact sent hundreds of thousands of legal immigrants here over the last ten years. Congress has never questioned the wisdom of permitting this immigration.

We could, of course, scrutinize visa applicants from some countries with greater care than we take in examining those from, say, Switzerland; it is even possible that Congress would curtail temporary visas in the wake of another attack. But it is politically inconceivable, in our equality-obsessed society, that we would ever return to the days prior to 1965 in which some regions of the world were allotted fewer green cards than others.

Reducing legal immigration from the Mideast is a sensible policy, but the only way this could ever happen would be the enactment of an immigration cap that would apply across the board—to all immigrants, wherever they might hail from. The same holds for efforts to deal with illegal immigration: Given limited resources, in a time of war, it makes sense—over the short term—to pursue with special vigor those immigration-law violators who are Middle Easterners. But over the long term, such a policy would be unfair and politically unsustainable. Reducing the overall immigration level is the wisest plan, for the decades to come.

# Immigration Controls That Hurt Scientific Exchange Should Be Removed

by *Nature Neuroscience*

**About the author:** Nature Neuroscience *is a multidisciplinary journal that publishes articles on molecular, cellular, systems, and cognitive neuroscience, psychophysics, computational modeling, and diseases of the nervous system.*

One of our editorial colleagues, an Australian citizen working in *Nature*'s New York office, set out on what should have been a one-day trip to Montreal for a prearranged visa interview. He found himself unable to reenter the United States for nine weeks. The reason for this unexpected delay: he was born in Malaysia, one of 26 countries on the US State Department's 'watch list' in the wake of the [September 11, 2001, terrorist] attacks. Incidents like this are becoming increasingly common, and the National Academy of Sciences (NAS) has . . . warned that the new immigration policies may have unintended detrimental effects on scientific research in the US.

## A Widespread Problem

In a statement issued . . . [in] December [2002], the NAS reported as a result of these restrictions that ". . . ongoing research collaborations have been hampered; that outstanding young scientists, engineers, and health researchers have been prevented from or delayed in entering this country; that important international conferences have been cancelled or negatively impacted; and that such conferences will be moved out of the United States in the future if the situation is not corrected." In one example cited by NAS, 90% of recent visa applications for young Pakistanis already accepted for graduate work by US universities were denied.

The problem seems to be widespread, and is not confined to scientists from 'high risk' countries. Obtaining a US visa typically involves two steps. The first step, processing the visa application, used to take only a few weeks but now involves a fairly predictable wait for 4 or 5 months. The second stage, which involves obtaining an entry stamp at a consulate outside the US, is much less predictable; this is partly because consular officials—who can face criminal penalties for admitting someone who subsequently commits a terrorist act— have wide latitude to decide what background checks are required for entry. As a result, applicants can be left stranded outside the US for an open-ended period, sometimes in the middle of their research programs. Delays of several months are not uncommon, and this can lead to serious disruption of career plans; one Swiss scientist with a visiting scholar position at UC Berkeley was delayed for so long that he was forced to cancel the position.

> *"The new immigration policies may have unintended detrimental effects on scientific research in the US."*

Some of these delays reflect a general clampdown in security procedures for all visitors to the US, but additional concerns arise for scientists with special expertise that could be misused for terrorist purposes. The Bush administration has created a new panel to screen foreign researchers who apply for visas to study 'sensitive topics'. This panel, called the Interagency Panel on Advanced Science Security (IPASS), will be composed of representatives from the Departments of State, Justice and Commerce, as well as representatives from the major science agencies. Meanwhile, in a sweeping response to the terrorist threat, the US Department of Agriculture has already announced that it will cease to apply for visas for foreign students and scientists to work in its labs, and that it will not apply for any extensions of current visas.

The need for tighter security seems indisputable in the wake of the 9/11 attacks, which were perpetrated by terrorists who had entered the US on temporary visas. But in designing countermeasures, it is also important not to undermine the openness that has made the US the world's leading scientific destination. The US scientific enterprise is substantially dependent on the contribution of foreign researchers. For example, according to 2000 figures from the National Science Foundation, 58% of all biology postdocs were on temporary visas; similarly, 23% of biology PhDs in 2001 were awarded to foreign students. Given the extent of this reliance, policies that adversely affect the ability of US labs to compete for foreign scientists could have lasting effects on scientific output.

## Streamlining the Process

The NAS statement suggested three mechanisms that could streamline the visa process for foreign scientists without compromising security concerns: reinstating a pre-clearance procedure for scientists with appropriate credentials;

instituting a special visa category for established scientists; and involving the US scientific community in identifying areas of research that raise special security concerns. These suggestions are now under discussion with the State Department, and the NAS describes the talks so far as "very useful and productive". Meanwhile, the NAS has also created a new web site (http://www7. nationalacademies.org/visas/index.html) to provide information for foreign scientists applying for visas; the site also includes a survey, intended to collect more accurate data and to assess the extent of the current problems.

Scientific self-interest should be a sufficient argument for seeking a carefully balanced solution. But there is another argument, which in the long run is perhaps even more compelling. The countries that represent the primary breeding grounds for terrorism are to a large extent excluded from the world scientific community. (For example, of the 1872 submissions received by *Nature Neuroscience* [in 2002], only six came from countries on the State Department's list.) This isolation can only increase if researchers from these countries are systematically denied contact with the West. Science is a potential liberalizing force for these countries; it offers an outlet for ambitious and talented people, a stimulus for contact with other countries, and a framework of shared values and beliefs that transcend national politics. Many commentators agree that the threat of terrorism will only disappear when there is substantial reform in the countries from which it originates. Science has the potential to contribute to this process, and it would be a shame if this were to be prevented by excessively stringent restrictions on international scientific exchange.

# Caps on Highly Skilled Immigrant Visas Should Be Removed

**by Suzette Brooks Masters and Ted Ruthizer**

**About the authors:** *Suzette Brooks Masters, an attorney, is a board member of the National Immigration Forum, which supports public policies that welcome immigrants and refugees and are fair and supportive to newcomers in the United States. Ted Ruthizer, a law professor at Columbia University, is a former president and general counsel of the American Immigration Lawyers Association.*

For almost 50 years the U.S. economy has benefited from the contributions of people admitted with the H-1B status, which permits qualified foreign national professionals to work for U.S. employers on a temporary basis. By using the H-1B visa, employers have been able to quickly plug holes in their domestic workforce with capable and often exceptional professionals from abroad in a wide range of fields, including information technology, finance, medicine, science, education, law, and accounting. Yet, as U.S. employers, large and small alike, struggle to find enough skilled professionals, particularly in the high-tech sector, the H-1B status is being strangled. Unnecessary and inadequate H-1B quotas have put this vital immigration status in jeopardy and threaten to undermine the competitiveness of U.S. companies in the global marketplace.

The puzzling question is why the use of H-1B professionals has been subject to such virulent attack. How is it that this long-established visa category can be championed by virtually all employers and by most economists who have studied its effects on the economy and, at the same time, be reviled by much of organized labor and labor's supporters in Congress and the executive branch?

To understand that enigma, one must examine the major questions—both factual and rhetorical—underlying the H-1B debate:

- Do H-1B professionals benefit the domestic economy?

- Do H-1B professionals displace U.S. workers or depress wages?
- Without a strict quota, will employers hire foreign nationals before U.S. citizens?
- Does the availability of H-1B professionals diminish the willingness of U.S. companies to train and educate our domestic workforce for technical and scientific positions?

Our study of each of those questions leads us to the firm conclusion that H-1B hiring has contributed significantly to the growth and continued good health of our economy and has helped, not harmed, the U.S. worker. Although labor organizations and their political allies have continued to perpetuate the myth of underpaid foreign professionals damaging our economy and destabilizing our domestic workforce, the facts tell us otherwise. The challenge for Congress is to move beyond this restrictionist mindset and recognize the important benefits of using foreign professionals to fill specific employment positions. That requires a rethinking of the numerical caps now crippling the H-1B status.

## A Boon to the U.S. Economy

The United States is the economic envy of the world. Our dynamic tradition of accepting and successfully integrating successive waves of immigrants has made us the beneficiary of the world's most talented and renowned research scientists, economists, engineers, mathematicians, computer scientists, and other professionals. Those immigrants have made major contributions to the U.S. economy, particularly in the high-tech sector. Recent studies that have measured the magnitude of those contributions have confirmed that immigration creates wealth and increases the size of the economy overall.

One of the most widely respected of those studies, a 1997 report by the National Research Council of the National Academy of Sciences, found that immigrants raise the incomes of U.S.-born workers by at least $10 billion per year. And some people believe that those estimates are understated because they do not account for the domestic economic impact of immigrant-owned businesses or of highly skilled foreign national workers on overall U.S. productivity. Over time, the benefits of immigration are even greater. James P. Smith, chairman of the National Research Council's Panel on Immigration and an economist at the

*"H-1B quotas have put this vital immigration status in jeopardy and threaten to undermine the competitiveness of U.S. companies in the global marketplace."*

RAND Corporation, testified in 1997 before the Immigration Subcommittee of the Senate Judiciary Committee that if the $10 billion annual gain from immigrants were discounted by a real interest rate of 3 percent, the net present value of the gains from immigrants who have arrived in the United States since 1980 would be $333 billion.

Of all the foreign workers coming to the United States, no category provides such an instant boost to the economy as do H-1B professionals. Although they are here no longer than six years, H-1B professionals, like their permanent counterparts, satisfy unmet labor needs and provide a diverse, skilled, and motivated labor supply to complement our domestic workforce and spur job creation. But unlike their permanent counterparts, H-1B professionals offer the very important advantage of enabling employers to meet immediate labor needs. Employers can hire H-1Bs in months or even weeks. In contrast, it can take four years or more to qualify a worker for permanent "green card" status.

With unemployment at a peacetime, post-war low of 4.1 percent, the resulting tight labor market has made the H-1B status even move important to U.S. companies of all stripes and sizes. In recent years, H-1B usage by financial and professional service firms has risen sharply, reflecting the increased globalization of those industries. Multinational companies often must draw on the skills and talents of professionals from their operations abroad. In information technology, management consulting, law, accounting, engineering, and telecommunications, companies are increasingly using international teams to work on transnational projects to meet the needs of their global clients.

Across the board, in virtually all the professions, skilled and talented foreign nationals bring fresh perspectives and special expertise to American companies. For example, in the important field of advertising, British nationals have led the way in introducing the important new discipline of account planning. In the 15 years

> *"In virtually all the professions, skilled and talented foreign nationals bring fresh perspectives and special expertise to American companies."*

since British account planners "exported" that new way of looking at advertising from the consumers' point of view, virtually all major U.S. advertising agencies have established account planning departments, which follow the precepts taught by the British account planners who first came here with the H-1B status. When French or German H-1B corporate lawyers use their knowledge of European civil law or EU law to analyze complex legal issues, they not only benefit their U.S. law firm employers but also enrich our economy in ways beyond simply filling a job for which competent professionals are in short supply. Similar examples abound in countless other fields, in which H-1Bs bring to their U.S. employers new ways of thinking about technology, processes, and problem solving.

## The Digital Work Force

Perhaps no industry presents a stronger case for increased usage of H-1Bs than does information technology (IT). The evidence is overwhelming that there is currently a serious shortage in the United States of IT professionals, one that is projected to become increasingly severe over the next several years. Two years ago, the Information Technology Association of America and Virginia Polytechnic Institute released preliminary findings on the shortage of IT workers, estimating that as of January 1998 there were 346,000 IT vacancies; there is no sign that the shortage has abated since then. Currently, the IT sector remains the most dynamic in the U.S. economy and is

> *"The allegation of significant H-1B fraud is simply unsupported by the facts."*

driving much of its growth, contributing more than one-third of our real economic growth between 1995 and 1997. The increase in the number of IT workers in the U.S. economy has vastly outpaced the overall U.S. job growth rate. For example, between 1983 and 1998 jobs for systems analysts and computer scientists soared by 433 percent, or nearly 15 times the comparable national rate of job growth of 30 percent.

The explosive growth of high-tech jobs will likely continue through the next decade. In its June 1999 report, "The Digital Work Force," the U.S. Department of Commerce's Office of Technology Policy [OTP] underscored the importance of the IT sector to the U.S. economy and noted that the need for IT workers cuts across all industries, from manufacturing, services, and health care to education and government. The OTP predicts that 1.4 million new workers, nearly 150,000 a year, will be required to meet the projected demand for core information technology workers in the United States between 1996 and 2006, and that the domestic pipeline of potential workers will not meet that demand. In November 1999 the U.S. Department of Labor projected that the five fastest growing occupations between 1998 and 2008 would all be in computer-related fields. Three of those occupations—systems analysts, computer engineers, and computer support specialists—were also among the top 15 in projected numerical growth. The Labor Department expected the total number of workers in those three core high-tech occupations to increase from 1,345,000 in 1998 to 2,685,000 in 2008, a 100 percent increase compared to a growth rate in overall employment of 14 percent. "The demand for computer-related occupations will continue to increase as a result of the rapid advances in computer technology and the continuing demand for new computer applications, including the Internet, Intranet, and World Wide Web applications," the Labor Department noted.

Information technology companies depend on H-1B professionals to compete in a rapidly changing marketplace. In 1995 about one-quarter of H-1B professionals were in IT-related fields. Not surprisingly, by 1997 approximately half of the H-1Bs were in IT-related fields. Several aspects of the way the IT industry functions account for its particular need for H-1B professionals. First, quick turnaround time inevitably drives employers to hire professionals who already possess the needed technical skills and experience and can work productively at once. Second, product proliferation creates demand, which changes suddenly and often, for specialized knowledge and skills. Combined, those pressures produce the need for "the right worker, with the right skills, at the right time [write the OTP]." Because of those constraints, if there is no readily available U.S. worker, the H-1B professional becomes critical to continued economic growth. Yet, despite the demonstrated contributions of those workers to America's welfare, the Clinton administration and some members of Congress have gone out of their way to make it difficult, and sometimes impossible, to hire H-1B professionals.

## Curtailing Availability

The H-1B visa category was designed to be an asset to American industry, and for almost 40 years there was no limit on the number of H-1B "nonimmigrant" petitions granted in any given year. In its 1992 report reviewing the history of the H-1B status, the U.S. General Accounting Office explained the economic benefit provided by H-1B professionals:

> One of the major purposes of nonimmigrant work-related visas is to enable U.S. businesses to compete in a global economy. Increasingly, U.S. businesses find themselves competing for international talent and for the "best and the brightest" around the world. The nonimmigrant visa program can be a bridge or a barrier to successful international competition.

What had been a bridge suddenly became a barrier with the passage of the Immigration Act of 1990. At the same time that Congress expanded the levels of permanent employment-based immigration (raising the annual maximum numerical quota from 54,000 to 140,000), it reduced the future availability of temporary H-1B professionals by imposing, for the first time, a cap on annual visas. The rationale driving the 1990 act's seemingly inconsistent expression of public policy was the erroneous assumption that, with an increase in the number of slots made available for permanent immigrants, there would be reduced demand for temporary professionals. And many members of Congress were swayed by organized labor's fears about the weak economic bargaining power of the temporary professionals and the possible displacement of U.S. workers. The 1990 law imposed a cap of 65,000 on the annual number of new H-1B professionals permitted entry into the United States and required U.S. employers hiring such foreign workers to make a variety of attestations to ensure that those hires would have no adverse effect on the wages and working conditions of U.S. workers.

> *"Hiring H-1Bs and educating and training domestic workers are not mutually exclusive but complementary."*

Employers were also prohibited from using foreign workers as strikebreakers and were required to notify their employees of the proposed hiring of a foreign temporary worker.

In 1997, when the cap was reached for the first time, U.S. employers began to clamor for more H-1B visas. In 1998 the cap was again reached, this time in May, only seven months into the fiscal year. Finally, in October 1998 Congress responded to the employer outcry by enacting the American Competitiveness and Workforce Improvement Act, which increased the number of H-1B professionals to 115,000 for fiscal years 1999 and 2000, and 107,500 for FY01. The new law also provided for a return to the 65,000 cap in FY02. Unfortunately, the increase soon proved insufficient. Because of pent-up demand and an economy chugging along in high gear, the increased numbers for FY99 were once again exhausted by the spring of 1999, months before the September 30 end of the fiscal year. The situation for FY00 seems even worse—the 115,000 cap is likely to be reached several months before the fiscal year ends. . . .

## Minimal Enforcement Problems

The most common argument against H-1Bs is that they allegedly displace U.S. workers and depress wages. In response, Congress has spun an elaborate web of laws resulting in complex regulations supposedly to protect native workers from any such impact. But nothing in theory, wage and job trends, or law enforcement data indicates that the H-1B status has a negative impact on the U.S. labor market.

> *"Current restrictions on H-1B visas are impeding employment and output in a rising number of regions and economic sectors."*

The U.S. Department of Labor [DOL], one of the major critics of the H-1B status, has carefully tracked the program's so-called abuses. We obtained and reviewed H-1B enforcement data from the Wage and Hour Division of DOL and were surprised by what we found. From 1991, at the inception of the H-1B caps and labor condition attestations, through September 30, 1999, DOL received a total of 448 complaints alleging underpayment of H-1B professionals, and other employer violations (an average of fewer than 60 complaints nationwide each year). Of those 448 complaints, only 304 resulted in a DOL investigation. During that period, nearly 525,000 H-1B nonimmigrant petitions were granted. . . . The complaint rate for a program supposedly rife with abuse is minuscule.

A violation was found in only 134 of the 159 DOL investigations that have been completed to date. Back wages found due over the entire eight-year period amounted to $2.7 million spread over 726 employees. That amount averages $337,500 a year in total underpayments, or less than $5 a year in underpayments for each H-1B visa issued during the period. In relation to the $4.2 trillion in total wage and salary disbursements paid to U.S. workers in 1998, the average annual underpayment to H-1Bs amounted to 0.000008 percent—or about 40 cents for every $50,000 paid in wages and salaries. With H-1B workers accounting for such a small share of total U.S. workers, the impact of these rare cases on the overall wage level is insignificant.

Infractions of DOL wage rules appear to be not only rare but random, with no discernible pattern of intentional abuse. Of the 134 violations, only 7 were determined to be "willful," an average of about one intentional violation per year. The fact that more than 94 percent of the small number of violations were unintentional demonstrates that the problem is not with employers but with a law that is needlessly complex, arbitrary, and cumbersome.

> *"America's economic health should not be jeopardized by an arbitrary quota on foreign-born professionals."*

Given all the attention lavished by H-1B critics on the "job shops" (i.e., companies providing temporary professional personnel to high-tech employers on a contract basis), one would expect to find large numbers of cases involving IT-sector employers failing to pay the prevailing wage. In fact, the authors' analysis of DOL enforcement data shows that, over the eight-year period in question, only 231 employees in the high-tech sector, now estimated to employ between 2 million and 3.5 million people, were owed back wages. This constitutes less than one-third of the total number of H-1B employees in all specialty occupations found by DOL to be due back wages.

What is most striking about the low level of enforcement activity is that an aggrieved party (i.e., the largely mythical American worker who loses a job to an underpaid temporary foreign worker) has but to make a call to DOL to start the ball rolling. Complaints don't require lawyers, simply a phone call. And DOL is champing at the bit to find abusive employers. In this environment, one would expect every "displaced" U.S. worker and every "underpaid" foreign worker to clamor for justice. Workers talk to one another, and job hopping and raiding are commonplace. If abuse were prevalent, it would be impossible to hide. The enforcement data simply do not support allegations of the displacement of U.S. workers or the underpayment of H-1B professionals by employers.

The tame enforcement picture contrasts sharply with the widespread but unproven accusations of pervasive fraud in the H-1B visa process. According to some opponents of the H-1B status, the alleged fraud is occasioned by employers who knowingly file visa petitions for persons who fail to meet the statutory criteria, prospective H-1B applicants who falsify their academic credentials, and government employees on the take who further those criminal acts. But the evidence of H-1B visa fraud is exclusively anecdotal. Given the small number of those visas available every year and the overwhelming need for such visas by legitimate employers complying with the law, vague, largely unsubstantiated allegations of abuse should not be accepted without hard evidence, and they must not obscure the very real benefits provided by this important category of visa holders.

In House Immigration Subcommittee hearings held on the topic of nonimmigrant visa fraud in May of 1999, senior Immigration and Naturalization Service official William Yates testified that "anecdotal reports by INS Service Centers indicate that INS has seen an increase in fraudulent attempts to obtain benefits in this category [H-1B]. These fraud schemes appear to be the result of those wishing to take advantage of the economic opportunities in the U.S." Given the small base number of proven frauds, the alleged increase hardly seems a vigorous call to action. In a similar vein, the inspector general of the U.S. Department of Justice, Michael R. Bromwich, testified that "there is very little hard data available to gauge the magnitude of visa fraud, a point noted by [the General Accounting Office] in its reports on this subject. . . . This lack of comprehensive statistics hinders the ability of the State Department and the INS to appropriately respond to visa fraud." Moreover, the three cases cited in the inspector general's testimony as ongoing fraud investigations all involved criminal activity by INS employees. No reasonable person condones immigration fraud of any type, but the allegation of significant H-1B fraud is simply unsupported by the facts. . . .

## H-1B Hiring Complements Training and Education

Another charge against the H-1B program is that it discourages U.S. companies from adapting to the domestic skills shortages by investing in training of the domestic workforce. In practice, however, American industry is pouring money into training programs and technical education. Hiring H-1Bs and educating and training domestic workers are not mutually exclusive but complementary: both are essential to preserving the competitive edge of U.S. companies in a global economy.

The reasons for training are obvious: retaining existing employees, keeping pace with new product lines and technological advances, and boosting skill levels of new hires. And U.S. companies are responding to the call for new training initiatives. According to Phyllis Eisen, executive director of the National Association of Manufacturers' Center for Workforce Success, U.S. industry currently invests between $60 billion and $80 billion in training annually. U.S. companies are not only training their own employees but educating America's youth in order to create a suitably trained workforce for the future.

On the basis of its 1998 survey on training issues, NAM's Center for Workforce Success reports that one-third of manufacturers offer programs to teach computer technology, and fully one-quarter of them are upgrading their workers' math and problem-solving skills. The vast majority of companies (more than 80 percent) also offers supplemental educational opportunities beyond remedial training. Half of survey respondents spend between 2 and 5 percent of their payroll on training, a huge jump since 1991. In

> *"Sound policy dictates that Congress should abolish the [H-1B] caps and let the market determine the need for H-1B professionals."*

the high-tech sector, companies spend even more on training, between 4 and 6 percent of payroll, according to NAM's Eisen. Microsoft, a company that petitions for many H-1B IT professionals, invests heavily in training its own employees ($54 million in FY98) and supports the use of technology in schools throughout the country. In FY97 it contributed nearly $250 million to promote those broad training efforts.

The need to train the next generation of U.S. workers and to retool current American workers to help meet the demand for professionals in the IT and other sectors makes training a high priority for U.S. companies. In a fiercely competitive global environment, H-1B professionals help U.S. companies remain in the game while they invest in their workforce and their future.

## Unfettering H-1B Hiring

Meanwhile, on Capitol Hill, Congress struggles to achieve consensus on whether and how much to raise the H-1B cap, largely ignoring the overwhelming evidence that attempts to "control" the H-1B inflow are not only unnecessary but counterproductive.

"Increase the H-1B cap" bills have been introduced in the Senate and the House and are awaiting action while the available FY00 visas evaporate. The American Competitiveness in the 21st Century Act, introduced in February 2000 by Sens. Phil Gramm (R-Tex.), Spencer Abraham (R-Mich.), Slade Gorton (R-Wash.), and Orrin Hatch (R-Utah), would raise the cap on H-1B visas to 195,000 in fiscal years 2000–02. It would exclude from the caps foreign-born workers employed by universities and those with advanced degrees.

Another proposal involves creation of a new immigration visa category (the so-called T visa) for foreign-born technology professionals, in recognition of the national shortage of qualified high-tech workers. Under the proposed BRAIN Act (H.R. 2687) introduced by Rep. Zoe Lofgren (D-Calif.) in August 1999, a foreign professional would need a bachelor's degree or higher in mathematics, science, engineering, or computer science and the offer of a job paying at least $60,000 a year to qualify for this new visa status. Eligibility would be limited to recent graduates of U.S. undergraduate or postgraduate programs who are currently in the United States on student visas. A similar Senate bill (S. 1645) was introduced in September 1999 by Sen. Charles Robb (D-Va.). Although the Lofgren and Robb bills acknowledge the need to fix the serious, chronic problem of too few visas, the $60,000 threshold seems arbitrarily drawn and too high an amount to cure the problem of insufficient numbers. Creating a new, separate category of visa would also require a whole new set of regulations, needlessly complicating the hiring process and introducing more delays and uncertainty into the system, rather than working within the already established H-1B procedures.

In late October 1999, Sen. John McCain (R-Ariz.) became the first member of Congress to propose doing away with the H-1B cap altogether. The 21st

Century Technology Resources and Commercial Leadership Act (S. 1804) would suspend the cap on H-1B nonimmigrants for the next six years, through FY06. It would also require the INS to give priority to processing H-1B petitions on behalf of students graduating from U.S. universities with advanced degrees in technical disciplines. Congress will likely consider some variation of these proposals in 2000.

## Letting the Market Decide

Should Senator McCain's bill become law, for the first time since 1991 the U.S. government would let the market determine how many H-1Bs were needed. Since the evidence does not support claims of job displacement, wage erosion, or failure to invest domestically in training, what is the real fear? That the floodgates will fly open and millions of H-1B professionals will invade our shores? That is extremely unlikely. Before 1990 there were no caps on H-1B entrants and the numbers were always modest. Even in the early days of caps, demand for H-1B professionals never reached the permissible limit. It was not until 1997 that the legislated cap of 65,000 was first met, a reflection of a strong economy's need for those valuable professionals.

The argument for raising the cap cuts across party and ideological lines. Laura D'Andrea Tyson, former chief economic adviser to President Clinton, made the case in a *Business Week* column [in 1999] that the current restrictions on H-1B visas are impeding employment and output in a rising number of regions and economic sectors. She pointed to evidence that immigrants have been a major source of job and wealth creation in Silicon Valley's thriving high-tech sector, bringing with them skills, creativity, human capital, and links to global markets. She concluded: "Conditions in the information technology sector indicate that it's time to raise the cap on H-1B visas yet again and to provide room for further increases as warranted. Silicon Valley's experience reveals that the results will be more jobs and higher income for both American and immigrant workers."

One of the great strengths of the American economy today is its openness—to the flow of goods, services, capital, and people. The warnings from left and right that more trade and immigration would throw native Americans out of work, destroy jobs, and drive down real wages have proven to be spectacularly wrong as economic expansion continues. In the last decade, trade and investment flows have reached record levels while the influx of legal immigrants has averaged close to 1 million per year. During that period, unemployment has fallen to a 30-year low, 15 million net new jobs have been created, real wages have been rising all across the income scale, and the current economic expansion has just set a record as the longest in U.S. history. Our openness to trade and immigration has been an integral part of our economic success.

America's economic health should not be jeopardized by an arbitrary quota on foreign-born professionals. It is time to return to U.S. employers the ability to fill gaps in their workforce with qualified foreign national professionals rapidly, subject to minimal regulation, and unhampered by artificially low numerical quotas. We advance neither U.S. workers nor the U.S. economy by denying our employers the ability to continue to bring to our shores the best professional talent available in the world. Sound policy dictates that Congress should abolish the caps and let the market determine the need for H-1B professionals.

# Organizations to Contact

The editors have compiled the following list of organizations concerned with the issues debated in this book. The descriptions are derived from materials provided by the organizations. All have publications or information available for interested readers. The list was compiled on the date of publication of the present volume; the information provided here may change. Be aware that many organizations take several weeks or longer to respond to inquiries, so allow as much time as possible.

**American-Arab Anti-Discrimination Committee (ADC)**
4201 Connecticut Ave. NW, Suite 300, Washington, DC 20008
(202) 244-2990 • fax: (202) 244-3196
e-mail: adc@adc.org • Web site: www.adc.org

ADC is a nonsectarian, nonpartisan civil rights organization dedicated to combating discrimination against people of Arab heritage and promoting intercultural awareness. It works to protect Arab American rights through a national network of chapters. The committee publishes the newsletter *ADC Times* ten times a year as well as an annual special report summarizing incidents of hate crimes, discrimination, and defamation against Arab Americans. ADC publishes current news, fact sheets, and articles, which are available on its Web site.

**American Civil Liberties Union (ACLU)**
125 Broad St., 18th Floor, New York, NY 10004
(212) 549-2585
Web site: www.aclu.org

The ACLU is a national organization that champions the rights found in the Declaration of Independence and the U.S. Constitution. The ACLU Immigrants' Rights Project works with refugees and immigrants facing deportation, and with immigrants in the workplace. It has published reports, position papers, and books that detail what freedoms immigrants and refugees have under the Constitution, some of which are available on its Web site.

**American Friends Service Committee (AFSC)**
1501 Cherry St., Philadelphia, PA 19102
(215) 241-7000 • fax: (215) 241-7275
e-mail: afscinfo@afsc.org • Web site: www.afsc.org

The AFSC is a Quaker organization that attempts to relieve human suffering and find new approaches to world peace and social justice through nonviolence. It lobbies against what it believes to be unfair immigration laws, especially sanctions criminalizing the employment of illegal immigrants. It has published *Human Rights Report: Voices from the Border*, which is available on its Web site.

**American Immigration Control (AIC) Foundation**
PO Box 525, Monterey, VA 24465
(540) 468-2022 • fax: (540) 468-2024
e-mail: aicfndn@cfw.com • Web site: www.aicfoundation.com

The AIC Foundation is an independent research and education organization that believes massive immigration, especially illegal immigration, is harming America. It calls for an end to illegal immigration and for stricter controls on legal immigration. The foundation publishes several pamphlets, monographs, and booklets, including Joseph L. Daleiden's *Selling Our Birthright* and Lawrence Auster's *Huddled Cliches* and *Erasing America: The Politics of the Borderless Nation.*

**American Immigration Lawyers Association (AILA)**
918 F St. NW, Washington, DC 20004
(202) 216-2400 • fax: (202) 783-7853
Web site: www.aila.org

AILA is a professional association of lawyers who work in the field of immigration and nationality law. It publishes the *AILA Immigration Journal* and compiles and distributes a continuously updated bibliography of government and private documents on immigration laws and regulations.

**Americans for Immigration Control (AIC)**
PO Box 738, Monterey, VA 24465
(540) 468-2023 • fax: (540) 468-2026
e-mail: aic@immigrationcontrol.com • Web site: www.immigrationcontrol.com

AIC is a lobbying organization that works to influence Congress to adopt legal reforms that would reduce U.S. immigration. It calls for increased funding for the U.S. Border Patrol and the deployment of military forces to prevent illegal immigration. It also supports sanctions against employers who hire illegal immigrants and opposes amnesty for such immigrants. AIC offers articles and brochures that state its position on immigration, some of which are available on its Web site.

**The Brookings Institution**
1775 Massachusetts Ave. NW, Washington, DC 20036
(202) 797-6000 • fax: (202) 797-6004
e-mail: brookinfo@brook.edu • Web site: www.brook.edu

The institution, founded in 1927, is a liberal research and education organization that publishes material on economics, government, and foreign policy. It publishes analyses of immigration issues in its quarterly journal, *Brookings Review*, and in various articles, books, commentary, reports, and speeches, some of which are available on its Web site.

**California Coalition for Immigration Reform (CCIR)**
PO Box 2744-117, Huntington Beach, CA 92649
(714) 665-2500 • fax: (714) 846-9682
e-mail: barb@ccir.net • Web site: www.ccir.net

CCIR is a grassroots volunteer organization representing Americans concerned with illegal immigration. It seeks to educate and inform the public and to effectively ensure enforcement of the nation's immigration laws. CCIR publishes alerts, bulletins, videotapes, and audiotapes, some of which are available on its Web site.

**Cato Institute**
1000 Massachusetts Ave. NW, Washington, DC 20001-5403
(202) 842-0200 • fax: (202) 842-3490
Web site: www.cato.org

The institute is a libertarian public policy research foundation dedicated to stimulating policy debate. It believes immigration is good for the U.S. economy and favors easing immigration restrictions. As well as various articles on immigration, the institute has published Julian L. Simon's book *The Economic Consequences of Immigration*. On its Web site the institute publishes studies and commentary on immigration issues.

## Center for Immigration Studies
1522 K St. NW, Suite 820, Washington, DC 20005-1202
(202) 466-8185 • fax: (202) 466-8076
e-mail: center@cis.org • Web site: www.cis.org

The center studies the effects of immigration on the economic, social, demographic, and environmental conditions in the United States. It believes that the large number of recent immigrants has become a burden on America and favors reforming immigration laws to make them more consistent with U.S. interests. The center publishes editorials, reports, and position papers.

## Council on American-Islamic Relations (CAIR)
453 New Jersey Ave. SE, Washington, DC 20003
(202) 488-8787 • fax: (202) 488-0833
e-mail: cair@cair-net.org • Web site: www.cair-net.org

CAIR is a nonprofit membership organization that presents an Islamic perspective on public policy issues and challenges the misrepresentation of Islam and Muslims. It publishes the quarterly newsletter *Faith in Action* and other publications on Muslims in the United States. Its Web site publishes statements condemning both the September 11, 2001, attacks and news releases on discrimination against Muslims and other civil rights issues.

## El Rescate
1313 W. Eighth St., Suite 200, Los Angeles, CA 90017
(213) 387-3284 • fax: (213) 387-9189
Web site: www.elrescate.org

El Rescate provides free legal and social services to Central American refugees. It is involved in federal litigation to uphold the constitutional rights of refugees and illegal immigrants. It compiles and distributes articles and information and publishes the newsletter *El Rescate*.

## Federation for American Immigration Reform (FAIR)
1666 Connecticut Ave. NW, Suite 400, Washington, DC 20009
(202) 328-7004 • fax: (202) 387-3447
e-mail: info@fairus.org • Web site: www.fairus.org

FAIR works to stop illegal immigration and to limit legal immigration. It believes that the growing flood of immigrants into the United States causes higher unemployment and taxes social services. FAIR publishes a monthly newsletter, reports, and position papers, including *Running in Place: Immigration and U.S. Energy Usage*, and *Invitation to Terror: How Our Immigration System Still Leaves America at Risk*, which are available on its Web site.

## Foundation for Economic Education, Inc. (FEE)
30 S. Broadway, Irvington-on-Hudson, NY 10533
(914) 591-7230 • (800) 960-4333
e-mail: fee@fee.org • Web site: www.fee.org

FEE publishes information and research in support of capitalism, free trade, and limited government. It occasionally publishes articles opposing government restrictions on immigration in its monthly magazine, *Ideas on Liberty*. Articles and commentary on immigration issues can be found using the FEE Web site's searchable database.

## The Heritage Foundation
214 Massachusetts Ave. NE, Washington, DC 20002-4999
(202) 546-4400 • fax: (202) 546-8328
e-mail: info@heritage.org • Web site: www.heritage.org

The foundation is a conservative public policy research institute. It has published articles pertaining to immigration in its Backgrounder series and its quarterly journal, *Policy Review*. Articles and reports on immigration can be found using the searchable database on its Web site.

## National Alliance Against Racist and Political Repression (NAARPR)
1325 S. Wabash Ave., Suite 105, Chicago, IL 60605
(312) 939-2750 • fax: (773) 929-2613
e-mail: info@naarpr.org • Web site: www.naarpr.org

NAARPR is a coalition of political, labor, church, civic, student, and community organizations that oppose the many forms of human rights repression in the United States. It seeks to end the harassment and deportation of illegal immigrant workers. The alliance publishes pamphlets and a quarterly newsletter, *The Organizer*.

## National Council of La Raza (NCLR)
1111 Nineteenth St. NW, Suite 1000, Washington, DC 20036
(202) 785-1670
Web site: www.nclr.org

NCLR is a national organization that seeks to improve opportunities for Americans of Hispanic descent. It conducts research on many issues, including immigration, and opposes restrictive immigration laws. The council publishes and distributes congressional testimony and policy reports, including *Unfinished Business: The Immigration Control and Reform Act of 1986* and *Unlocking the Golden Door: Hispanics and the Citizenship Process*.

## National Immigration Forum
50 F St., Suite 300, Washington, DC 20002
(202) 347-0047
e-mail: info@immigrationforum.org • Web site: www.immigrationforum.org

The forum believes that immigration strengthens America and that welfare benefits do not attract illegal immigrants. It supports effective measures aimed at curbing illegal immigration and promotes programs and policies that help refugees and immigrants assimilate into American society. The forum publishes the annual *Immigration Policy Handbook* as well as editorials, press releases, and fact sheets, many of which are available using the Web site's searchable database.

## National Network for Immigrant and Refugee Rights
310 Eighth St., Suite 303, Oakland, CA 94607
(510) 465-1984 • fax: (510) 465-1885
e-mail: nnirr@nnirr.org • Web site: www.nnirr.org

The network includes community, church, labor, and legal groups committed to the cause of equal rights for all immigrants. These groups work to end discrimination and unfair treatment of illegal immigrants and refugees. The network aims to strengthen and coordinate educational efforts among immigration advocates nationwide. It publishes reports, including *From the Borderline to the Colorline: A Report on Anti-Immigrant Racism in the United States*, and a monthly newsletter, *Network News*, recent issues of which are available on its Web site.

**Negative Population Growth, Inc. (NPG)**
2861 Duke St., Suite 35, Alexandria, VA 22314
(703) 370-9510 • fax: (703) 370-9514
e-mail: npg@npg.org • Web site: www.npg.org

NPG believes that world population must be reduced and that the United States is already overpopulated. It calls for an end to illegal immigration and an annual cap on legal immigration of 200,000 people. This would achieve "zero net migration" because 200,000 people exit the country each year, according to NPG. NPG frequently publishes position papers on population and immigration in its *NPG Forum*. It also publishes a quarterly newsletter, *Population and Resource Outlook*, recent issues of which are available on its Web site.

**The Rockford Institute**
928 N. Main St., Rockford, IL 61103
(815) 964-5053 • fax: (815) 964-9403
e-mail: info@rockfordinstitute.org • Web site: www.chroniclesmagazine.org

The institute is a conservative research center that studies capitalism, religion, and liberty. It has published numerous articles questioning immigration and legalization policies in its monthly magazine, *Chronicles*, recent issues of which are available on its Web site.

**U.S. Citizenship and Immigration Service (USCIS)**
U.S. Department of Homeland Security
20 Massachusetts Ave. NW, Washington, DC 20529
Web site: www.uscis.gov

The USCIS, an agency of the Department of Homeland Security, is charged with administrative and management functions and responsibilities that were once in the former Immigration and Naturalization Service, including the enforcing of immigration laws and regulations, as well as administering immigrant-related services including the granting of asylum and refugee status. It produces numerous reports and evaluations on selected programs. Statistics and information on immigration and immigration laws, and other materials are available on its Web site.

# Bibliography

**Books**

| | |
|---|---|
| Dale Anderson | *Arriving at Ellis Island.* Milwaukee, WI: Gareth Stevens, Inc., 2002. |
| Nicholas Blake and Raza Husain | *Immigration, Asylum, and Human Rights.* New York: Oxford University Press, 2002. |
| George J. Borjas | *Heaven's Door: Immigration Policy and the American Economy.* Princeton, NJ: Princeton University Press, 1999. |
| Stephen Castles and Mark J. Miller | *The Age of Migration.* Basingstoke, England: Palgrave Macmillan, 2003. |
| Wayne A. Cornelius, Thomas J. Espenshade, and Idean Salehyan, eds. | *International Migration of the Highly Skilled.* San Diego: Center for Comparative Immigration Studies, 2001. |
| Roger Daniels | *Guarding the Golden Door: American Immigration Policy and Immigrants Since 1882.* New York: Hill and Wang, 2004. |
| Roger Daniels and Otis L. Graham | *Debating American Immigration, 1882–Present.* Lanham, MD: Rowman & Littlefield, 2001. |
| Debra L. Delaet | *U.S. Immigration Policy in an Age of Rights.* Westport, CT: Praeger, 2000. |
| Michael A.E. Dummett | *On Immigration and Refugees.* New York: Routledge, 2001. |
| Jonathan Friedman and Shalini Randeria, eds. | *Worlds on the Move: Globalization, Migration, and Cultural Security.* New York: Palgrave Macmillan, 2004. |
| Donna R. Gabaccia and Colin Wayne Leach, eds. | *Immigrant Life in the U.S.: Multi-Disciplinary Perspectives.* New York: Routledge, 2004. |
| Scipio Garling and Ira Mehlman | *The Environmentalist's Guide to Sensible Immigration Policy.* Washington, DC: Federation for American Immigration Reform, 1999. |
| Victor Davis Hanson | *Mexifornia: A State of Becoming.* San Francisco: Encounter Books, 2003. |
| Nigel Harris | *Thinking the Unthinkable: The Immigration Myth Exposed.* New York: I.B. Tauris, 2002. |

| Helene Hayes | *U.S. Immigration Policy and the Undocumented: Ambivalent Laws, Furtive Lies.* Westport, CT: Praeger, 2001. |
| Arthur C. Helton | *The Price of Indifference: Refugees and Humanitarian Action in the New Century.* New York: Oxford University Press, 2002. |
| Samuel P. Huntington | *Who Are We? The Challenges to America's Identity.* New York: Simon & Schuster, 2004. |
| Tamar Jacoby | *Reinventing the Melting Pot: The New Immigrants and What It Means to Be American.* New York: Basic Books, 2004. |
| Kevin R. Johnson | *The "Huddled Masses" Myth: Immigration and Civil Rights.* Philadelphia: Temple University Press, 2004. |
| David Kyle and Rey Koslowski, eds. | *Global Human Smuggling: Comparative Perspectives.* Baltimore: Johns Hopkins University Press, 2001. |
| Gallya Lahav | *Immigration and Politics in the New Europe: Reinventing Borders.* New York: Cambridge University Press, 2004. |
| Ruben Martinez | *Crossing Over: A Mexican Family on the Migrant Trail.* New York: Picador, 2002. |
| Joseph Nevins and Mike Davis | *Operation Gatekeeper: The Rise of the 'Illegal Alien' and Remaking of the U.S.-Mexico Boundary.* New York: Routledge, 2002. |
| Eva Østergaard-Nielson | *International Migration and Sending Countries: Perceptions, Policies, and Transnational Relations.* New York: Palgrave Macmillan, 2003. |
| John S.W. Park | *Elusive Citizenship: Immigration, Asian Americans, and the Paradox of Civil Rights.* New York: New York University Press, 2004. |
| Mei Ling Rein et al., eds. | *Immigration and Illegal Aliens: Burden or Blessing?* Wylie, TX: Information Plus, 1999. |
| Peter D. Salins | *Assimilation, American Style.* New York: Basic Books, 2000. |
| Saskia Sassen | *Guests and Aliens.* New York: Norton, 2000. |
| Michael Teitelbaum | *Threatened Peoples, Threatened Borders: World Migration and U.S. Policy.* New York: Norton, 2000. |
| Maura I. Toro-Morn and Marixsa Alicea, eds. | *Migration and Immigration: A Global View.* Westport, CT: Greenwood Press, 2004. |
| Julie R. Watts | *Immigration Policy and the Challenge of Globalization: Unions and Employers in Unlikely Alliance.* Ithaca, NY: Cornell University Press, 2002. |
| Michael Welch | *Retained: Immigration Laws and the Expanding INS Jail Complex.* Philadelphia: Temple University Press, 2002. |

**Periodicals**

| *America* | "Refugees on Hold," March 11, 2002. |

# Bibliography

| | |
|---|---|
| Melinda Ammann | "Breast Men: Mexican Immigrants Want to Fillet Our Chickens. The INS Is Determined to Stop Them," *Reason*, July 2002. |
| John Attarian | "The Wrong Answer: Immigration Is Not the Right Way to Fix Social Security," *Social Contract*, Summer 2003. |
| Gabrielle Banks | "Politicking the Border," *Colorlines*, Fall 2003. |
| George J. Borjas | "Making It Worse," *National Review*, February 2, 2004. |
| Robert J. Bresler | "Immigration: The Sleeping Time Bomb," *USA Today Magazine*, July 2002. |
| Steven A. Camarota and Mark Krikorian | "A Myth Dies Hard," *National Review*, February 21, 2000. |
| Jeff Chapman and Jared Bernstein | "Immigration and Poverty: How Are They Linked?" *Monthly Labor Review*, April 2003. |
| Rebecca L. Clark and Scott A. Anderson | "Illegal Aliens in American Prisons," *Crime & Justice International*, October/November 2001. |
| Santiago Creel | "Migration and National Security After 9/11," *Origins*, August 28, 2003. |
| Peter Duignan | "Do Immigrants Benefit America?" *World & I*, February 2004. |
| *Economist* | "Opening the Door," November 2, 2002. |
| James R. Edwards | "The Business Case for Immigration Reform: A Fresh Look for America's Future," *Executive Speeches*, August/September 2002. |
| Michael Finkel | "Desperate Passage," *New York Times Magazine*, June 18, 2000. |
| Andy Fixmer | "Immigrants' Woes Provide Fat Paychecks for 'Notarios,'" *Los Angeles Business Journal*, March 8, 2004. |
| Arnoldo Garcia | "Special Registration and the War on Immigrants," *Left Turn*, May/June 2003. |
| Daniel Golden | "No Green Card Means American Education Is a Win-Lose Prospect," *Wall Street Journal*, June 22, 2000. |
| Bruce Goldstein | "Guest Worker Schemes and Broken Dreams," *Dollars & Sense*, March/April 2004. |
| William Norman Grigg | "Stealth Invasion," *New American*, April 5, 2004. |
| Kimberly Hamilton and Elizabeth Grieco | "Measuring the Impact of Rich Country Immigration Policy on Poor Country Development," *Migration Policy Institute*, November 6, 2002. |
| Justin Heet | "The Economic Benefits of Immigration," *American Outlook*, Winter 2003. |
| Tamar Jacoby | "About Those Huddled Masses," *Wall Street Journal*, June 24, 2004. |
| Tamar Jacoby | "Too Many Immigrants?" *Commentary*, April 2002. |

Joe D. Jones "Immigration Demands Realistic Consideration," *Mississippi Business Journal*, January 13, 2003.

Mark Krikorian "The Security Costs of Immigration," *American Outlook*, Winter 2003.

Tikva Lecker "Foreign Aid as a Discipline on Illegal Immigration," *International Advances in Economic Research*, August 2000.

Marsha Lillie-Blanton and Julie Hudman "Untangling the Web: Race/Ethnicity, Immigration, and the Nation's Health," *American Journal of Public Health*, November 2001.

Lee G. Madland "Population/Immigration: One Problem, Indivisible," *Social Contract*, Summer 2003.

Michelle Malkin "No Divine Right," *American Legion*, April 2004.

Maria Margaronis "Europe's Unwelcome Guests," *Nation*, May 27, 2002.

Tim McGirk "Border Clash," *Time*, June 26, 2000.

Nicholas V. Montalto "Halt the War on Immigrants and Immigration," *NJBiz*, January 20, 2003.

John O'Sullivan "Ideologues Without Borders: A Global Attack on Assimilation," *National Review*, September 30, 2002.

John O'Sullivan "Invasion of a Certain Kind: A Big Question for the West," *National Review*, April 30, 2001.

Lorrie Rank "Gays and Lesbians in the U.S. Immigration Process," *Peace Review*, December 2002.

Stephan-Gotz Richter "The Immigration Safety Valve—Keeping a Lid on Inflation," *Foreign Affairs*, March/April 2000.

Alisdair Rogers "Global Migration," *Geography Review*, January 2001.

Phyllis Schlafly "America Must Choose: Open Borders or Civil Liberties," *Phyllis Schlafly Report*, November 2002.

Phyllis Schlafly "What the Global Economy Costs Americans," *Phyllis Schlafly Report*, June 2003.

John Simons "Even in a Recession, the U.S. Economy Depends on Immigration," *Fortune*, November 26, 2001.

Peter Skerry "Citizenship Begins at Home: A New Approach to the Civic Integration of Immigrants, *Responsive Community*, Winter 2003–2004.

Howard Sutherland "Amnesty Insanity," *American Conservative*, February 16, 2004.

Jeffrey Tayler "Another French Revolution," *Harper's*, November 2000.

Russell Taylor "Hardship at Home, Hardship Abroad: The Migration 'System' Doesn't Work," *UN Chronicle*, March–May 2003.

Stephen Webster "Fade to Brown: Immigration and the End of White America," *American Renaissance*, April 2003.

# Bibliography

Alison Stein Wellner    "The Newest American Families: Hispanic and Asian Immigrants Bring a Traditional Family Structure with Them," *Forecast*, April 2003.

Thomas G. Wenski    "The Immigration Reform That Is Needed," *Origins*, February 26, 2004.

Thomas E. Woods    "Fathers Knew Best: The Founders' Words Refute the 'Nation of Immigrants' Myth," *American Conservative*, February 16, 2004.

# Index

# Index